The Year of Chaos

D1388709

Leabharlann Ráth Maonais
Rathmines Library
01-2228466

By the same author

Non-fiction

The Trouble with Guns

I Was a Teenage Catholic

The Telling Year

Empty Pulpits

Under His Roof

On My Own Two Wheels

Gerry Adams: An Unauthorised Life

Fifty Years On: The Troubles and the Struggle for Change in Northern

Ireland

Fiction

Terry Brankin Has a Gun

The Year of Chaos

*Northern Ireland on the
Brink of Civil War, 1971–72*

Malachi O'Doherty

Atlantic Books
London

First published in hardback in Great Britain in 2021 by Atlantic Books, an imprint of Atlantic Books Ltd.

Copyright © Malachi O'Doherty, 2021

The moral right of Malachi O'Doherty to be identified as the author of this work has been asserted by him in accordance with the Copyright, Designs and Patents Act of 1988.

All rights reserved. No part of this publication may be reproduced, stored in a retrieval system, or transmitted in any form or by any means, electronic, mechanical, photocopying, recording, or otherwise, without the prior permission of both the copyright owner and the above publisher of this book.

The picture credits on p. 359 constitute an extension of this copyright page.

Every effort has been made to trace or contact all copyright-holders. The publishers will be pleased to make good any omissions or rectify any mistakes brought to their attention at the earliest opportunity.

10 9 8 7 6 5 4 3 2 1

A CIP catalogue record for this book is available from the British Library.

Hardback ISBN: 978 1 83895 122 1
Trade paperback ISBN: 978 1 83895 121 4
E-book ISBN: 978 1 83895 123 8

Printed in Great Britain by Bell and Bain Ltd, Glasgow

Atlantic Books
An imprint of Atlantic Books Ltd
Ormond House
26–27 Boswell Street
London
WC1N 3JZ

www.atlantic-books.co.uk

For Maureen

Contents

The Year of Chaos

Prologue

Cities and countries can be traumatised, just as people can. My home city Belfast suffered a huge psychological and emotional shock in August 1969. After months of protests by the civil-rights movement, and increasing violence on the streets as the police opposed these marches, an enormous gun battle erupted near the city centre.

I was there that night.

I couldn't work out what was happening. I realised afterwards that many of those in the heat of it didn't know either.

Protestant mobs came down onto the catholic Falls Road, perhaps realistically anticipating that rioters there would invade their streets. So protestants and catholics fired on each other and burnt buildings. The police opened up with Browning machine guns mounted on armoured cars. Later it emerged that they thought they were confronting an IRA uprising.

Then British soldiers came in to restore order and things were calm for a few months, relatively so anyway.

Leabharlanna Poiblí Chathair Baile Átha Cliath
Dublin City Public Libraries

But, stunned by what had happened, many in the following weeks and months gathered into groups and acquired weapons for the next recurrence.

And organisations existed that were ready to receive them, like the Irish Republican Army (IRA) and the Ulster Volunteer Force (UVF), defence committees, vigilante groups.

From a state of shock following the gun battle of August 1969 a gradual recovery of composure in the city turned into an expectation of more trouble and, for some, an eagerness for trouble.

Those few who had the legacy in their families of past violent eruptions framed the political visions of republicanism and loyalism that would establish the paramilitary camps.

Some who were just hurt and angry and confused wanted the satisfaction of taking some control.

So, from that trauma the violence grew slowly through the following year, 1970.

A major irritant in the original violence had been the Northern Ireland state itself, its confrontation with protest, brutal and incompetent policing. It could all have been managed differently.

And that is true of how the next two years of gradual escalation were managed until we reached the year of chaos, the pinnacle of violence, the bloodiest months and the prospect of all-out civil war.

Children who hardly understood what the trouble was about faced into an adulthood in which they felt they had to be ready to fight, to kill and to die.

You will meet some of those kids in this book. They have

shared their stories with me in close private recorded interviews, most but not all acknowledging that their lives went awry in those horrific years, as did my own. We are the generation that remembers and can talk about it with the clarity of deep impressions made but also with the comfort of distance and, for now, the absence of fear of each other.

Introduction

At this time I lived in Riverdale. This was a small housing estate built in the fifties on what was then the western fringe of Belfast, beyond the terminus for the number 12 bus serving the Falls Road and Andersonstown. The bus stopped at the Gaelic Athletic Association sports ground at Casement Park, named after Sir Roger Casement, a British diplomat who had tried to smuggle guns to Irish revolutionaries from Germany during the Great War and was executed for his treason.

This didn't make him a bad person from the perspective of my family. My twin brother Roger was named after him. This was the only English-sounding name in a family of six children, most of whose names came from Gaelic mythology.

When we moved to Belfast from Ballycastle in 1956 I was sent to school at the Casement Park ground where classes were held in the changing rooms. I can still smell the space, the damp concrete and must. This was not due to any failure of the Stormont government to provide a school building for catholics. The Church had decided to run its own system –

largely paid for by the state – and had not yet built enough schools for an expanding population.

Every week at Mass my parents were asked to pay into the School Building Fund and also to pay towards the upkeep of the church.

We did, in time, get a very nice school building, the Holy Child. It opened in 1959. But already it was too small for the expanding catholic population in the new housing estates around us. The boys' side of the Holy Child was dedicated to the nineteenth-century Italian Dominic Savio who had mortified his flesh out of devotion to God and died at the age of fourteen. The girls' side was dedicated to Maria Goretti, born in Italy in 1890, who had been murdered at the age of twelve for refusing the sexual advances of her killer. But she died forgiving him. She even visited him in a dream and gave him lilies.

The models we were offered were children who had accepted death with good grace.

One of the hymns we sang at that time, 'Faith of Our Fathers', prayed that future generations might lose their lives like the martyrs of the Church. 'How sweet would be our children's fate, if they, like them, could die for thee.'

These shocking details require the corrective that most people did not really want their children to die. Nor did we anticipate that in later years there would be abundant opportunities to die for the faith, be tortured and killed for acknowledging that you were a catholic. Still, martyrdom was engrained in our culture and this referred as often to dying for Ireland as dying in defence of catholicism. In fact, we thought of them as more or less the same thing.

So, set that culture as part of the backdrop of life on a new housing estate on the edge of Belfast in the fifties in which young people will either grow away from that tradition or add to it. A young man reaching his teens in the sixties might have to choose between Bob Dylan or the Beatles and the role models of catholic nationalist Ireland, between the great secular rebellion and the hoary past.

Unfortunately, chauvinism was getting a revival through the 1966 fiftieth anniversary commemorations of the Easter Rising. Reflecting on this during the Covid-19 pandemic in 2021 throws up a little forgotten detail about the Irish war of independence waged from 1919 to 1921: it coincided with a flu pandemic that killed 23,000 Irish people. There is no mention of those flu deaths in the doleful songs of martyrdom and estrangement that were being revived in the sixties and added to by vigorous upbeat new rebel songs.

Take two young men of that time, Gerry Adams and Joe McCann. Were they rebels or conformists? Close friends, they were civil-rights protesters and militant republicans. They would go their separate ways after the 1970 split in the IRA but they had no disagreement on the right of Irish people to shoot British soldiers or local policemen, to blow up shops and pubs, the unification of the island into a single Irish jurisdiction still being worth killing and dying for.

McCann's militancy was consistent in his eyes with his devotion to God as a lay Franciscan, Adams's with his regular attendance at Mass.

And this at a time when the secularising of Ireland was starting as a revolt among young people against constraints their parents had found acceptable. It was that young generation which hollowed out the congregations, but nationalism did not wane in the same way. It secularised too.

The Provisional IRA was a new organisation but it had emerged from a long tradition. As a youth I had read the history of the IRA and had my imagination peopled with heroic guerrillas like Sean Treacy and Tom Barry. I suppose they were not exceptional people in their time, but books about the period previously known as the Troubles, that is, between 1916 and 1922, presented their ambushes on the Royal Irish Constabulary and the Black and Tans as heroic and unreservedly constructive contributions to peace and freedom for the Irish people. I had some idea that my parents' generation remembered some of these men more selectively. Michael Collins, the head of the IRA, was remembered as a military genius who had penetrated British intelligence and then ordered the executions of agents.

Still, that had entailed gunmen going into a man's bedroom and shooting him dead in front of his wife.

Dan Breen had started off the shooting war in 1919 simply by shooting dead two policemen. My mother said, 'I don't know why you are reading a book by that lout.' Dan Breen may have been a lout but he was Michael Collins's lout.

But now the IRA were my neighbours and people who had lately moved into the estate, and it was difficult for me to imagine that they would be written up as heroes in the future, though some indeed would be.

Successive IRA leaders were impassioned catholics and ruthless killers but the average bloke on operations – I'd never call him a foot soldier – would as likely be the bully who scoffed at you when you walked to school. It is often said that these were ordinary decent people who never would have seen the inside of a prison were it not for the political mess that generated the violence, but actually a lot of them would have done.

At first it had not seemed likely that the IRA would organise on a large scale. Once in 1970 a vigilante rebuked me for dismantling a makeshift barricade so that my friend's car could get through to my house. 'Next time it will be the IRA that you have to deal with,' he said, and he might as well have been threatening me with the Viet Cong or the Red Brigade at that time. He would have known that the words had the power to shock because they had been retrieved from history but I had no great fear then that the movement itself would come alive. What I hadn't worked out was that the IRA when it re-emerged would be this same man and his friends.

What I had not noticed, although there were signs around me in my childhood, was that the IRA did still exist, though it was small.

A cluster of families had preserved a long tradition. They had customs and resources that a freshly devised military project would not have had. Other factions would form to establish paramilitary command structures and run campaigns and they fell apart into internal feuding. The same plague ate into the loyalist groups, which rarely had stable leadership for long. The IRA tradition had the DNA for organisation. They did not have to study how Palestinians, for instance, ran a people's army, preserved it intact and integrated it with a wider community. There were older people in the movement who understood these things and who had learnt from their parents and grandparents. They also had easy access to American support groups and others who could get them guns and money.

Some of those families had roots going back to the Fenians of the nineteenth century. Gerry Adams's uncle Dominic had sent Brendan Behan to England as a young bomber in the forties. Republicans from west Belfast had been interned in Frongoch camp in North Wales after the Easter Rising of 1916.

And another thing I had not understood was that within these families the hopes for a future war were kept alive. This was a culture within a culture. Chauvinistic and catholic and nationalist as many of us were through our schooling, our home reading and our religious practices, there were others for whom this was much more serious. There was even intermarriage between these families. Gerry Adams's parents had married within that cluster of families, an Adams with a Hannaway. He married into another such family, the McArdles, and his sister Margaret married Mickey McCorry, of another of those families. Immigrant members of those same families in the United States and Canada retained their connections. In those families, having been to jail was an honour in the way graduation from university was for others.

So there was almost a skeleton standing army ready to be activated and an officer caste in place. A story is told of how Brother Murphy, the principal of St Mary's Christian Brothers' Grammar School in Barrack Street near the centre of Belfast, watched the 1966 Easter Rising commemorative parade go past and spotted Gerry Adams, a former pupil, stewarding the marchers. He said, 'I see, at least we have the officers.'

In a few short years, hundreds more young men from the catholic communities of Belfast would join the IRA and those officers would be in place to receive and organise them.

In contrast, the unionist Ulster Defence Association (UDA) modelled its drilling routines on the Boys' Brigade, patching an army together with local community resources and drawing no doubt on the experiences of the Royal Ulster Constabulary (RUC) and the Ulster Special Constabulary, known as the B Specials, too. It was an evolution from street fighting for some and vigilante patrolling for others, coming together and establishing a new street army, pooling skills from the British army and the manufacturing industries to make guns, badges and knives.

They defined themselves as an army defending the Union with Britain, providing extra muscle against the IRA beyond what the state could sanction. Usually this would translate in action into killing random catholics, perhaps in the hope that terrorising the catholic community would drive it into rejecting the IRA.

The republicans defined their project as one of defending the catholic community and advancing a war to push Britain out of Ireland. These were both fake agendas. The IRA would do more to endanger the catholic community than to protect it. And it hadn't the remotest prospect of defeating the British army because it was so much smaller. What it could do was build a movement in opposition to the army.

If Northern Ireland – the six-county state, as nationalists called it – needed the army on the streets to preserve it then it was easier to argue that it had no right to exist, that there would at least have to be major constitutional change.

The IRA's outright demand for a united Ireland presented the British with an unanswerable challenge, created a level of violence that could only be managed, never quashed, never appeased with a political concession. Demanding the impossible put the British in an impossible position too.

The Boy Soldiers

For some it started in childhood.

For them it wasn't about demanding or resisting constitutional change.

At fourteen Tommy Andrews was a gang leader in north Belfast. He enjoyed rioting and 'fenian bashing'. 'Fenian' was a common term for a catholic or someone with catholic lineage. He had a simple test for the stranger: 'Spell "Harry".'

If someone cornered by his gang started with Haitch rather than Aitch, that was enough to warrant laying into him.

Tommy says now that he was not politically minded but that he was angry.

Two years earlier his family had lived on the Moyard estate at the top of the Whiterock Road, among catholic neighbours. The violence of August 1969 had prompted catholics and protestants across much of the city to leave their homes and move closer to people among whom they felt safer. Word had also reached the family that Tommy's uncle had been shot during a riot closer to the city centre.

He saw his mother 'in hysterics'. He says he was deeply disturbed and cried without knowing why he was crying.

There was turmoil now in the city. His family felt unsafe. Areas were homogenising as catholic or protestant. In some cases your neighbours, in a community that might make you feel like a vulnerable minority, would want you to stay, would want to dissociate themselves from the raging sectarianism of the time. But would they be able to protect you? There were others of their own community homeless now, sleeping as refugees in church halls and schools. Didn't it make more sense for the house of a protestant in a catholic area to be given up for another catholic, when the protestant would be better off in a protestant area anyway? Even a friend on the other side would want that for you. Sectarianism wasn't always bitter and cruel; sometimes it was simply practical, in everyone's interest.

All over town people were moving out of their homes in areas where they felt unsafe. And if you talk to those people now, many will tell you that it was not their protestant or catholic neighbours who were insisting they leave but people from outside the area. Vigilante groups were trying to find homes for people evicted in another part of town and they would seek out a solitary catholic or protestant family in an otherwise homogeneous street and tell them to leave and make room for another homeless family, perhaps to swap.

The Andrews family moved in with Tommy's grandmother on the West Circular Road. From Tommy's granny's bedroom he had a view over the whole of the city. When there was violence he could see the burning buildings.

A year later the family moved onto the Highfield estate, and from there Tommy was able to lead attacks on the community in Moyard that he had had to leave.

*

I was eighteen when the huge riots consumed parts of Belfast in August 1969. I had grown up so far without knowing serious sectarian violence. Unlike Tommy Andrews I did not come to my teens with a settled understanding that I had a sectarian war to fight.

My family was not threatened during the '69 riots, though two bars my father managed were burnt out and he was unemployed for a few weeks. We had not been excessively unsettled by the tumult on the wind, the noise of distant bother whether gunshots or raucous shouting. Nor had the arrival of armed soldiers on our streets felt like a threat. Tommy Andrews, when I meet him now as a surprisingly placid older man, talks about being frightened, crying without knowing why he was crying, and in making sense of his world he responded as others around him did, first by rioting, later by joining the Ulster Defence Association, which would arm young men to shoot random catholics, first in back alleys, later in their homes.

I wonder if those who were just twelve or fourteen when the violence started were more likely to absorb a tradition of rioting and sectarian hostility as their normality. If chaos comes with puberty, does it feel intrinsic to the changes that are affecting everything else in your life? Whether you are going to be rioting on the streets or not, you are still going to feel unsettled by hormones and be a menace to someone.

Maybe it is the world that you see when you come through puberty that you settle on as normal and negotiable, and for boys who discovered masturbation and the petrol bomb at the same time, rioting is just what you do, what you suppose everyone does.

Or maybe violence is an attractive option when you have not yet worked out how to direct those new energies, a comfort for your hard edges. This deepening war was fired up by boys who, had they not had battles to wage, would perhaps have been fighting and destroying anyway.

That's what many of them, like Tommy, were doing, before loyalist paramilitary discipline redirected their love of trouble.

This was the early days of the Troubles, during a two-year period of gradual escalation towards the worst of the violence. There were weeks and months at a time of peace, with just a few bombings and fewer killings.

Paramilitary groups were trying to gather weaponry and explosives and to recruit new members but for now much of the violence was among young people like Tommy Andrews, rioting, attacking strangers. Some of those young people would soon become serious paramilitaries in leadership roles on the streets and in prison.

Anthony McIntyre was twelve years old when the violence erupted on the Falls Road. He speaks now as a writer and left-wing activist in Dublin who believes the IRA campaign was pointless. I've known him for about twenty-five years, since he left the IRA and got driven out of Ballymurphy by pickets at his home who protested against his frank critique. He says he had no political ideas when he got involved. It was about being with your mates. Like others, the shock of the violence of August '69 made a deep impression on him.

On the morning after much of the burning, probably 15 August, he and a friend walked over to the Falls Road from the Ormeau Road where they lived.

'We found something. We never knew what it was but we brought it back with us to the Ormeau Road. We were all sitting on the railway line between Donegall Pass and the railway bridge. Then the unmerciful bang of the thing. I presume it was a detonator, but I remember all these wee pricks over my legs and the ringing in my ears.

'We were sitting around it poking at it and wondering what it was. Just glad we didn't have our hands on it.'

He was a boy soldier before long, inducted into the youth wing of the Official IRA. This was what was left of the IRA after the Provisionals broke away in 1970; it was a socialist organisation. Not that he thinks that he should be compared to the boy soldiers who have been fighting in various African wars. He wasn't forced to join. He was enthusiastic.

'I remember rioting the night before internment in the Falls area. It was amazing. It was exciting. Right close-quarter fighting with brits and then every house in the street open so that you could run in and then the brits were coming in after us, houses of people we didn't know, and out and over the back walls. And this was really exciting. Batons were snapping, lashing at our feet as we were trying to get up.'

This was not the playful antic that his laughing about it today suggests.

'People would have thrown petrol bombs. There were also nail bombs being thrown. And the bang of the nail bomb sent a real surge of adrenalin through you but it was deafening, as if it went off right at your feet.

'Then we were fighting the brits all down Leeson Street and there was a place called Varna Gap and the next thing the British army were at the top of the street. The IRA pulled in. They were in two cars and they took rifles out and they were pointing up the street. It was like being a spectator to a film. You didn't sense the danger.' On that occasion the gunmen from the cars did not open fire, perhaps as well for themselves.

There were many young protestants from different parts of the city who evolved in that year or two through the same stages, from being members of rival gangs. Beano Niblock and Tommy Andrews, from different parts of the city, recall how the 'tartan gangs' would meet by appointment for a fight, perhaps in the Botanic Gardens. When the Ulster '71 Exhibition was staged there to mark the fiftieth anniversary of the state of Northern Ireland it was disrupted by two protestant gangs in different tartan scarves charging across the lawns at each other with hammers and clubs. These gangs later coalesced to fight catholics and from that stage merged into loyalist paramilitary organisations and took up guns. Some would be recruited at first into the adult paramilitary groups as young helpers.

Tommy Andrews was one of the first members of a gang called the Ulster Boot Boys. They wore a tartan scarf as part of their uniform. The first tartan gang had been formed on the Shankill Road with a red tartan; the Ulster Boot Boys adopted a brown tartan.

No one ordered them to do that.

Eddie Kinner from the lower Shankill tells a similar story. I first met Eddie in the mid nineties when we were both invited to speak to trainee police officers as part of a Community Awareness Programme. His gang saw the Shankill tartan boys in their scarves and picked another tartan for themselves.

Beano Niblock's gang in east Belfast did the same. They were just the boys that hung around a corner and they gave themselves a brand. The scarf wearing gave the impression of them all being part of a citywide organisation, the tartan seeming more a uniform than a trend. Then tartan gangs grew up around the city, all in protestant areas, all at first fighting among themselves and then turning their anger on catholics.

Tommy says one of his gang was called Thor because he carried a hammer. Beano Niblock says that he went to gang fights with a steel comb. He has scars from the fights. 'I got injured in a few of the fights, hit with a hammer, stabbed. Broken bottle stuck into me and stuff like that. That happened me quite a lot. The scar on my chin I got from rioting with catholics on Short Strand but the scars I have in my head and the side of my head were from other protestant gangs.'

Beano writes poetry now and urges young protestants not to get caught up in violence. In one poem, he writes of waking to 'thoughts of a base nature that shudder me fully awake'.

Eddie Kinner says that one of his gang acquired a pistol, a zip gun. 'Two tartan members had been in Borstal and one of them got out one weekend for parole and he didn't want to go back so he asked the tartan guy to shoot him in the arm with the zip gun. He shot him in the arm.

'Two weeks later the other one was out. He wanted shot in the leg so that he would not have to go back. He got shot in the leg. This was on the pretence that they were shot by republicans. And Nokie (Noel) Shaw then came down. He was the UVF – later killed.

'He said, "Knock it on the head; youse are bringing attention to us."'

One of Eddie's favourite games was tricking people into rioting. 'Our entertainment would have been opening the pub doors on a Friday and Saturday night and shouting, "Quick, the taigs [catholics] are coming up Percy Street." And you'd have had these drunk people running out of the bars running down Percy Street expecting a crowd coming up. People then at the other end seen these drunks coming down and a riot just erupted.'

This was at a time when the streets of Belfast were mostly policed by armed soldiers, ordered into the city in 1969 to restore order after the first major rioting in which guns were used.

Tommy Andrews says, 'We were constantly being arrested by the army. The army had a barracks in Springmartin and I can remember oftentimes being arrested by different soldiers between the Scotch regiments, the paratroopers, whatever regiment would have been there at the time. You could have been lifted off the street during the riots and sometimes not even rioting. I don't know why, they would have picked us up and brought us to the Springmartin barracks and gave us a hard time. They just kept us and slapped us about.'

He was legally a child at the time but he says the army never sent for his mother, as the law required, just beat him about for a while and let him go.

'There was one time that they lifted me off the street and brought me to Springmartin, slapped me about a bit, then took me for a ride in the back of a Saracen [armoured vehicle], two or three of us. I can't remember who the other kids were. I could guess.

'They took us for a run in the back of the Saracen, closed all the traps in it, told us they were going to throw us out in Ballymurphy [a catholic area]. We were hearing what sounded like stones hitting the Saracen and then all of a sudden they just opened the back doors and kicked us out. But where they kicked us out was up the mountain. We thought we were getting kicked out in the middle of Ballymurphy.'

The initiative in absorbing these gangs into the paramilitaries was taken by the paramilitaries themselves, as much to impose order on their areas as to expand recruitment. It was a merger that both sides were happy with for it brought the young tartans into a system that protected them from each other. The first concern of the paramilitaries was to stop rioting between protestants.

Eddie Kinner had been a victim of the gang fighting. One gang had invaded the Shankill looking for two members of his gang. They caught one of them and gave him a beating. Later, when Eddie was on his own, he was spotted and attacked.

He would need protection. An invitation came to join the Young Citizen Volunteers (YCV), an armed group. As a member he would have 'backings'. He would be safe from any threat of attack from other protestants. So he joined.

He was fifteen.

Anthony McIntyre joined the Fianna, the youth wing of the Official IRA, at fourteen.

'It was just a case of going in and putting your hand on a flag and saying some oath, then that was you in. It was a great feeling. You didn't feel you were doing any wrong. I always felt that the other side were doing the wrong. I suppose it was as natural for me to join a group like that as it was for somebody from the unionist community to join the police.'

He was still at school, often rioting and also having to attend lectures provided by the IRA.

'They used to do engineering meetings – that's what they were called. They were teaching us about bombs and guns. They had this lesson they called DRINK. Designation, Range, Indication, Number of rounds, Kind of fire.

'That stuck in my mind.'

And he fought the tartan boys.

'They used to try to come into our area. One night the Woodstock Tartan tried to take over the Hatfield Bar. We were fighting with them every week on the Ormeau Road. One time stickies [the Official IRA] shot one called Elder in the leg in the Hatfield Bar.'

Once, in a clash with the tartans in Donegall Pass, a protestant area close to where he lived, Anthony McIntyre fell into a trap and was nearly killed.

'They tried to kidnap me on Donegall Pass with Noel McGuinness. They had lured us into one of the side streets and we went down and chased them and then an older guy came out with a gun and we bolted. We were lucky. 'Cos it was exciting then.'

He says, 'The guy who tried to get me was later convicted for killing Norman Hutchinson, a seventeen-year-old protestant, son of an RUC member who mixed with catholics in the lower Ormeau. This guy shot him in the stomach. My father found him and put a hankie over the wound and we got him an ambulance and stood over him. The next morning we heard that he had died.'

As McIntyre remembers, it the life of a rioter was separate to a degree from his role as a member of the Fianna. He would act on his own initiative as a rioter, alongside his responsibilities as a boy under IRA orders.

'A Fianna boy's responsibility was to run the local slua, and I was on the staff. The slua is the company. You had your own autonomous existence but you were always subject to the IRA. You were organising riots, finding arms and finding dumps, houses where people would keep stuff, securing nail bombs, wee bits and pieces, acid for acid bombs, the usual things, going to discussions, taking part in protests, going on marches. We were busy fools. A lot of it was meetings but it was a life I liked and I thought I was doing the right thing.'

Eddie Kinner says, 'The first meeting of YCV that I attended they asked for volunteers for operations and I didn't volunteer for anything. And the guy that had asked me along said to me after the meeting, "Why didn't you volunteer for anything?" My response was, "Well, I expect to be trained before I do anything." So the training process did begin. I was handling weapons early enough. I'd be given weapons to store.'

But a paramilitary commander or quartermaster who orders

a youngster to mind guns can't always get them back when he wants them.

'Once I had a weapon in the house and nobody else knew about it and two of the other YCVs had been in a hurry and hadn't been able to get a hold of me and they had called at the house and asked my da for the weapon. So I'm on my way back home and a motorbike pulls in and the two guys said, "We were trying to find you but your da got it for us."

'I went to the house shiting myself, expecting my da to go bananas at me. He just called me to the side. He says, "Next time you have anything like that in the house make sure I know about it." He's coming at it from the perspective that he'd be the one getting charged.'

The gangs were unashamedly sectarian. Beano Niblock says, 'There was that attitude, if they are not with you they're against you. So you had that mass intimidation, putting people out of their houses. There was a catholic chapel on the Woodstock Road, St Anthony's. It's still there. In the Ravenhill, lots of catholics lived in that Lagan Village area. They went to St Augustine's. There was a catholic school called Lagan Village as well that closed in the sixties. So you had a nucleus of catholic families, and once it died down in '69 most of them stayed. Or they moved a few streets away up past My Lady's Road.

'But then by the time 1971 came round, people were saying, you see those fuckers we didn't get in '69, get them out now.'

Beano developed skills as a bomb maker even before he joined the paramilitaries. He had learnt how to make nail bombs which he and his gang-mates took to riots.

'Did they work? Mostly. You were throwing them in riot situations. Sometimes you were more danger to yourself than others. Manufacturing them was a real dodgy process as well. I had accidents with them and lived to tell the tale. But others weren't so lucky.'

He was caught making bombs just before his seventeenth birthday.

'They caught me actually putting a fuse into one of the bombs. My sister was getting married in June and she had rented a wee house and she and her future husband were fixing it up. And it had a wee outhouse out the back. I used the outhouse as a wee store. She didn't know. I came home from work one night and wanted to get a couple of bombs out because people were looking for them for the weekend. This was a Thursday. I'd bring them down to the house for somebody calling for them. I had a couple of crates of petrol bombs and these wee blast bombs and I was putting the fuse in one of them and I heard a wee noise, the click of a gun and I turned round and saw two uniformed constables. I don't know if they'd seen me climbing over the wall or whatever. Had to get my mum.

'So they kept me overnight and charged me. I appeared in court in September. Usually they just gave you continuing bail but if there was no one to sign your bail you got remand. I didn't know about this. I went to court one day and got remanded in custody and I said, I'm on bail. So it ended up I did a week in Compound Seven in Long Kesh and that was a hell of an experience, and then I got bail again.'

Long Kesh was a new prison camp that had been improvised from an old air force base to accommodate internees after August 1971.

Eddie Kinner was also moving from gang antics to serious crime. He says, 'On one occasion when I had joined the YCVs we were meeting to go out on a robbery so I had taken the morning off work. I was standing at a bar waiting for the others to arrive and my da came walking down the street and I bolted, near shiting myself.'

He sharpened up his act fairly quickly.

All four of these men, and many others, regret their teenage violence and their more serious commitment to full-on adult paramilitary warfare. All served long prison sentences. But they felt – or say they felt – that they were doing the right thing. And they were endorsed in their violence by people who were older than them.

William Craig, the former Stormont minister of home affairs who banned the first civil-rights marches in 1968, had formed the Ulster Vanguard Movement and staged huge rallies of his supporters around Northern Ireland in 1972.

Beano Niblock says, 'Vanguard was a turning point because they rallied people and they used the tartan gang as like a vanguard really. We turned up at the rallies in our denims with our tartan scarves on and were lined up like soldiers and inspected. You had that feeling of high esteem. People were saying, "These lads are our future."'

Beano was on bail on that charge of making bombs when he paraded with his gang before Craig and other senior unionists, business people and clergy.

Yet not every young rioter joined the paramilitaries.

Beano says, 'I seen guys who would have clubbed you over a girl yet they wouldn't get involved. They had the wit to say it wasn't for them. I had a very close friend who went to a different grammar school – he went to Grosvenor. He didn't join up and years later I had a drink with him and he was asking me about being in prison and I said, "I have always wanted to ask you a question but never had the opportunity. Why did you not join?" We were in our forties.

'He said, "It was dead simple. See when the riots were at their height, once you heard a bottle being smashed, everybody ran out. There was a particularly heavy riot and it lasted ages and it was great but one of my neighbours saw me and told my da. I went home that night. My da didn't say anything. He pulled me out of the chair and he beat the fuck out of me. He said, if I catch you down the bottom of that road again I'll bust your back. I didn't join the paramilitaries because I was scared of my da."

'How basic can you get?'

*

Those of us who were just a little older had memories that told us this was not normal. To be honest, I had not been a normal vandal or street fighter in my difficult years. The difference between the young man who will join a militia and set out to kill people and one who won't is not as simple as hormonal edginess, but it is not as simple as political conviction either.

Around me, many men and women of my own age did join the IRA. They too started their violent careers through rioting and later put themselves under command structures, took orders and killed or helped others to kill.

I knew them.

I was at school with some of them.

I wasn't like Beano's friend, who stayed out of the rioting because he was afraid of his father. I think my father would have supported me if I had joined the IRA. Probably he would have been happier if I had been an activist who didn't kill people or risk getting killed, though we all did take risks just by living there. He knew the young IRA men in the street, knew them better than I did. I argued with him about the IRA and told him flatly that I held them in contempt for bombing the city centre where I worked every day. He wasn't able to have a clear argument without losing his temper anyway so I don't know exactly what he wanted of me. He was of a generation that didn't doubt the basic republican cause. He had grown up by the Irish border. Born before it was put in place, he inevitably saw it only as a violation. He had no doubt that Irish people had a right to fight to remove that border and unite their country.

Not for him the argument that the border was a compromise to resolve a division between people; it was simply a foreign, British imposition.

'Well, even so,' I argued with him, 'how has bombing the bus station helped?'

And maybe I was just the more conventional rebel defying my father. The young men of the IRA and the loyalist groups were often adopting the values of their fathers. They were essentially conservative.

Beano and Eddie and Tommy describe communities in which virtually everyone, as they recall, supported loyalist violence. Beano says that when he was in jail the butcher and the grocer brought gifts for him to his mother.

Yet that doesn't quite fit with other parts of their stories, the father who battered a son spotted rioting; Beano's own mother from whom he had to hide his bomb making; Eddie, 'shiting' himself for fear his father would see him taking a day off work to scout for bank robbers.

Tommy Andrews's family urged him to join the army so that he would be away from the influence of loyalist paramilitaries.

No one was a seasoned bomber or sniper yet. The main experience they had at that time was rioting, perhaps firing shots from the fringe of a riot. Some had responsibility for arms dumps.

And yet these organisations had fierce internal discipline which members accepted. One guy told us one night that he had to report for a punishment. He had taken guns from a dump and gone into a drinking club and waved them around, acting the lig.

'It will be a beating. Hopefully it will just be a beating.'

I suggested that he would be better off getting out of the country to save himself but he took pride in his readiness to take his punishment, even if it was to be a bullet in the leg, for he had submitted himself to the discipline of his officers and he had let them down.

Once a thin and fraught young man in the company declared that he was a member of the Provisional IRA.

We all thought the Provisionals were religious lunatics trying to establish a catholic and Gaelic Ireland, the sort of Ireland the Christian Brothers would have approved of. In our company at that time the Provisionals were regarded as eccentric chauvinists. Later I got a message from him that he would like to meet me. We met in a bar and he told me that his cumann, or club, was running an educational programme on Irish culture and asked me if I had any books I could spare for them.

I gave him a few including P. W. Joyce's *Old Celtic Romances*. I never heard from him again. Perhaps he went stag hunting over the mountains in the hopes of being lured into a glade by a woman of the Shee. I hope so.

Gearing Up

There was a two-year period between the colossal eruption of violence in August 1969 and the introduction of internment without trial which triggered the escalation into a year of chaos. That violence in August '69 had come after a year of street violence around civil-rights marches that had been banned by the government and attacked by the police and by loyalists. In one horrible night the police opened up with Browning machine guns in Belfast, mostly firing over the heads of rioters.

Eddie Kinner, a child, watched that from a distance and believed that the machine guns mounted on armoured cars were the IRA's and that they were attacking the protestant Shankill where he lived. That is how ill-informed his understanding was of the war he was entering. In jail, years later, he met others who told him the police tracer bullets lighting the sky that night were not the IRA's after all. So the threat was never as big as he had imagined it to be.

Belfast was traumatised in August '69 but measures were taken quickly to impose order. A peace line barricade was erected by the army to divide the Shankill and the Falls. It is still there today, much stronger, much higher.

The police were disarmed. An auxiliary police force, the all-protestant B Specials, was disbanded. Many former members were absorbed into a new local British army regiment which was established to give locals a role in defence, in the hope that catholics would join. And for about six months there was very little violence – only minor rioting.

At the same time, vigilante groups were formed in catholic and protestant areas, and the IRA split to create the more militant Provisional movement contrasting with the socialist leadership of the Official IRA which had not armed for the clash it had provoked. Both wings recruited and imported arms with enthusiasm, anticipating war.

I watched the riots.

I had a friend called Rocky who lived in the lower Falls. Rocky had taken a bullet through thick muscle at the back of his neck. He was proud of the scars, like holes for a bolt like the one through the neck of Frankenstein's monster. The bullet had come from a police gun fired at him during the '69 riots.

One night in 1970 he said he had something to show me. He took me first to his family home and gave me a dark jumper to put on. Then he led me into the Divis Flats complex from behind and up a stairwell onto a balcony. Dozens of people had gathered there, all in dark clothing and all keeping still and quiet.

Out on the main road, Divis Street, a few rioters were taunting soldiers with stone throwing. It was a trap.

When the boys ran back into the flats complex soldiers with batons ran in after them. The area below us was as wide as an arena and as soon as the soldiers were within range a huge shout went up from around me and everyone threw an empty bottle at them. The bottles seemed to form a single glistening mass crackling in the air over them and to shower down upon them.

I had not thrown one, nor would I have done.

When I walked through other confrontations on my way home that night, I did so with the confidence of the innocent and was not stopped. In one street a group of boys lined up to fight the soldiers and a woman on her doorstep scowled at them to go home and give everyone a bit of peace.

That year the army announced that petrol bombers might be shot dead. The government passed a law creating a mandatory six-month sentence for disorderly behaviour.

I was often in the court watching one friend or another face trial and learnt that I had been lucky to walk through riots unscathed, for it was obvious that the soldiers were often making easy arrests of bystanders. That was a shock for respectable catholic families, to have sons going to jail.

In the spring of 1970 Provisional republicans in Ballymurphy organised nightly riots. Ballymurphy is a housing estate at the foot of the Belfast Hills, not far from the Moyard estate where Tommy Andrews grew up. I frequently walked up there to watch the riots. A line of soldiers across the main Springfield Road would confront dozens of young men hurling stones, bottles and petrol bombs at them. It all looked orchestrated.

That year the army used CS gas, which created an awful tightening in the chest. The defence against it was to soak a handkerchief in a mix of vinegar and water and hold it over your nose.

One night, on the way to watch the riot, I saw a woman tug at her husband's arm and plead with him not to go up onto the road to join in. On another, a line of women formed up across the road, between the soldiers and the rioters.

On yet another night, the riot stopped so that people could go home and watch Celtic play for the European Cup.

On a bright Friday evening in July 1970 I heard that there was a big riot on the Falls Road. The army had raided houses for arms and crowds had confronted them. The area was peaceful when I walked around the streets. Many houses had a bucket of water and vinegar at the front doorstep for people to use if they inhaled the gas. The sting of it was still hanging in the air. There was almost a carnival atmosphere with people on the street.

A man in a brown corduroy jacket passed me. He had a rifle under the jacket, its barrel pointing to the ground. He looked like a student or a teacher, not like the usual street fighter.

A helicopter passed overhead with a loudhailer announcing that the area would be placed under curfew. I got over a wall down a side street and on the other side faced ranks of soldiers crouching with their rifles, waiting for the order to go in. I walked right past them.

When I got home I heard the gunfire in the still night air.

*

Those were dangerous times and yet when I cast my mind back to 1970 I remember enthusiasm and long summer days. A young man of nineteen or twenty found the trouble thrilling. We knew that the country was changing rapidly and we gathered in bars to discuss revolution, the scale of change, the humiliation of an old order and formulae for restructuring the constitution, whether by a federation of Britain and Ireland or with Ireland standing alone like a Cuba at the edge of Europe supported by her friends in the East.

I never thought that I would affect the pace or pattern of change but I did feel that we were all being carried on a high wave to a new shore. We were young men and women drinking pints in the afternoon in an old Belfast pub where past revolutionaries had gathered, hiding from the yeomen, and we felt we were part of something.

Sinister things were going on around us that we barely comprehended. One day, in the same pub where we met for these fulsome conversations and speculations, three Scottish soldiers felt safe enough in those early years of the Troubles to drink and chat with strangers at the bar. One of those strangers was himself a former British soldier. He had boxed for the Parachute Regiment. His name, Pat O'Kane. He is believed to have killed those soldiers, two brothers and a friend, the youngest just seventeen years old.

A car took them to a mountain road over Belfast. Their bodies were found still warm, bundled together. They had their flies open, so they had probably lined up at a ditch for a slash together and been shot from behind.

I think we thought of that as an exceptional event, out of character with the revolutionary spirit in the city. This was more brutal than we imagined our revolution would be.

This was before it all became too awful, more awful than most of us anticipated.

*

For those of us who had not been put out of our homes or jobs but who had maybe had a few minor adventures to lend plausibility to a story about being close to the heat for a moment, this was a time when the talk was lively and the future alluring. The Troubles had not yet become a perpetual irritant and spoiler of sleep.

One of my friends talked of how he had got laid on a French holiday. He impressed the girls he'd met with his stories about '*la guerre*'. He told me that the way to impress new acquaintances was simply to say, '*La guerre, c'est très mauvaise.*'

We were young and having adult conversations, men and women together. Some in the company were members of republican clubs or the Catholic Ex-Servicemen's Association (CESA), set up for the defence of catholic communities. Some were journalists from America or France.

My friend Philip told me how the CESA took him and others away disguised as a football team for arms training.

The future weakness in the CESA was that it wasn't up for a fight with other paramilitaries and too easily had its weapons purloined by others who were more eager to use them. What the old catholic soldiers and disillusioned Ulster Defence Regiment (UDR) men who joined them had planned for was simply to create a defensive militia that would be on hand if catholics were attacked.

Every paramilitary group had its drinking clubs and these

O'Neill, Jack

Until:	Mon 22 Nov 2021
Patron barcode	20006001488488
Pickup location	Wicklow Bray
Notice type	...
Item barcode	DCPL8000070636
Author	O'Doherty, Malachi, 1951- author
Title:	The year of chaos : Northern Ireland on the brink of Civil War, 1971-72 / Malachi O'Doherty.
Hold note	

were popular as people became more wary of going into town to socialise. The government also raised the demand for illicit booze by closing pubs when there was trouble, acting on the shallow theory that violence on the street grew out of excessive drinking, being blind to any suggestion that bad government was fundamental to the problem.

Another trope picked up by the media at the time was the idea of the 'long hot summer'. Rioting, they presumed, was 'recreational'. And there was something in that, but as a comprehensive theory it didn't explain why people were gathering to fight the army on the streets of Belfast but not in Liverpool or Hull.

There was a buzz about the city.

Those who had served their six-month sentences for disorderly behaviour, with two months' remission, were received back with fascination for their stories about prison life. Families had parties for boys coming home or getting out on parole, and the parish priest and the boys' teachers would call at the house to affirm their regard for them and their belief in their innocence.

I remember one man telling me about his brother home from jail. 'He forgets to shut the bog door when he's having a shite, he's so used now to doing it into a bucket in front of his cellmate.'

I had sent books and magazines to friends in jail and some of this reading material had been turned away as too radical. They told me that the prison library was full of cheap novels, westerns and crime thrillers. I visited the prison and sat in the musty waiting area with other friends and relatives of prisoners.

There was a display cabinet there of inmates' handiwork, little purses made of leather, cut and punched and stitched. None of it was very impressive. In those days prisoners wore a cheap brown uniform made of a cloth like rough muslin and had their hair cut short.

I had a column in a local weekly newspaper at that time but I did not write about the forthcoming revolution or the coteries in the bars planning manifestos and rallies. I wrote about the disco scene, the teenage angsts around love and male rivalry. I was trying to be funny. There might have been a revolution on the streets but I was more interested in being part of the sexual revolution that we were only reading about.

Some of the people who joined the discussions then were serious paramilitaries, though they had not done much at this stage. If Pat O'Kane, as suspected, had killed the three Scottish soldiers, he was likely to be an exception in the IRA at that time, having perhaps killed before in Aden or Cyprus where he had served as a British soldier. We were at the start of a period of trouble that would last for three decades, at a time when few, if any, of those who would drive that violence had taken another's life.

Like Beano Niblock, they were experimenting with bombs, and sometimes those bombs would blow up on them and cut their revolutionary careers horribly short. Count the IRA dead in the first years of the Troubles and you will see that half of them died in accidents, premature explosions or shooting accidents.

One of them was a boy I had been to school with, Tony Henderson. At twelve, Tony and I were friends at a summer school in Donegal, sent away to an Irish-speaking area for three and a half weeks to learn the language through stern lessons and absorption. He and I were the homesick ones, the children in the group, the ones who didn't understand the dirty jokes of the big boys. At fifteen, Tony was a wee hard man in winklepicker shoes who said fuck a lot. At sixteen, he was drinking from a bottle of beer on the street. He was taking on the trappings of gruff manhood as fast as he could and scowling at my warm greeting perhaps because it reminded him of his softer youth. And at twenty, he was a member of the IRA getting a military funeral, with a colour party of boys in berets and tunics marching in step on each side of his cortège. He can't have done much to warrant the military honours since the war had hardly begun.

In those days a family home might be a bomb-making factory. Thomas McCool and two other IRA men were making a bomb in his home in Derry in June 1970. He was mixing sodium chlorate with petrol or paraffin. McCool and Joe Coyle died in the house when the blast ripped through them, perhaps killing them before they could be conscious of the mistake that had triggered it. One of the men survived another eleven days. McCool's daughters were upstairs in bed at the time. Carol was four years old. Bernadette was nine. They died of their injuries within hours, probably never having had a moment's comprehension of how stupid their father had been.

McCool had been in the IRA in the fifties and wasn't new to having inflammable materials in his home. In 1957 he was arrested and charged with possessing guns, ammunition, grenades and explosives, according to the tribute written for him by the IRA in a catalogue of the dead, *Tírghrá*.[1] He had refused to recognise the court as having a legitimate right to try him and was sentenced then to twelve years' imprisonment; he was out five years later after the IRA ended the border campaign in 1962.

The tribute to him says that serious rioting had broken out after the arrest of Bernadette Devlin, an independent MP and civil-rights campaigner, for her part in the 1969 riots. Tommy and Joe Coyle had gone to Tommy's house to make petrol bombs.

Joe Coyle is remembered in *Tírghrá* as a keen gardener who bred budgies. He was in Tommy McCool's house 'preparing to resist British incursions with the only means available'.

Tommy Carlin, the other IRA man who died there, 'used to make and sell toffee apples and clove rock from the kitchen'. This experience had perhaps given him more confidence in his cookery skills than was appropriate in the circumstances. *Tírghrá* says: 'Even as he lay dying from the severe burns caused by the explosion and fire, he managed to retain his sense of humour.' Some achievement after incinerating two little girls.

Tommy McCool's diligence as a bomb maker earned him a hero's regard from the IRA. That he might have shown more concern for his children than to be making a bomb in their home didn't taint that regard. If the IRA didn't show as much reverence for the members who blew themselves up as it did for those whose bombs did what was expected of them then the lists of the honoured martyrs of those years would not be even half as long. Eight members of the Provisional IRA and

one member of the Officials died in accidents between the
start of the Troubles and the introduction of internment in
August 1971. They blew themselves up or crashed their cars
or took a bullet in a training exercise. The British army was,
at this stage, a little less successful in reducing IRA numbers,
having killed six of them.

*

Tony Rosato was an exception in that he got involved in the
republican movement while studying at Ruskin College, an
adult education institute affiliated to Oxford University. He
had been active in other protests. Indeed, when republicans
were marching in Easter 1966 to commemorate the 1916
Easter Rising which triggered the war for independence,
Tony thought there were more important concerns to deal
with. He preferred to join one of the Aldermaston marches
demanding unilateral nuclear disarmament.

'The fiftieth anniversary? We considered that bullshit.
That was nationalist politics. We were internationalists. More
interested in the Vietnam War and CND [Campaign for Nuclear
Disarmament]. We couldn't take seriously the politics here.
We had moved on from the old sectarianism.'

He involved himself in the Oxford Union and got a political
lesson from Gerry Fitt, the Republican Labour MP for West
Belfast, when he picked him up in a taxi to bring him to a
debate. This was shortly after the rioting in Derry when the
police attacked a civil-rights march. Fitt had been one of those
struck by a police baton and had appeared on television with
blood streaming down his face.

Tony recalls, 'In the taxi, Fitt put a plaster on his head so that he could point to it during a speech and say, "This is British democracy." Over a wound that had long healed.'

While in Oxford Tony attended meetings of a Sinn Féin group in Cowley, in the east of the city. When he returned to Ireland the Cowley group told him to report to headquarters in Dublin rather than to the IRA in the North. There he met Roy Johnson, one of the strategists for the Official IRA, from which the Provisionals had broken away, averse to their socialist politics.

'Johnson said he would like me to establish a republican club at Queen's University in Belfast.'

And that's what he did. This attracted visits from leading members of the Provisional IRA trying to persuade his members to defect to them but he stayed with the rump of the original organisation, now to be called the Officials or, more colloquially, the stickies or the sticks. This wasn't because they had 'stuck' with the old leadership but because their commemorative Easter lilies in 1970 had adhesive backs.

'My wife at the time was a girl from South Derry so I was well in with the South Derry IRA and all of those guys were Officials. My brothers were in People's Democracy.' PD, as it was called, was a student protest movement.

Tony's republican club raised money for the IRA.

'We organised two concerts at Queen's. At the first concert we made over three hundred quid and I brought it over to Ton Street to Liam McMillen [an IRA leader] and Liam McMillen said, "Fuck me, you've got this money without a gun." He told me that they had staged bank robberies and had got less money risking volunteers and guns.'

Tony and other members also joined a rifle club at the university.

'We were protected by the Ulster Defence Regiment up the Malone Road on target practice with subsidised ammunition, 2p a round.'

He gave lectures to the IRA volunteers including members of the Fianna like Anthony McIntyre. McIntyre recalls, 'Tony, like a lot of the sticks, looked like a teacher. They would always talk about this that and the other. We had the young rioter's view of the world. Fuck that talk about the economy and – it was all shit to us. Makes perfect sense now but then it didn't. Tony was always taking discussions, or he was at them, and it was all above our heads.'

*

While Tony Rosato, anticipating war, aligned himself with the Official Republican Movement, a young man from the Falls Road called Tommy Gorman went with the Provisionals. I first saw Tommy as an IRA man operating from a safe house across the street from my home, and I stayed out of his way. Like Anthony McIntyre, he was not strongly motivated by ideology and says now that he barely remembers his swearing-in ceremony, which was held by somebody called Montgomery in a house in Iveagh, a street off the Falls Road. He was twenty-three at the time.

He did want political change and a united Ireland but says even now that the value of the IRA campaign was that it would help to illustrate for people that they lived in an unfree society. Had the civil-rights demands been met, this suggests, that would have been enough for him.

He says, 'My reasoning was that we had tried protest and peaceful means and getting our balls beat in and that was it. I joined the IRA then. We had gone as far as we could with the civil-rights protesting.'

The Provisional movement was much more doctrinaire in its public declarations than were new recruits like Gorman. Billy McKee, a senior founding member in Belfast, was a Mass-going catholic, one of the old regime who thought it was entirely appropriate to say the rosary at IRA gatherings. The united Ireland that the leadership of the time envisaged was one which was catholic and Gaelic. That leadership was affronted by the thinking of the Officials.

But while ideology defined the difference between the two IRAs of 1970, the trigger for the split had been their eagerness for war in the North. The Provisionals claimed that the Officials had left the catholic people undefended, as if they imagined that an even larger battle on the Falls Road in August '69 would have made catholic people safer.

The Provisionals' approach, at least in their propaganda, was founded on an understanding that the British government would concede defeat by a few hundred armed guerrilla fighters.

Tommy Gorman had been on the Falls Road during the rioting of August '69.

'The whole riot was going on and at one point I slipped and fell and I crept into the doorway of a shop. The cops were running up and they were firing their Sten guns into the ground. And I said to myself, what the fuck are they doing that for? But I learnt later that they shot into the ground so that if anyone was going to be hit by the bullets, they wouldn't be able to trace the bullet to any particular gun.' The theory sounds plausible, though another might be that the police were trying to scatter rioters with gunfire while reducing the risk of actually killing anyone.

And an alternative theory of revolution might argue that a long war of wearing down British morale would coax political concessions, and this is the theory that the later actions of the Provisionals, or provos, imply that they followed.

Tommy's family illustrates the diversity of the catholics in Belfast at that time. It was not a uniformly republican community yearning for a united Ireland. While Tommy joined the IRA, one of his brothers joined the Royal Ulster Constabulary and another, Charlie, joined the British army.

He says, 'Our Jack was in the RUC. Where we lived in Iveagh there were several policemen and there was one in particular our Jackie spoke with. Jackie was a good runner, and he said, "Jackie, you get in there and join the athletics club and stuff like that. It'll be good for you." And he joined it because he was a great runner and that was his life.'

Jack Gorman's membership of the police force unnerved the RUC more than the IRA. Tommy says that a police station in Keady, County Armagh, put up a wanted poster for him, [Tommy] and that the poster warned that he might be disguised as a police officer, wearing his brother's uniform.

'He wasn't provo minded. He married a protestant woman. He didn't know what I was up to.'

Tommy says he was hardly aware of the difference between the Officials and the Provisionals.

'I was working. Somebody said, would you make bombs? I

said there's no problem. I was the only one volunteered to do them. I had no fear of them. We were always running about trying to do something because there was still a shortage of weapons. You did what you could. That was it. It was very quiet at that time. We were trying to get things done in the hope of getting some fucking weaponry.'

That weaponry was coming.

*

As it became clearer that the backdrop of murder and explosions would be part of our lives into the future, I felt a sickening disappointment. Anthony McIntyre says it was exciting. Beano Niblock and Tommy Andrews had found purpose in their lives at the age at which one looks for purpose. They were going to war.

I had already found purpose and the prospect of fulfilling it was being taken away from me. The city was becoming inaccessible. The prospect of having a career, learning the job in a peaceful context, was dying. Ironically, the job I wanted to do was journalism and journalists from around the world would come into Belfast to see the rioting and the aftermath of bombings and report from their hotels, but I was too young to brave the world in that way, too inept still as a journalist to be much use anyway.

I woke each morning to an anxiety that I had to shake off, and the only way to shake off anxiety was to get busy. Easy enough for McIntyre or Niblock who fancied a riot, Eddie Kinner who had to go and hold up a policeman and steal his gun, Tony Rosato who had a class to take or money to raise for the cause.

I would be a cub reporter with fillers to write, stories from provincial papers to rework into the style of our paper, this between bomb scare evacuations and startling news reports that would enliven the other journalists round the newsroom table.

I had grown up within a context that I had presumed was stable and enduring. It wasn't a very interesting one: a large family, the Catholic Church, a fairly drab education, a housing estate on the edge of an industrial city, fields to play in and summers that returned every year. When the trappings of war are all around you in a place you thought you knew as different, when there is real danger that if you go to work you may be injured or killed by a bomb or that someone might step out in front of you and shoot you, you hardly feel you have the language even to voice your horror, for those words belong to the comics you read, the films on television. You don't normally use those words in the same space in which you count your change for a bus ticket, shiver in icy rain or kiss a girl at a gable wall.

What had changed? Everything had changed. I woke in the morning to a vague anxiety that crystallised into fuller realisation that this wasn't the world I knew. Nothing in my past had prepared me to live like this, though these were the streets I had always known – only now there was a barricade on the corner and soldiers on the main road in their armoured vehicles, the box-like 'Pigs' and big Saracens which were almost like tanks. And the news said that a boy just like me was found in a back alley with a bullet in his head.

And even still, *Coronation Street* was on the telly, like a taunt.

Internment

Internment had been planned for. The anticipated date for its introduction had been 15 September 1971 or thereafter. A soldier I met on my travels once challenged me on my use of the word 'raid' to describe the army invasion of housing estates around Belfast for the mass arrests – five weeks earlier than planned – on 9 August. The term used in an official document, stamped 'Secret' but now available through the Public Record Office of Northern Ireland, is 'swoop'.

That document, entitled 'Contingency Plan for Internment',[1] outlines the thorough administrative preparations that were under way.

Arrests were to be made by the police with the support of the army. The hope was that the first 'swoop' would capture between 300 and 350 men, though the document warned of the prospect of as few as fifty actually being caught.

Accommodation was being prepared for these initial 'detainees' and their 'custodians'. They would be detained first and then either charged, released or have internment orders issued against them. The accommodation would be in Armagh Prison, where eighty-five prisoners could be taken in at seventy-two hours' notice, though prisoners would have to be lodged first at Crumlin Road Gaol in Belfast.

The document adds: 'There will be room in "HMS Maidstone" for 150 detainees or internees at 48 hours' notice. This will give time for troops to be moved out.' Soldiers would be ejected from their bunks and moved elsewhere so that the people they had arrested would be able to use them. 'Within a further fortnight accommodation can be provided for a total of 300, but only on a short-term basis.'

The army and police were to be further inconvenienced. 'In addition, up to 100 arrested persons can be accommodated initially in local police and army guardrooms, or at Ballykelly [an army base].' These places are referred to as interrogation centres.

A 'provisional list' of detainees had been prepared. The diligent civil servant who compiled this plan may have noted the pun, most of those on the list being suspected members of the Provisional IRA, though also of the Official IRA and other groups like People's Democracy. No loyalists were to be arrested at this stage.

As many as possible of the detainees were to be 'dealt with' at interrogation centres. Others would be distributed between prisons and the prison ship HMS *Maidstone* while a camp at Long Kesh outside Belfast was being prepared for them.

What this suggests to me is that, aside from being an ill-conceived idea, internment was rushed through, six weeks ahead of the intended time, without the material preparations having been in place.

Someone had panicked. I suspect that the Stormont government foresaw a possible escalation of violence in Derry around a loyalist Apprentice Boys parade scheduled for 12 August and felt it could not ban the parade without simultaneously moving strongly against the IRA to placate any sense of an injustice being inflicted on the Loyal Orders.

When it came, it came quickly and before preparations were complete.

The adjutant of the Ulster Defence Regiment based at Ballykinlar camp in County Down was summoned back from leave to find that a Royal Artillery regiment had arrived overnight to build an interrogation centre. Soldiers had erected a perimeter fence around much of his compound and an officer was demanding keys to several buildings. According to John Potter's book on the UDR, *A Testimony to Courage*,[2] when the adjutant refused to give them up soldiers simply broke in and took over.

The contingency plan set out that the Ministry of Home Affairs in Belfast would be responsible for the accommodation of detainees held in the prisons and would not require extra staffing. Those held in the *Maidstone* would be the responsibility of the Ministry of Defence (MOD). The hutted camp at Long Kesh, when it was ready for internees, would be provided by the MOD at a rent to be negotiated by the Commissioner of Valuation and the Lands' Officer. The Ministry of Home Affairs would be responsible for paying the agreed rent, building the perimeter fences and other installations and returning it to the MOD in a fit condition when it was no longer needed.

The plan also noted that no action would be required internationally. The European Commission of Human Rights, part of the Council of Europe, recognised the right of a signatory government to introduce internment during an emergency. That confidence would be challenged later. The government of the Irish Republic had already decided not to intern terrorist suspects because it thought that opt-out from normal human rights standards did not apply.

Internment would be directed only at republicans for this could be justified on the grounds that they sought to destroy the state. At this point there seemed to be no legal basis for interning loyalists who had no such intention.

This was made clear in a letter dated 18 August 1971 to Assistant Chief Constable David Johnston from the Government Security Unit at Stormont. The author said it would not even be legal to intern known members of the IRA who were not active: 'the Minister will want to justify a decision to intern on the grounds that the person being interned has taken part in an armed conspiracy and that if he were to remain at large he would be a threat not merely to law and order but to the security of the State.'[3]

The 'Contingency Plan for Internment' recognised that the government would have to facilitate International Red Cross inspections of Long Kesh and prepare itself for petitions to be lodged to the European Commission of Human Rights.

And that covered nearly everything, except for a brief paragraph at the end of the document:

Apart from international pressures and the reactions of Parliament and the news media, there will remain two possibilities –

1. demonstrations and riots, and

2. a stepping-up of terrorist activity.

Contingency plans will be needed for both these eventualities.

That's the part they should have given more thought to.

*

They came in their armoured cars into housing estates in cities and towns. They kicked in front doors, charged upstairs and dragged men from their beds.

The first internment raids against IRA suspects on 9 August 1971 lifted 337 men.

Amnesty International's first report on injustices in the United Kingdom, published two months later, was its investigation into the conduct of the police and the army during those raids and their treatment of the arrested. They rarely gave men more than five minutes to get ready, hug their wives and children, use the toilet. There was a practical reason for this haste. The Provisional IRA had grown rapidly in recent months and was now well armed so raiding parties had reason to fear being fired on.

The Amnesty report looked at the cases of twelve of the original detainees lifted on that first day. It said, 'Certain of the older (over 60 years) men in this group were brutalised to such a degree that they could not properly walk or speak upon arrival at prison.' The report describes how the 'prison' was usually a gymnasium or an exercise hall. Soldiers confiscated the shoes of arrested men and kept them waiting for hours and then made them run 'across rough ground strewn with broken glass' to the vehicles that would take them to Crumlin Road Gaol.

According to the report, 'The beatings and verbal abuse in these cases were clearly of such an unsophisticated type that it cannot be supposed that they were employed to ease the future extortion of information from the detainees.'

This was just soldiers enjoying themselves as hoodlums would, though some thought went into the abuse.

One of the men broke out in a rash after being beaten and was told in front of the other men, by someone claiming to be a doctor, that he had a venereal disease. He then had his whole body shaved.

But there were more serious cases than these. Some men were dealt with more systematically and are still represented by Amnesty in their ongoing efforts to get acknowledgement that they were tortured. Campaigners call them 'the hooded men'. They were beaten and forced to do exercises at Palace Barracks, where Tony Rosato was held when he was arrested later. These appear to have been men whom the army was more confident were actual IRA men, as indeed some were. One of the amusements the soldiers had with them was to make them run on the spot while urinating.

But if there was special treatment for the known 'players', this implies an understanding that most of those arrested were less of a threat.

Then on the morning of 11 August, before dawn, soldiers handcuffed the men, put hoods over their heads and took them into helicopters. They led some of the prisoners to believe that they were to be thrown out when they were high in the air.

There were reports at the time that some men were indeed thrown out of helicopters just a few feet off the ground while believing that they were over the Irish Sea, but this detail, though often repeated since, is not included in the Amnesty report.

At the interrogation centre they were brought to, soldiers ordered the men to strip naked and to put on overalls and hoods. They made them stand spreadeagled against a wall, beat them if they moved or fell and all the while subjected them to 'a strange noise, likened by some to the hissing of steam, by others to the noise of an operating air compressor'. Perhaps the rhythm that some detected in the 'white noise' was their own heartbeats amplified by the stress.

They were sparsely fed and one of them lost thirteen pounds in weight in the week of his interrogation.

*

I woke up on the morning of the introduction of internment to a bright summer's day with an almost carnival atmosphere in the air, as young men eagerly mobilised for rioting. The main raids had all finished by then.

I saw men in vans bring crates of petrol bombs to groups of rioters preparing to fight the army. I spotted Tommy Gorman at Riverdale Park South with a group of young men. I knew he wasn't from the area and assumed that he was an IRA man posted there to organise a riot. He was an unlikely looking street fighter, in a clean and pressed striped shirt, and had the appearance of someone who was well cared for at home. He was in his twenties but was small, like me, and had a soft boyish manner about him. In no other context would I have thought him fearsome. I knew some of the other young men who had joined the IRA as snarly, abrasive types, best avoided. I walked through the little mob to cross Finaghy Road to the shops and walking back saw an army vehicle come up the road. I ran back home where my sister Brid was and heard the first firings of rubber bullets.

Brid was frantic and suddenly boys fleeing from the army were running through our garden. I had no impulse to help them but I was afraid they would draw the soldiers after them and endanger us all. I opened the living room window and roared at them to fuck off. Anthony McIntyre and Tommy Gorman will tell stories about how people left their doors open so that he and his rioter friends could run through and out the back to safety. He would not have found my door open for him.

Then I heard two shots, distinctly rifle fire.

The soldiers appear not to have been on a mission to arrest anybody. They had been passing through and had been invited to have a ruck and they had taken it, killed someone and moved on.

The boy they shot was Frank McGuinness.

Tommy Gorman says, 'God love him. I was standing right beside him and I thought he was only winged. We lifted him up. The wound was just like a wee slit here [under the arm].

I says it's OK, but apparently it was inside him and rattled everywhere. That confounded everything. You say to yourself, this is it. That was the first time I had seen somebody killed. It was frightening. And I was angry as well.'

I knew Frank McGuinness. We lived on neighbouring streets. I didn't know him so well that I had been out drinking with him, but when we fell in alongside each other walking up the street we chatted.

Tommy Gorman, unlike Frank, was a known IRA man and thinks the bullet might have been intended for him.

'I wouldn't blow myself up to say that maybe the soldier was trying to shoot me. I knew the family but Frank wasn't in the IRA. Just like all the other kids.'

*

Anthony McIntyre went rioting that day again, back to the Falls Road.

'I was in the Fianna at the time but I went over on my own bat. I was with a friend, Noel, and the two of us rioted all day. We were on a lorry that was set across McDonnell Street at the corner of Albert Street and when brits went past in Saracens we were hammering them. We were told by the brits that afternoon – one read out that rioters will be shot and we threw bottles at him as he was announcing this. In the course of the day tiredness kicked in and we headed back to the Ormeau Road, quite knackered.'

Beano Niblock and his loyalist friends had a quiet day.

'I lived right beside the Short Strand, at the bottom of the Woodstock Road just before it joined the Short Strand.

I lived in Hamilton Place. My mum said, there's something happening here. I went out round the corner. All the lights had been knocked out. The troops were moving into the top of Short Strand.

'It was a great thing to me. Up till then it had seemed that the police were ineffective. Strong-arm tactics were needed and this seemed to be it. In hindsight it was probably the worst thing they ever done because it was a recruitment drive for the IRA.'

There was warfare all over Belfast that week.

One night, Anthony McIntyre, at fourteen years old, under Official IRA orders, joined a major battle in the Markets area of Belfast.

'I was involved in what became known as the battle of Inglis's Bakery. The whole IRA had it surrounded and a gun battle started. And I was with a guy called Vincent Robinson. I was sent along to assist him as a member of the Fianna. We were down beside the old scrapyard.'

Robinson was later shot dead by the IRA.

'Vincent was probably only seventeen but I thought he was a big guy. He was armed and the two of us sat there all night with the gun battle going on all over the Markets. And we sat there at the barricade and he would have thrown a bomb in the event that they would breach our end.'

That gun battle became part of the mythology of the Official IRA. In their newspaper, the *United Irishman,* they claimed that they had 'carried out an action for nine hours, inflicting several fatalities on the enemy while suffering none'.[4]

The army recorded no losses.

McIntyre and Robinson had sat by a barricade all night listening to the gunfire and contributed nothing to the battle itself. One of the IRA men, Joe McCann, posed for a photographer called Ciaran Donnelly during the action and the picture has since been widely reproduced in histories of the period.

Only one person is known to have been killed that night in the proximity of the shooting and that was twenty-one-year-old William McKavanagh, a catholic who was not a member of the IRA. Daylight revealed his body next day in McAuley Street, in the same area as the battle. He had run from soldiers who had tried to detain him and one of them shot him in the back.

Most of the deaths in the days after the first internment raids were in Ballymurphy where there had been a huge amount of gunfire. Soldiers killed six people there on the first day. One was a priest, Hugh Mullan, who had gone out onto waste ground to help a wounded man. He was brought down by rifle fire from the roof of a block of flats in the neighbouring Springmartin estate. Young Frank Quinn, just nineteen, died beside him and a fifty-year-old mother of eight, Joan Connolly, was shot dead from the Henry Taggart Memorial Hall by soldiers billeted there during a gun battle; she had been looking for her children. Daniel Teggart and Joseph Murray died there too. Mr Teggart was a forty-four-year-old catholic and the father of ten children. Joseph Murray was forty-one and had nine children.

Years later, their cases were combined with other killings by the army in the following days into a campaign for recognition of what was called the 'Ballymurphy Massacre'. That none of the dead were armed suggests strongly that soldiers were careless or even wilfully murderous.

Others who died on that first day included a nineteen-year-old soldier called Malcolm Hutton. He was in the Green Howards regiment and was shot by an IRA sniper in Ardoyne in north Belfast, where there was also a massive amount of rioting and population displacement. Soldiers shot and killed a sixteen-year-old boy called Leo McGuigan. He had been near a house from which the IRA had fired on soldiers.

When McGuigan and a wounded friend were being taken away in a car to hospital, a soldier lined his sights on them and was deterred by passers-by from firing again.

A soldier shot Sarah Worthington, a protestant woman of fifty. She was inside her house at Velsheda Park in Ardoyne during the gun battle.

Another soldier shot and killed fourteen-year-old Des Healey at a riot on the Stewartstown Road, about a mile from where Frank McGuinness was killed. And, outside Belfast, an army sniper killed thirty-one-year-old Hugh Herron. The IRA killed Winston Donnell, a local part-time soldier in the recently formed Ulster Defence Regiment. This was at Clady on the Tyrone–Donegal border.

Fifteen deaths in a single day was carnage on a scale not previously experienced during the Troubles. By 12 August the army around Northern Ireland had shot dead nineteen people, ten of them in Ballymurphy.

And none of the killings by soldiers are free of the suspicion that they were unwarranted, even criminal.

For example, William Ferris, a protestant, died on the Crumlin Road. He was the back-seat passenger in a car, coming home from work. The car had been approaching a checkpoint and the driver appears to have been confused about whether he was being ordered to stop or to proceed. He made the wrong call and a soldier shot at the car. The counsel for the army at an inquest said that it had been a 'tragic error' and one for which the soldier who fired the shot will 'feel very deeply'.

Confusion about cars led to two other killings. John Beattie was only seventeen and driving his father's van. Soldiers claimed to have thought the van was giving cover to snipers. By contrast, Norman Watson, a fifty-three-year-old draper, was shot dead in Armagh at the wheel of his car beside his wife because the soldiers, by their version, thought nearby gunfire was giving cover to the car. And it does appear that cars were used in support of snipers, as when one IRA gunman killed Paul Challenor, a twenty-two-year-old soldier in the Royal Horse Artillery. On that occasion a car flashed its lights to warn off civilians just before the gunman struck.

There were also in that week two apparently blatant sectarian murders of protestants by the IRA. These were the murder of William Atwell, killed by a nail bomb thrown into the Mackie's factory, and William Stronge in the Oldpark area, who was shot by a sniper while helping neighbours to move out of their home to safety.

Angelina Fusco, later a top BBC producer in News and Current Affairs, was just a child then, a catholic in a street with protestant neighbours, living less than a mile from Tommy Andrews, and remembers the time before the riots.

'We had, I suppose, an idyllic childhood. It was a cul de sac street. You could walk to school at St John's in Colinward Street. We played on the hills behind us. My aunt lived with her children in Springfield Park so basically we spent summers roaming the hills and collecting wild roses and making perfume and...'

And assuming that life would go on like that forever in Dunboyne Park.

The geography of the area was changing with the growth of new housing estates. After the upsurge of violence in '69 those estates had little chance of being well mixed. The pattern of violence would decide which fell to the protestants, which to the catholics.

Angelina recalls, 'We had an Orange Hall at the bottom of the street. I saw my daddy cine-filming parades and then the army coming onto the streets. He filmed those as well. And then we got a couple of calls to the house. I didn't understand them but the language was nasty. I told my mummy some of the words. I didn't really understand what bastards were, or fenians.'

But the Fuscos held out. Theirs was a nice middle-class home with a garden and a recent extension. It was their own, not a rental property. It was not easy to contemplate giving it up.

Angelina says, 'What was lovely about that street was that it was mixed. There was a policeman and somebody who used to put up a union flag on the twelfth of July. There were protestants and catholics and the houses were good houses.'

But other neighbours were deciding to leave.

'We had been away on holidays and had come back. Some

of our neighbours were moving out. I could see lorries and vans and heard a discussion between my mother and father but didn't understand it. My best friend in the street – her family started moving out and the children were there. One day there was virtually nobody in the street except us. I have a vague recollection of a row or discussion about whether we should go. And the other argument that this is my home and I am not leaving.'

But principles and legal deeds don't keep you safe.

*

Anne Tannahill, later an eminent publisher in Belfast, was a protestant living in a mixed area between the catholic and protestant parts of the Lenadoon estate. The Ulster Defence Association visited her and urged her to leave for her own safety. They told her they had a 'lovely wee house' for her in Monkstown.

She says, 'It was as if people thought it perverse to want to resist this deep polarisation and to stay with neighbours you knew and had befriended, if those neighbours were "the other sort".'

Angelina Fusco was too young to fully comprehend what was happening. She says she recognised the gunfire from the neighbouring estates because her father loved westerns.

'We were the last two children that I know who were in the street. All of a sudden my mum and dad said, "Let's go, let's go." So we ran out. It was dark. We ran across the street. We ran across the street to neighbours, Mr and Mrs McClean and the big collie dog, Rover. And we just ran across the street into the

Reaves's house. I didn't know where we were going. We went down behind their garden into the garden of the house at the front of the Springfield Road where my dad's car was. We got into the car. I think it was a white Viva. And we drove off in the dark of night. There was Mummy and Daddy, Mr McClean, Mrs McClean, Caroline and me and a big dog who was so hot and panting. This was really uncomfortable. And we ended up somewhere near Stockman's Lane in Andersonstown with some of Mr McClean's relatives.

'And basically that night completely changed and transformed my life. At the same time my aunts and uncle were being put out of Springfield Park. I had just had my eleventh birthday.'

At this time Anne Tannahill still lived in the Lenadoon estate on the westernmost part of west Belfast, below Black Mountain. This was an estate I had seen being built when I was at school in the sixties. It extended into beautiful countryside we had often passed through as children in our walks to Colin Glen or up towards the quarry at the top of the mountain. The estate had been conceived of as an experiment in bringing catholic and protestant families together as neighbours. Anne was a protestant.

She recalls, 'We were very happy with the house and we believed in the experiment, feeling that the old ghettoisation had to change if there was to be any progress. We got on extremely well with our neighbours, both catholic and protestant (our next-door neighbours on both sides were catholic). We all had young children who played together and most of us thought it was a pity when they inevitably went to separate schools when they were five.'

Whatever ambition the Housing Trust had to merge the historically divided communities, few, if any, at this stage were thinking of merging the schools.

When sectarian violence erupted in August 1969, to such an extent that the army had to be mobilised on the streets, some of the more level-headed catholics and protestants of Lenadoon tried to stick together.

'When Bombay Street was burnt out and things got very tense in our area (young lads attacking each other etc.), the catholic and protestant men walked the streets together to break up situations before they got out of hand. Some of the women, including myself, also worked voluntarily with the refugees in the St Oliver Plunkett School on the Glen Road, collecting blankets and clothes for them and running story-time sessions for the youngest children.'

Anne and her husband Brian tried to stay on, as much to resist the consolidation of sectarian communities as to preserve a home they loved.

That night in Lenadoon after a tense day of enduring the rattle of gunfire nearby and in the distance, Brian went to a meeting in the community hall with their neighbours to support each other.

Anne says, 'We woke the next morning to find that some of the protestants who had been the most vocal at the meeting about not moving were already loaded up and gone or going, helped by the local loyalists, who had loaded their furniture onto flatbed lorries, wrecked the empty houses and drove them away, singing, I kid you not, "We shall not be moved".

'There followed a week when we and a few protestant neighbours held grimly on, wanting to stay in the mixed area we believed in. This in spite of loyalists coming to the door and offering to move us to a Housing Trust house in Mallusk. We knew such houses were only empty because catholic families had been forced out and we kept refusing. On the other hand, there were quite a few refugee women with children at their skirts knocking and asking when we were moving. When we said we weren't going, they would say incredulously, "But we heard you were protestants!" and look nervously over their shoulders at men in black leather jackets (who were using whistles, not guns, but we were certain were IRA).'

Even the British army expected Anne and Brian to move out.

'During that same week, an officer and two soldiers came to say there was going to be an offensive up into our area the next day and they "wouldn't be able to discriminate". We decided we had to move and next day tried to get the Housing Trust to rehouse us. They said they couldn't. At that stage they had been completely overwhelmed and had more or less thrown in the towel. We were at our wits' end and only after Brian and the presbyterian minister having a sit-in in the Trust's Seymour Hill office did they relent and give us the keys to an eighth-floor flat on the River Road.

'The next day we moved in chaotic circumstances. Furniture removers had been refusing to come to the area since internment day and there was no way we were going to ask the UDA for help. A friend of ours, Harry Carson, had a very small van and he and Brian made numerous journeys to the flat while me and my father and sister hastily scrambled together the stuff to

be moved. During this time, about five different women came
to the door to ask if they could have the house. Law-abiding
to the last, I phoned the Housing Trust to ask them to send
someone for the keys and was told there was no way they were
going to go "up there" and that I should make the decision as
to who got the house. When the next woman knocked, I told
her the house was hers once we had cleared it. She thanked
me and God and asked if she could put one of her chairs in
our hall (I assume to establish her right of possession).

'I went on the next trip to the flat and when I got back the
woman and her children were in the house in the middle of all
the chaos. It turned out my father had taken pity on them sitting
on the garden wall and had invited them in. I was raging at him
but it turned out for the best, as she heard us worrying about how
we were going to move the final items, which were too big for
the van. She said her brothers had a bigger van and got them to
deliver our stuff to the flat. They were petrified to be anywhere
near loyalist Seymour Hill, but they did it in double quick time.
When we were finally leaving, several of our catholic neighbours
came to us and we all wept on each other's necks.'

There was a massive increase in violence after internment.
A measure that had been meant to curtail and deplete the IRA
had equipped it with a further argument for its legitimacy and
an opportunity to make the governments in London and Belfast
look brutal and incompetent. All the republican militants had
to do to invalidate the whole project was to demonstrate that
their organisation had survived the effort to close it down. The
Provisionals made their point by staging a press conference
in west Belfast for their chief of staff.

This was the first time most of us had seen Joe Cahill. He sat at a table in a secondary school, a man of fifty in a cloth cap, looking like a docker or a barman, dressed for the dog track or the bookies and not for war, with television cameras, photographers and reporters around him. The most wanted man in the country had been able to summon the media to meet him without the security forces knowing. And he told them that not a tenth of the men detained had been members of his organisation.

But the political damage was not limited to the elevation of the IRA. The constitutional nationalists of the Social Democratic and Labour Party (SDLP), on the day before the emergence of Joe Cahill, had called a campaign of civil disobedience in protest against internment. A component of that would be a rent and rates strike.

My own family joined in. We had a printed notice taped to a downstairs window. I don't know how my parents managed when the money they owed was called in two years later, when the SDLP was in a short-lived power-sharing executive. I hope they had been putting some aside.

A secret report to the taoiseach (the head of government in the Irish Republic) on 16 October 1971, now in the National Archives of Ireland, claimed that political leadership in catholic areas of Belfast and Derry had shifted to the IRA. I think this overstated the changed climate. The SDLP would, for another thirty years, garner more votes in those areas than Sinn Féin or supporters of the IRA. The name of the person making the report has been redacted in the archives but it must have been somebody of significance to be reporting directly to the taoiseach.

The writer said that 'since the visit last month of [redacted] the minority population [i.e. the catholics] in Belfast and Derry had come under IRA control. There was now little chance of weaning away support from the IRA, in those areas, in favour of non-violent political leaders.'[5]

This report writer's sources blamed the army for being insensitive to complaints of brutal behaviour. 'Its leadership had changed from an independent man who had standards and an appreciation of the limitations of military solutions (Farrar-Hockley) to a mere carrier-out of orders (Ford).' This refers to Major General Anthony Farrar-Hockley who had been commander of land forces in Northern Ireland and had been superseded by General Robert Ford.

The writer said, 'Army conduct on the ground had become progressively intolerable.' Access to senior officers had now ended and complaints were being taken by juniors and not followed up. In effect, the army had given up caring what people thought of them.

One of the early detainees was Tony Rosato. With the first wave of raids in catholic areas he had gone on the run but he says that the Belfast Officer Commanding (OC) of the Official IRA, Liam McMillen, ordered him to go back home.

'Most of what I was doing was vetting new applicants and intelligence gathering. There had to be six seminars on political awareness that they had to do and if anyone was overtly sectarian they were out.' These were the lectures that Anthony McIntyre thought so little of. He perhaps hadn't realised that he was being vetted.

One night Rosato was at home with his wife in Sandymount

Street in Belfast. His brother Eamonn was also there and two other women. Special Branch raided the house and took them all away. He had been trained in what to expect and how to respond to it.

'We were taken away for three days. There was an interesting series of interrogations. I knew as much about the interrogation technique as the bloody idiots who were dealing it out. Basically it was no sleep, deprivation, standing against a wall, sometimes sitting facing a wall, sound treatment, all that. Beatings now and again.'

Another detainee called Liam Shannon was beside him at the wall. Shannon had been reported missing and no acknowledgement had been made that he was in state custody.

Rosato says, 'He whispered his name to me. Someone came into the room and it was thump thump thump. Next thing I heard was a click and Shannon was screaming. He was dragged out for interrogation. Some time after that someone came in behind me and I felt the cold steel of a gun barrel at the back of my head. And I thought, fuck they are going to do the same thing with me. I braced myself but there wasn't a click, there was an explosion. They fired a blank into the back of my head. My head hit the wall.'

He has been diagnosed as having post-traumatic stress disorder but regards the alertness the condition leaves him with as an asset. 'The cops didn't realise the favour they did me. My reaction speed from that day has increased.'

The behaviour of his army and police interrogators, as he recalls it, was bizarre and childish.

'On one occasion they held my brother against a wall and they were sticking pins in his back. I thought that was terrible. On another occasion I was brought into a mess room where soldiers were eating. I was given a paper tissue to dry plastic knives and forks and paper plates that these bastards are eating off. The paper disintegrates and these characters are effing and blinding at me, look what you've done to our drying cloth.

'Two soldiers came over and produced a porn mag. Look at the tits on that, as good as Ann Marie's (my wife). They were trying to provoke me into thumping one of them but that incident really jarred me.'

He believes that the police were more interested in friends of his who were members of the Provisional IRA. And though the two factions were at odds with each other, and had feuded, they sometimes co-operated. One group had had weaponry but no appropriate ammunition and another had ammunition but no guns to fire it, so they made an exchange to suit both of them. They had just made that swap before the raid on Rosato's home.

In Palace Barracks one of the interrogators introduced himself as Sergeant Pine. 'That's what he called himself. You go into an interrogation room. You are marched there by a uniformed cop. You are standing there. Sergeant Pine says, why are you standing? Because if you try to sit down you are thumped by all the other guys. I said I was always told to stand and after three nights without sleep it's difficult. He says, Tony, sit down.

'This is how he started; let me tell you something, if there was an all Ireland tomorrow, I would be the first member of the

RUC to join the Garda Síochána [the Irish Republic police].

'So he was presenting himself as the intellectual cop.'

Rosato, proud of his training, tried to demonstrate that he had some control over the dynamic between them.

'You've no watch, the windows are blackened out. You are in a room with an interrogator and you let him feel comfortable. I said, Sergeant, what time is it?

'Oh, it's ten past three in the morning.

'I said, you're a liar. I could hear the Bangor train. That ended our conversation. The whole objective was to disorientate us.'

He and his brother Eamonn were released after a few days.

'My brother and I met at the reception area where we were led out. Next thing I am grabbed by these two thugs from Lurgan, Special Branch men. One of them had veins in his nose. "Right, Castlereagh Roundabout, twelve o'clock Saturday morning. You be there or you're fucked." This was standard, trying to turn people and make them into informers.'

He says that he and Eamonn were taken away in an unmarked police car and dropped off on the Shankill Road, a protestant area where at that time they were in some danger of being killed or beaten up by the likes of Tommy Andrews or Eddie Kinner if they spotted them.

Something similar happened to me around that time.

I had been with friends in a car in Ardoyne, a catholic area in north Belfast, looking for a party. We were stopped by a joint police and army patrol and I was taken in the back of a police vehicle while a soldier got into my friend's car and instructed him to drive to the Shankill, to a police station on Tennent Street. In the police Land Rover, one of the cops started prodding me. He was beside me and was poking something into me below the ribs. This seemed to me such a transparent attempt to provoke me to anger that I wondered if it had really worked on others. I wasn't angry but I was curious and wary. I felt that I was learning that a policeman in uniform might be not just more mischievous than I expected but also more stupid.

I said, 'I don't know why you are poking at me but please stop.' It was not the reaction he wanted. The others facing us gave him a disapproving look. I presume he was hoping that I would retaliate with an elbow and give him an excuse to get stuck into me.

At the station I met my friends. We were individually brought before a bored army officer, asked superficial questions and then released onto the Shankill. Fortunately, we had a car and could get out of the area quickly.

When Tony Rosato was released he was able to make media appearances to describe his treatment. He was a member of the Student Representative Council at Queen's University, 'so there was a whole machine ready to greet me when I got out. I got a few hours' sleep and then there were interviews arranged with the media at the Students' Union.'

The *Sunday Times* took up his story. 'A journalist asked me if I would be willing to swear my account to the commissioner of oaths. I had to go to McMillen [the Official IRA's Belfast OC] to get permission to do that because there was a policy of non-co-operation. McMillen said, Right.

'That changed everything for me. I was then a clear target for loyalists and I had to get out.'

So he was representing himself to the media as a totally innocent student who had been tortured by the police and army in their crackdown against the IRA yet he had sought the permission of the IRA to make his case. In fairness, he would argue that even as someone under IRA orders he was entitled to his basic human rights and should not have been tortured.

*

Internment had produced three grounds for massive disaffection between the catholic community and the British state. One was the suspension of human rights entailed in the internment policy, though this had supposedly been verified as consistent with the European Commission of Human Rights. The second was the readiness of soldiers to shoot people dead in situations where that did not seem reasonable, and the third was the brutality employed by police and soldiers in interrogation of detainees.

Interestingly, it was not until decades later that the shootings became a central focus of protest, and even then the campaign and subsequent inquiry focused only on the killings in Ballymurphy. It is difficult to explain why the killings should not have drawn more anger at the time and it probably comes down to the fact that innocent people shot dead in the street will not have the political backup that members of a paramilitary organisation will have.

The families of the dead were not able to organise their outrage, and perhaps, in some cases, did not want to. At a time when anger was leading to more killing, the innocent and the uninvolved might have felt under a moral onus to keep silent.

I don't know what I would have done if someone close to me had been shot dead by a soldier after a misunderstanding at a checkpoint. I would have blamed the soldier, disputed his right to open fire, but I would also have resented the paramilitaries stirring up the trouble that brought that reckless and heartless soldier onto the street in the first place.

Internment was also an irritant within the sectarian conflict, the acrimony between protestant and catholic communities. This was partly because much of the militant response to the army raids was in Ardoyne, on interfaces. Where I was, in Riverdale, there was no immediately adjacent protestant community that might join in the mayhem to attack catholics and burn them out of their homes. The tension was simply between the IRA and the army, with those like me who wanted no part of it staying indoors or getting out of town.

Another sectarian irritant was that no protestant loyalists were scooped in the first raids. This was despite the fact that loyalist activism had been increasing.

We have already heard from Tommy Andrews and Beano Niblock how they were attacking catholics. Beano Niblock remembers it well.

'By that stage, the fourteen year olds who were at the back of the crowd in '69 had pushed themselves forward and were more militant. I took part in that, intimidation, breaking windows, scratching cars. Throwing fireworks and shouting at people going to work and that. That was expected of you if you were part of the gang.'

We also know that the army and police knew the young people's identities so they presumably were acquainted with older loyalists around them and could have arrested them if they had chosen to.

On the more organised adult level, loyalism still expressed itself until then through vigilantism. Men patrolled the streets of their areas checking on the behaviour of strangers.

Sometimes these men were not excessively threatening.

Once my sister Brid asked me to accompany her to the Shankill Road to her boyfriend's home. I foolishly stood outside at a street corner while she was in the house. A man approached me and questioned me about what I was doing there, with a confident air of authority and the right to know who I was and what I was doing. My answers satisfied him and he left me alone after that.

But nationalists and the Irish government believed that the vigilantes were dangerous. John Hume, a leading member of the SDLP, picked up a rumour that the Northern Ireland prime minister Brian Faulkner had plans for them. Hume believed that Faulkner, who led the Ulster Unionist Party, was going to consult the British prime minister Edward Heath on a plan to legalise the vigilantes and give them a formal role.

The Irish Republic's Department of Foreign Affairs wrote to the British ambassador to protest. Department secretary Hugh McCann reported his action to the taoiseach: 'I emphasised the folly of any step which would give even the slightest cover of legitimacy to the Protestant vigilantes.' He believed that the catholics had every right to fear that such vigilantes would lead attacks on them and this 'in turn would lead to demands for creating similar forces in the Catholic areas'.[6]

None of this confirms that Faulkner did in fact propose to

'legitimise' the vigilantes, but clearly the Irish believed so and the ambassador in replying did not deny it.

Many of those angered by the internment arrests, the torture and the killings took their complaints to the Irish government. With Ireland partitioned into British and Irish territories the Irish government had no jurisdiction in Northern Ireland. When individual cases were brought before the taoiseach Jack Lynch he was advised by his own Department of Foreign Affairs to be cautious, to 'continue to attack the policy of internment on the broad front and not make representations in individual cases'.[7]

This may partly explain the failure to muster sufficient anger over the killing of civilians by the army. To take up one case as a clear murder of an innocent person but not another case about which they were less certain might have led the Irish into appearing to make unfounded distinctions between the guilt and innocence of victims. There was also a danger that they would only be representing people who had access to channels of protest or suggesting, by supporting only some, that internment was legitimate in the cases of other people whom they did not champion.

This briefing to the taoiseach's private secretary on 16 November 1971 is a clear warning that he should not allow himself to be manipulated by political activists, but from this distance in time it is striking that the language used, even internally, mirrors the analysis of the IRA itself, that Ireland should be a single jurisdiction. It not only avoids naming the northern state as Northern Ireland; it even avoids naming the Irish Republic, the country whose 'Foreign Affairs' interests the writer of the letter was employed to advance: '… as far as we know practically all internees are Irish citizens and it would not be right to differentiate between them and, in particular, to distinguish between 26-county and 6-county [Irish Republic and Northern Ireland] residents.'

The Irish Republic was in the curious position of seeking to defend the republican ideology and to criticise British measures against the IRA while wishing at the same time to dissociate itself from the IRA and to condemn its actions.

Consider that message to the British ambassador to head off any proposal from Faulkner that the vigilantes be legitimised. There is another issue raised in it, the question of whether the British are entitled to search vessels in Irish waters.

Hugh McCann's report says, 'The Ambassador then mentioned to me that he had received word from London that the British Navy might be undertaking some searches of vessels off the Northern coast shortly as there were two suspects in mind.'[8]

Presumably these 'suspects' were vessels that might have been bringing weaponry to the IRA, which would have been a concern to the Irish as well. Still, McCann's response would have heartened those gun runners: 'I immediately expressed the hope that London was not so foolish at this critical time to start resuming searches in Carlingford Lough or anywhere near our waters. The Ambassador assured me that this was not the case.'

The Irish would have difficulty getting the British government to accept that their primary interest was to stabilise the '6-county' state and to improve relations with Britain when

they couldn't even bring themselves to name the state that
was to be stabilised.

The Catholic Church in Northern Ireland was in a similar
bind. Three hundred and fifty priests had signed a letter to
the taoiseach protesting against the abuse of detainees by the
Northern Irish police, the RUC and the British army.

> We… are convinced that brutality, physical and mental
> torture and psychological pressures have been inflicted
> on men arrested under the Special Powers Act on the
> ninth of August and subsequently…
>
> We base our conviction on substantial medical evidence,
> on the testimony of priests who saw the injuries, and
> on the statements of men whose truthfulness is already
> known to us through our pastoral work.[9]

The letter said that 'the authorities' had yet to account for
why twelve men, including Liam Shannon, had gone missing for
periods. It continued: 'We call for a public, impartial, judicial
tribunal to expose the full truth of what has been done to
people arrested since August ninth under the Special Powers
Act, and to ensure the punishment of those responsible and
redress for the victims.'

So IRA suspects under detention were having their interests
defended by the Irish Republic and by the Catholic Church
and other nationalist parties. And this complexity in the
whole balance of interests within the mayhem was created by
internment.

It was impossible for nationalist parties, the Church and civil-rights activists to ignore the abuses by the state and the British army. Britain could not isolate the IRA by compromising civil rights and could not win full support from the Irish government or the other nationalist parties while suspects were detained without trial and beaten in custody, while civilians were being shot dead on the streets and soldiers absolved of those killings, and while the state was more equivocal about loyalist violence, even if, so far, it was a lesser threat.

One of Those Things That Happen in War

It took one man to carry the coffin of Angela Gallagher: her father. She was just eighteen months old. She could walk with the aid of the little trolley in which she pushed her doll around. She was behind that little trolley when she was going with her sister Paula to the shop on the corner. Paula was eight. They had been visiting their granny and she had given them money for sweets.

At the same time two men sat in a shiny grey Ford Cortina in nearby Iveagh Drive. These were small narrow streets hardly fit for the motor car. One of the men, dressed in a smart business suit, had a rifle. He got out on his own and placed himself in a concealed position, with a line of fire in mind.

It was a common event for British army foot patrols to move around the area. They were always on guard against possible attack. The sniper presumably wore that suit to look less like an urban terrorist. Bob Monkhouse once told a joke about how you recognise an officer in the IRA, by the gold braid on his donkey jacket. Brits who thought like that were easily deceived.

'I heard a big bang in my ear,' wee Paula said later. 'My duffle coat and dress swinged open. Something went through them.'

The bullet had ricocheted.

Paula tried to pick Angela up, but 'She was too heavy for me. I asked another girl to lift her. She carried her to the corner.'

The man in the business suit rushed back to the car. The driver was waiting with the engine running. They would be too easily hemmed in if they didn't move quickly. They drove out of the street, onto the Falls Road and headed west for less than a mile. They burnt the car in the Whiterock area. Witnesses told the police that the driver had a beard and that the man in the suit had wavy fair hair.

They had just killed a baby.

The country was outraged.

David Bleakley, the minister for community relations, said that those responsible should be treated 'like the lepers they are. They deserve neither comfort nor shelter – only cold contempt and utter rejection.' The taoiseach, Jack Lynch, said, 'Nothing – no motive, no ideal – can excuse this killing of the innocent or the innocents.' Like Bleakley, he made no allowance for Angela not having been the intended target. 'Cannot even this shameful act bring home to these men of violence the evil of the course they have taken? The sacrifice of this innocent life must surely convince them of the futility of their actions. The sympathy of the whole country goes out to the parents and family of this child.' Pope Paul VI said, 'We hope this innocent blood may be worthy to beseech from God a true and just reconciliation among the people.'

And when republicans sought to interject and remind people that this was an accident, the sort of thing that happens inevitably from time to time in a war, they were divided among themselves on whether or not that was the decent thing to say.

John Shaw of the Press Association had phoned Ruairí Ó Brádaigh, the president of Sinn Féin, at home – he was as easily contactable as that. Ó Brádaigh said the death of wee Angela was 'one of the hazards of urban guerrilla warfare... one of those unfortunate accidents.'

Apparently even his own comrades on the IRA army council were angered by those words though they were literally true. If the IRA was going to continue with its campaign it had to accept that it would kill innocent men, women and children down the years and it had surely reconciled itself to that inevitability.

Seán MacStíofáin was one of the leaders of the Provisional IRA, now its chief of staff, and was considered a fanatic. He was presumed to be a bit more ardent because he was English and had more to prove. His original name was John Stephenson. But when he heard the words that Ó Brádaigh had used, he called him and berated him for his insensitivity.

And the Official IRA, the stickies, who would kill innocents themselves, grasped for the moral high ground and said, 'We do not subscribe to the policy of those who attempt to excuse death and injury to innocent civilians as the fortunes of war.'

This tone of outrage echoed down the years as the appropriate response of the uninvolved but perhaps it would have been more fruitful to debate Ó Brádaigh's words than to condemn them. Why was MacStíofáin appalled by them? Surely not because he disagreed with them. He may have thought they were insensitive when the country was in shock but he may also have felt that they were too candid, that they stated too clearly the terms on which IRA supporters were assenting to the campaign. One of those terms was that still more innocent children would get killed because, if you fire shots in city streets or plant bombs in shopping centres, you will inevitably kill more than you intend to. If you absolutely cannot accept the death of Angela then you should not be endorsing the IRA campaign and cheering in shebeens when you hear a bomb or gunshots in the night.

Angela's father travelled from the funeral Mass to the cemetery in a black hearse with the coffin across his lap. A journalist for a unionist newspaper, the *News Letter,* reported that he sat with his head in his hands, weeping.

The piece also mentions that at the end of the short service at the graveside, led by Rev. Dr Montague, mourners went to the republican plot to see the graves of recently killed IRA members, to pay their respects to the fresh names. Maybe they had just gone there out of curiosity. The reporter reached the worst possible interpretation: 'Little Angela had been forgotten except by the family circle.' This is a cruel comment from a writer who cannot have known what was in the minds of those people. The propaganda objective was presumably to tarnish the whole community of west Belfast with some responsibility for the IRA.

The news story about the police investigation, on the same page, set itself the opposite objective: to argue that the people of west Belfast did not support the IRA and would help the security forces to catch the killer. It reported that the police had said that a large number of people had already volunteered information.

That contrast seems to illustrate the difference between simple prejudice and considered propaganda. The journalist who saw only republican sympathisers among the mourners had no empathy with that community. That report carries no details of the actual church service, the sermon or the prayers said at the graveside. Presumably it was written by a protestant journalist who did not actually go into the church, whether out of religious principle or simple discomfort among catholics; someone who probably could not identify catholic prayers anyway.

The writer who said that the police were pleased with the information volunteered to them was contradicting the claims of the IRA that they spoke for the community, even using their own language against them, implying that another kind of volunteer lived among them, one who would step forward to help the police and was eager to undermine the republican campaign.

*

A commonly used image for describing the relationship between paramilitaries and the communities from which they emerged was that of a fish in water. The terrorist needed a genial environment in which to operate, enough people willing to look the other way or more actively facilitate attacks, or if not attacks at least escapes.

The flaw in this theory is that it assumes that the water is more or less as it always was, an environment which by nature is conducive to the operations of the IRA or loyalist paramilitaries. What it overlooks is how the paramilitaries nurture the symbiotic relationship between their secret activists and the neighbours.

Compare the war for independence and the Troubles with the largest IRA campaign in between, which was organised in rural areas and conducted as guerrilla attacks in the fifties. Bands of men sneaked through fields to firing positions and shot at rural police stations, sometimes killing someone, sometimes getting killed. This border campaign produced its martyrs and its songs. But it did not arouse widespread support. It was not grounded in a real community whose interests it could share and it never gained approval. It ended in 1962, ten years before the worst violence of the whole Troubles period. The IRA then blamed its failure on lack of interest. The people had been distracted from the national cause. It seemed inconceivable that less than a decade later the IRA could be back running a much larger campaign with massive popular sympathy.

The water the fish moved in was not a static pool in which the fish could easily breed. Conditions in the water itself changed from generation to generation in response to political storms and state reactions. What the IRA had failed to grasp in the fifties campaign was that the movement had to be organically related to a community to thrive. It had to grow virally.

The IRA of 1962 was a fish in sterile water but the IRA of 1972 moved in genial murk that had been stirred up.

In that earlier campaign republicans had sought to stay out of the cities and to avoid a sectarian conflagration, but that removed the IRA from people who might become dependent on it or implicated in its purposes. It overlooked the horrific reality that sectarianism was the energy that would inflame conflict and draw recruits.

And a Britain that understood that dynamic might have strategised differently.

The IRA and the loyalists did not just need people who endorsed their methods and their project. They needed people, many more people, who would indulge them a little, who, on hearing of an atrocity, might say, if only to themselves, well, you can understand why they did that.

The narrative around internment from the start was that the British had made a massive mistake. And people who themselves would never have dreamed of going out and shooting a soldier might still harbour the thought that the soldier had it coming to him.

*

The police were an early target of choice for both the provos and the stickies.

After the reform of policing recommended by the Hunt Report that followed the chaotic rioting of August '69 and the standing down of the Ulster Special Constabulary (B Specials), a wholly protestant force, the British thought that catholics might be more willing to support and join a local regiment of the British army, which recruited a mix of catholics and protestants, so the Ulster Defence Regiment was set up in the hope it might enjoy a level of support that the RUC and the Specials had not even sought.

There was a logic to this. The B Specials had been run by the Northern Irish state since the twenties in order to form a line of defence against the IRA and they had a reputation for sectarian brutality. Some of that was exaggerated. I have, in fact, met some of the men who were members and officers of the B Specials and found them to be perfectly civil people, but then I have also found former loyalist killers to be decent chaps too.

The logical response from the IRA was to target UDR members and to prioritise the killing of its catholic members, so that the UDR would lose both its catholics and its temper and come to be viewed as a sectarian and truculent body.

The IRA sought to present itself as a legitimate army fighting a just war. So while an attack on the police or army might involve a couple of kids in denims and Doc Martens calling at a man's home and shooting him on his doorstep, the iconic imagery of the IRA in propaganda was of men in uniform, with berets. They would be guards of honour at funerals of dead members, marching in step alongside the coffin. A colour party would take orders to present arms and fire shots over the cortège.

Neighbours might speak of the dead man as a thug but the busy myth makers would describe him in terms which emphasised his virtues.

Anthony McIntyre, still a stickie, was part of the colour party for Paddy McAdorey, a provo. The British army had shot him dead in Ardoyne on the morning of the first internment raids. At that stage, the two wings of the IRA were functioning amicably together and the stickies provided the guard of honour.

McAdorey had left school at fifteen, served an apprenticeship as a wood machinist and then joined the merchant navy where he was an assistant cook. Those details come from *Tírghrá*, which also mentions how he loved music, dancing and football. The book says he was constantly harassed by the police after joining the republican movement but there is no indication of what role he played within the IRA or whether or not he was armed when shot. The death notices in the *Irish News* at the time, placed by his comrades, described him as a lieutenant in C Company of the third battalion of the IRA's Belfast Brigade. The police would hardly have been doing their own job if they had not been harassing him.

*

The IRA conducted vigilante patrols which claimed the right to stop your car, question you about your movements and order you to go home. Given that behaviour of this kind by the police and the army was one of the irritants that alienated people from the state, it seems paradoxical that the IRA chose to advance their prestige by the same method. In essence they were mimicking the state. They would have had a legitimate concern that loyalists might drive a bomb into a catholic area but, to a local boy on the receiving end of this, having your own neighbour ask you your name and address was like the enactment of a ritual. There were stories told of B Specials and, later, UDR men treating known neighbours in the same formal way, so it looked to me as if they were enjoying their authority so much that they would rather deploy it stupidly than set it aside.

One night, coming back from work, the taxi I was in was stopped at an IRA checkpoint on the Falls Road. I got out and spoke to the man in charge and asked him to let me have a look at his gun. The stock was a hollow metal frame rather than polished wood. He had no fear of being picked off by an army sniper. I don't know why.

Later the IRA would shoot people who broke through their checkpoints, just as the British army did. And they would reserve the right to arrest and interrogate those they suspected of violating their laws, in particular those they took for informers, and executing them.

But soft power was important too.

*

The IRA was now a reality inside the housing estates of Belfast and Derry and they had to be dealt with. The first example of this was during the movement of refugees. The IRA might put a protestant family out of their home in a mainly catholic area, then help a catholic family move into that house, usually one similarly intimidated by loyalists. The paramilitaries on both sides were, in effect, left free to allocate houses, and those tenancies were retroactively made legitimate by the Housing Trust. Rent books were issued and electricity supplies turned on.

Anne Tannahill's family refused to be part of that system, rejected housing offers made by loyalists and demanded to be rehoused properly and officially. Eventually the Housing Trust gave them a flat in Dunmurry.

That extension of paramilitary influence into communities included the running of shebeens, illegal drinking clubs where the booze was cheaper – often because it had been stolen – where the entertainment was rebel songs and where collections raised money for weapons and the support of prisoners' families. This was another way in which organisations set up to attack the state developed links with the communities around them.

And after internment a whole host of partial allies became available to the IRA wings; political and legal and media organisations which would never have actually endorsed the IRA became involved in causes that concerned them too. The injustices of the state had to be addressed. Journalists had legitimate stories to tell about state abuses but in telling them gave propaganda advantages to the paramilitaries.

What the government needed to do at that time was to create some social distance between the community and the IRA, not to make the water murkier itself. It needed to devise ways of addressing terrorism without imposing on the communities. Maybe that wouldn't have been possible and I can't personally think of such a possible strategy. The wider community wasn't just the water that the fish moved in. It was water that the state moved in too, the space in which it had to compete for respect. This would be impossible when some in the army and the police were treating people as the enemy when those people were maybe struggling with their loyalties and might have been won over.

Perhaps the United Nations might have been invited in, then British soldiers could have patrolled in protestant areas and Irish soldiers could have patrolled catholic areas, all of them in the blue beret. Patrick Hillery, Ireland's minister for external affairs, raised the idea with Britain in 1969 and was told sharply that he had no right to discuss purely British concerns. Britain would have seen that as ceding sovereignty and a de facto repartition, but given that the violence would continue for thirty years the price of enduring it and settling terms was going to be very high anyway.

Imagination in the early seventies was limited by the expectation that the trouble would soon burn out, this despite the fact that generations of British leadership had wrestled with what they called the Irish Question. In 1922 Churchill had bemoaned the tedium of having to deal with Ireland. 'But as the deluge [of the Great War] subsides and the waters fall short,' he said, 'we see the dreary steeples of Fermanagh and Tyrone emerging once again. The integrity of their quarrel is one of the few institutions that has been unaltered in the cataclysm which has swept the world.'[1]

Any historian or politician with an historic overview should have been able to see that trouble in Belfast was recurring. When reference was made to this in the media it was usually with an air of despair, like that in Churchill's comment. It affirmed a sense that the Irish are just innately unlike us; that they harbour grievances for centuries unlike ordinary civilised people. So the insight was squandered, bundled up as prejudice and viewed as simply irritating. No one was there to say, look, if this is an historic problem, it is not going to be lightly settled by shooting a few people and interning a few others, even if we could manage to confine ourselves to shooting and interning only the right people; this problem is going to be with us for decades and into the next century so it requires new thinking.

That historic view informed the approach taken by the nationalist parties and Dublin, which, unlike Britain and the unionists, wanted to revise big mistakes and remake the relationships between governments, parties and communities. The Northern Irish prime minister Brian Faulkner and his boss in London, Ted Heath, on the other hand, wanted to stabilise a ferment with firm authority. Dublin and the SDLP said we can at least clear the water and stop churning it, and then we will see the fish. In the autumn of 1971, Britain and the unionists had no interest in such an approach.

Summitry

Within weeks of the first internment raids Britain's Conservative prime minister Edward Heath was planning a summit with Jack Lynch, the taoiseach, and a later one to include the Northern Ireland prime minister Brian Faulkner. This would be the first summit of the three leaders in forty-five years, back when the Republic was still the Free State and James Craig was the prime minister of Northern Ireland.

Heath and Lynch met first at Chequers on 6–7 September 1971 to clarify their positions to each other.

Heath started off by saying that he wanted a full and free discussion and that he believed that the Irish had misunderstood what the British were trying to do in Northern Ireland. He said that the economy was being damaged. That would inevitably affect the economy of the Republic. Lives were being lost and both countries were about to enter the European Economic Community (EEC) together, what would eventually become the European Union. 'We would be in an intolerable position if we had to bring this present serious problem in with us.'[1]

So Heath seems to have anticipated the prospect of bringing the Troubles to an end fairly quickly.

But a breakthrough was needed to prevent an escalation of the violence.

Jack Lynch felt that Heath needed a history lesson. He argued that the island of Ireland had had partition imposed on it. At that point Heath might have thumped the table and said, hang on, you guys agreed to it and signed a treaty. He either missed the moment or just didn't want to get drawn into that argument. Lynch said that partition was the root cause of violence because it required that efforts had to be made to keep the unionists in power. He said that a third of the population of the North wanted a united Ireland. Everybody in the Republic also wanted a united Ireland, and most wanted it to be brought about peacefully.

He said that exclusion of the nationalists from power had led to protests by the civil-rights movement and then ultimately to the IRA campaign. The British had made things worse when they might have had a calming effect and now the 'minority' – meaning the catholics – saw the IRA as its protectors.

His theory was that if peaceful nationalist politicians could be shown to be effective, they would draw support away from the IRA and that would end the violence.

This was the same argument that would underpin the peace process twenty years later, that if nationalist interests and the prospect of a united Ireland could be advanced by peaceful politics, the IRA campaign could be ended. But it is very unlikely that in September 1971 Heath or Lynch thought their successors would still be having this debate so far into the future. Perhaps if they had foreseen that prospect they would have been minded to apply more radical measures to solve the problem.

Lynch agreed with Heath that it would not be good to bring this problem with them into the EEC. He said he thought that joining the EEC would help to bring about a united Ireland but he had always been careful not to 'play this up'. What was important for now was to stress that an attempt at a military solution would make things worse. Instead, Stormont would have to change into something in which nationalists could have an active ruling part.

Lynch described the IRA as 'a by-product of the situation' and asked Heath to state clearly that the unification of Ireland would have to be the ultimate solution and promise to work towards that, adding, 'this would be enormously helpful'.

Here Lynch had over-reached himself. In the peace talks of 1998, Sinn Féin would come back to the demand that the British would be 'persuaders' for Irish unity and Britain flatly and persistently refused. Lynch, like the IRA, had yet to learn that uniting Ireland against the wishes of the majority of people in Northern Ireland was simply impossible.

Harold Wilson, as leader of the Opposition, hadn't grasped this either. He was hatching a plan to announce a clear intention to unite Ireland but he too would find in time that he could not deliver on it.

The Irish record of that Chequers meeting says that Heath agreed with Lynch that membership of the EEC would indeed lead to a final solution of the Irish problem but he wasn't specific about what that solution might be. In the meantime, he said, the way for nationalists to get a share of power was to give up their fixation with the border and fight elections on other concerns.

Heath said the army was wrongly accused of coming to the aid of the unionists, that it was doing everything possible to prevent alienation of catholics. Indeed, the media was constantly asking why the army couldn't be tougher. He insisted that Britain was not seeking a military solution to the whole political problem but was simply trying to deal with republican urban guerrillas.

And, he said, Brian Faulkner, the Ulster Unionist prime minister of Northern Ireland, deserved more credit for his efforts, particularly the reform of local government.

Lynch came back at that to argue that fifty years of unionists in power had made Faulkner's government arrogant. Having the minority in perpetual opposition was not comparable to Westminster's style of democracy, where the Opposition had a realistic expectation of governing in the future.

Then he raised the fear of a protestant backlash against the IRA campaign and nationalist protest. A third of the gun clubs in Northern Ireland had been formed after the abolition of the B Specials. There were twice as many licensed guns in the North as in the Republic, per head of population. Lynch said there was a strong fear now that the protestant militants were so well equipped that they could 'wipe out' the catholics.

Who would protect them?

But then again, said Lynch, maybe this vision of a protestant backlash was being built up by the British to scare us.

Loyalists were in fact building up their organisations and

arming them in a growing anticipation of civil war. This Chequers meeting was in September 1971, the same month in which Tommy Andrews went to a community hall to be recruited into the UDA, the Ulster Defence Association, on a promise that he was willing to kill.

And some of those legally held guns were already being stolen for the Ulster Volunteer Force by Eddie Kinner. The protestant backlash was on its way but it was not coming in a form envisaged by fearful catholics at that time, with the police and the UDR sweeping through housing estates murdering all around them like Cromwell's forces. It was building slowly as the occasional murder of a catholic in a side street, someone taken away at a road block, when recognised as a catholic, and shot in the head.

Heath told Lynch that he thought that the danger of a protestant backlash was very real. He said that that very afternoon 20,000 protestant shipyard workers would meet to discuss ways of putting an end to the bombings. But he assured Lynch that Faulkner would act against the protestant militants and that no further gun clubs would be licensed.

Lynch then set out the demands of the SDLP: an end to internment and the prosecution of suspects against whom a charge can be made; a commission of appointed officials to replace Stormont – Heath sniffed at that because the SDLP had already withdrawn from a commission established to replace the gerrymandered Derry City Council. There would also have to be negotiations on a new means of governing Northern Ireland with the Irish government at the table along with the British, the unionists and representatives of the parliamentary

Opposition. And if these negotiations produced a settlement then representatives of the minority – the catholics – would be able to undermine the IRA by winning support away from them.

Heath rejected all of this: a commission would be undemocratic and a fifty-fifty division of power between nationalists and unionists would not be fair. The unionist majority was a simple democratic reality that would have to be respected.

Both men continued to talk over the issues on which they disagreed even when it was already clear that they disagreed on so much that there was no prospect of a settlement between them.

They went on to discuss internment, which Heath said he had been reluctant to introduce. He believed that the allegations of brutality by the army were excessive.

Interestingly, there was no discussion about the killings by the army. The 'Ballymurphy Massacre', which became the focus of a major inquiry in 2019, wasn't raised at all. Lynch told Heath that he was under pressure from his own opposition and from minority representatives in the North to make complaints before the European Commission of Human Rights in Strasbourg. He said he doubted that internment was justified as a derogation from the European Convention on Human Rights because this was only allowed for when the security of the state was threatened and that was not the case. Northern Ireland was not the UK state.

But Lynch was on weak ground too because he had himself threatened internment and he had been a member of the

Irish government which had interned IRA members in 1956 and 1957. And it had worked then to suppress the IRA. Heath reminded Lynch that that policy had worked because both parts of Ireland had introduced it at the same time, suggesting that it would work now if the Irish applied it too.

Heath would come to doubt, if he did not do so already, that Lynch was doing enough to defeat the IRA. Lynch refused to accept that he was 'turning a blind eye'.

They would meet again at the end of the month, 27–28 September, and Brian Faulkner, the prime minister of Northern Ireland, would join them.

*

Before the larger summit, the Department of Foreign Affairs in Dublin prepared a briefing document for Lynch outlining the Irish government's objections to the conduct of security in the North. The department wanted to equip the taoiseach with arguments to show that Stormont was not managing the crisis fairly, to accuse Britain and the unionists of an eagerness to appease the majority (meaning the unionists) and repress the minority (the non-unionist or catholic community). The briefing document listed twenty-two items of evidence of this discrimination and stated that the views of the Irish government on almost every point had already been expressed to the British government, some of them several times.

Top of the list is the Falls Road curfew of July 1970, when, after rioting, people in the square mile of the lower Falls were confined to their homes and their houses were searched for arms. During that curfew the army had fired 1,385 CS gas grenades, killed three people and recovered dozens of illegally held weapons belonging to the Official IRA.

A woman closely related to Gerry Adams retrieved some guns from the area during the curfew and wheeled them out in a pram. She claims that a soldier even helped her struggle with the pram when she negotiated a kerbstone and made no remark on the weight of the baby. But republican lore is full of stories about guns in prams.

Tony Rosato, who was there and moved in and out of the area several times while it was supposedly in lockdown, remembers the curfew not as crushing repression but as a victory for the Official IRA: 'We emerged re-energised, stronger and most importantly with increased PR with the people of the Falls.'

The Irish had complained about the appointment of John Taylor, a noted hardliner, as Northern Ireland minister of home affairs and of several other right-wing unionists to cabinet positions. The briefing notes for Lynch said there had been a failure to carry out adequate arms searches in unionist areas and to prosecute in obvious cases of incitement to hatred.

The Irish government was angered by the failure of the British to set up an inquiry into shootings in Derry that had prompted the SDLP to withdraw from Stormont. This refers to the killings of Seamus Cusack and Desmond Beattie during protests in the Bogside. The SDLP was appalled by these shootings and regarded them as murder but it is curious that none of the more recent questionable killings by the army in Belfast featured in the document. This may have had something to do with John Hume's greater willingness to brief the Irish government. Hume's base was Derry and his Belfast colleagues in the SDLP did not want to work through Lynch and his Fianna Fail party, which they regarded as conservative.

On the very day of Heath's first meeting at Chequers with Lynch the army shot dead Annette McGavigan, a fourteen-year-old girl, in Derry. There had been rioting. Annette had been gathering up rubber bullets fired by the army. But some reports say the riot was over and she was standing at a corner eating an iced lolly when a soldier shot her in the back of the head. She was wearing her school uniform at the time. She is memorialised on a gable mural in the Bogside. The army clearly wasn't exercising any particular care not to inflame relations even at a sensitive time.

Another issue of concern in the briefing notes was the widespread rearming of the police. They had been disarmed after the Hunt Report into the policing of protests and riots during 1969. Now they were carrying guns again on the street because they were likely targets of the IRA. And catholics resigned from the UDR in large numbers after the Falls curfew and again after internment, some undoubtedly intimidated by the IRA and scoffed at by their neighbours, but many likely also dissociating themselves from the British army and its awful behaviour.

Lynch was also getting advice from people who claimed to represent the views of the catholic community in Belfast. He got a message from Minority Rights Association members Fr Padraig Murphy and Tom Conaty. They were both members of the Belfast Citizens' Defence Committee but they were also middle-class catholics who would not have been under any suspicion of subversion or association with the IRA factions.

Their message passed through an emissary to the taoiseach was plain: 'Any settlement package offered by the British which did not include the ending of internment had no chance of acceptance by even moderate minority opinion.'[2]

And even if internment was scrapped as part of a settlement, they said, the RUC would have to be reformed lest they jeopardise it. But care should be taken that any deal made at the next summit in Chequers would not be presented as a concession to the IRA: 'Every effort must be made to sell a settlement package as a response to moderate grievance and not to the campaign of violence.'

In the event of such a settlement, Fr Murphy and Tom Conaty guaranteed, with the help of the SDLP, to 'mount an offensive designed to alienate the bulk of the minority from the violent wing – who are clearly tolerated at present'.

What is striking about this is its confidence that the British were about to make an offer of some kind and that there was a realistic prospect of the ending of internment being part of it. Further, the presumption that good citizens like the catholic clergy and catholic middle-class business people could undermine and invalidate the IRA was ambitious. And Heath, if not Lynch, would surely have been right in asking why, if these people could woo catholics away from the IRA in the event of a settlement, they couldn't do it now, unless they saw some advantage to their own position in allowing the violence to continue. There was just the faintest whiff of a protection racket in this.

*

At their second meeting, Heath and Lynch talked in the morning before Faulkner joined them.

Formally, this was a high-powered summit at an official residence for the prime minister that made him look like royalty. World leaders saw it as an honour to be received inside the 400-year-old mansion sheltered by woodland at the foot of the Chilterns. Heath had already hosted Indira Gandhi and Richard Nixon there, like a smug imperialist reminding the former colonies of what they had given up. A picture from the time shows Nixon looking candidly impressed. Chequers reminds the former colonial that British power at least has historic precedence. Only Mrs Gandhi would have been able to boast bigger, older, more ornate buildings back home. Heath might have hoped that Lynch would be humbled by grandeur, reminded by every artefact in the sixteenth-century house of Ireland's less secure grounding in history.

Heath made it clear from the start that he appreciated Faulkner's efforts and he framed the key challenge of their talks as simply getting the SDLP 'off the hook' of their boycott of the Stormont parliament. The party had walked out in protest against army violence and were refusing to return until internment was ended. Heath hoped that they might be persuaded to retake their seats if they could be shown that internment was being administered fairly and impartially.

Lynch didn't see it that way at all. He went in again still looking for a united Ireland.

Neither man's objective was realistic, be it getting the SDLP to assent to internment or persuading the British government to commit itself to ending the Union of Great Britain and Northern Ireland.

Lynch at least hoped to get Heath to see that he was the man he had to deal with, not Faulkner. He argued that they were equal in standing as heads of state while Faulkner was only the prime minister of a devolved region.

But Heath was not for bartering sovereignty over Northern Ireland. He saw Lynch not as an Irish leader with a negotiable claim to Northern Ireland but simply as a neighbour who might have useful influence over the truculent republicans or at least the obdurate nationalists of the SDLP.

The two men were also, unfortunately, equal in their distance from the problem and in their failure to realise the scale of it. But that's easy to say fifty years later. Heath and Lynch seem to have thought that they were dealing with a challenge that might be resolved before Christmas.

There were good indications that the men might find some common ground with each other. They were about the same age, in their mid-fifties. Both had working-class roots, though Heath had made it to Oxford and Lynch had come to law as a mature student at University College Cork. Both were sportsmen. Lynch had been a hurler, Heath a yachtsman. It was difficult for any Irish person to hear empathy in Heath's accent, which was so plummy that it was mocked by the Monty Python team and described by his own biographer John Campbell as having undergone 'drastic alteration' at Oxford. It was not the accent of his father or brothers.

In this affectation Heath and Faulkner were much more alike. They both spoke as if they had a gobstopper in the back of their throats. But there were grounds for supposing that Lynch might have got on better with Faulkner than he did. Faulkner was educated in Dublin and was a personal friend of the son of W. B. Yeats. He had also, like Lynch, studied law but, unlike him, had not completed his studies, instead devoting his energies to his family's shirt factory.

Faulkner was also a horseman and a hunter, a love that would unfortunately be the death of him in a riding accident during a stag hunt in 1977. At the time of the talks Faulkner lived much of the time in a cabin on an island in Strangford Lough, which, fortunately for him, the IRA did not know about. So they were all men with some hinterland to them, physically fit, fond of the outdoors and largely remade, living lives that could not have been foreseen for them in childhood. They were all born at a time of war and had lived through the Second World War, though maybe that experience divided Lynch from the other two since Ireland had remained neutral.

Only one of the men had actually been a soldier. Heath, who had been an officer in the Royal Artillery and taken part in the Normandy landings, had once had command of a firing squad that executed a Polish soldier convicted of rape and murder. So he was also probably the only one of the three who had ever actually killed anyone.

*

Both Lynch and Faulkner had sat in governments which had had to deal with a previous IRA campaign in the fifties. Both had endorsed hardline positions; Faulkner as minister of home affairs in the North had used internment then and so had the government of which Lynch was part. Taoiseach Eamon de Valera, who had fought the British as a young man, introduced internment in support of Faulkner's effort then and between them they had crushed the IRA. He did this following an IRA murder of a Northern Irish policeman. De Valera had led the anti-treaty forces in opposition to the Anglo-Irish Treaty in 1921, the year Faulkner was born. This was the IRA from which the Provisionals claimed their lineage. Yet this same de Valera had introduced internment and gone on to become president of Ireland.

Faulkner had a right to wonder why co-operation that had been available from de Valera was not available now from Lynch. De Valera's journey from being an active revolutionary to a scourge of the IRA was surely longer than the one that Lynch was being urged to make.

My generation – and I was a boy of twenty – had been taken by surprise by the violence. For me, past periods of trouble like this were history that I read about in books. For both Lynch and Faulkner this was old familiar bother raising its ugly head again.

Lynch had already established a good relationship with one of Faulkner's predecessors, Terence O'Neill, so you would think that if they had sat down and talked personally they might have come to a shared understanding of each other's limitations. Maybe the formality of the surroundings in Chequers and the aloof bearing of Heath made that more difficult than it would have been if they had met in a nice country hotel on the Irish border.

None of these men are alive now to take questions on their failure even to come to a shared understanding of the nature of the problem, let alone to agree on a resolution. But we have the Irish government's record of the meetings in the National Archives and they describe how the three leaders of the UK, Northern Ireland and the Irish Republic, all of them men of immense political experience and a deep acquaintance with war and danger, spent a day and a lunch break circling each other with proposals that had no prospect of being accepted, and no chance of securing peace if they had been.

This was the highest level, best-informed debate at the time on how to secure peace and stability in Northern Ireland. In the information and figures that each brought to the table we can read valuable statistics on weaponry, security measures, legal and constitutional considerations, but the sad part of it is how shallow the discussion seems now, looking back from decades later.

Personal backgrounds, family histories and inclinations were not going to help in these negotiations. And the range of ideas that they were capable of mustering between them barely touched on those on which later compromises were built.

One can see now what an education the following decades of violence were to be when untenable ideas were being advanced by heads of state at that time, like the prospect of the catholic community accepting internment or of a British government committing itself to easing Northern Ireland out of the UK.

While this summitry was going on, the home secretary Reginald Maudling – perhaps unjustly best remembered for describing Northern Ireland as 'bloody awful' – was meeting peaceful parties and organisations to explore ideas on how the minority catholic community could be integrated into political life. Maudling had no interest in meeting Sinn Féin, which was a negligibly small party at the time, and the SDLP was refusing to sit down with him. Heath wanted to get the SDLP into those talks and use them as the means by which changes could be devised.

They explored ideas like special courts to handle the internees, proportional representation for the election of a Northern Ireland parliament, perhaps a list system whereby voters might give every candidate a vote, if they wish, but in order of preference. But Heath said he and Mrs Gandhi had talked about the list system and she told him she found it a nightmare.

Lynch said that it was surely possible to devise an acceptable arrangement for the sharing of ministerial posts on the basis of the proportions of the two communities and for the alternating of certain ministerial portfolios between representatives from each community.

This is precisely the formula that was ultimately arrived at in the Sunningdale Agreement of 1973 and refined in the Good Friday Agreement in 1998. Heath and Faulkner both dismissed it at the summit as impractical and undemocratic.

Maudling had raised the same thought in a parliamentary debate the previous week but only to emphasise the difficulty with it:

There are great and strong arguments for a broadly-based Government, particularly in a country faced with acute problems. On the other hand, government makes no reality unless there is collective cabinet responsibility, and one cannot create a cohesive Government if people do not denounce violence or if people are not prepared to accept the will of the majority on the fundamental point about the border which succeeding Governments have always accepted in this country.[3]

But Maudling had already accepted that something had to be done to make Northern Ireland governable with the inclusion of the minority:

> In effect our system in this country works in practice by giving almost unlimited powers for a few years to the party that happens to possess a temporary majority in the House of Commons. This is acceptable because the party in government changes. But one must recognize that there are different circumstances in a country where the majority does not change. I look forward, as I am sure we all do, to the time when the political battles of Northern Ireland are fought between Conservative and Labour and not between Catholic and Protestant; there will not be a lasting solution in Northern Ireland until that is so. In the meantime, it will obviously continue for a long while on the present sectarian basis.

There is a clarity to Maudling's thinking here that contrasts with Heath's more limited, less adventurous approach.

When Faulkner joined the talks Heath immediately paid a compliment to the people of Northern Ireland for not taking the law into their own hands, the way he said the people of Manchester and Edinburgh would be sure to do if confronted in the same way by murder and bombing. It was a strange thing to say. It suggested that a popular uprising against the IRA in the unionist community would be a reasonable thing to expect and seemed to flatter Faulkner that he was leading a people who were so much more mature and restrained than the English and the Scottish.

Was he trying to spook Lynch with the threat that if Faulkner could not appease his own people a protestant backlash was all that a reasonable person could expect?

Faulkner saw three points on which they all agreed: their condemnation of violence; their desire for greater co-operation between North and South; and their recognition of the need for reform. He said the civil-rights protests had had genuine grievances but unfortunately the IRA had returned.

He would not agree that there was an urgent need for constitutional change in Northern Ireland. Northern Ireland had been in place for fifty years and there had only twice been major outbreaks of IRA activity.

The priority was security.

It had been inevitable that there would be an escalation of violence after internment but, Faulkner said, it was beginning to work because 200 people who had been involved with the violence were now contained. He recognised that Lynch could not replicate the stand de Valera had taken fourteen years earlier and introduce internment in the South, without political difficulty for himself, but he looked forward to working with him.

At this stage, Faulkner was coming across as practical and reasonable, demonstrating that he had no animus against the Irish Republic, patronising the taoiseach a little perhaps, suggesting that he wasn't the man de Valera had been, and promising that reform would follow a security solution and dismissing criticism of internment as having deepened the crisis.

Lynch's response, that he had it on good authority that the IRA campaign could be stopped if internment was ended, didn't impress Faulkner or Heath.

Faulkner, on the other hand, did impress Heath with specifics. He had set up an advisory committee that could examine internees and recommend release. But he had no doubt that all 219 internees currently held were active trouble-makers. He said twenty of them were teenagers, eighty-four were aged between twenty and thirty, the largest number – 101 – were aged between thirty and fifty, and only fourteen were over fifty. Forty of them had previously been interned in the fifties campaign and the majority of them were skilled people.

He also had intelligence which showed that the IRA was 'losing steam'. Catholics were now coming forward with information about arms dumps. This hadn't been happening before internment.

Heath reminded Lynch how the Dublin government itself had threatened internment just a year before and that Lynch had said that that threat had been effective. Lynch said that he had considered internment because a small republican group called Saor Eire had been involved in several murders, including that of Garda Richard Fallon. They shot him during a bank robbery when he confronted them unarmed.

There had also been threats to kidnap members of the Irish government. Lynch, on his own patch, was facing a serious threat.

The Irish had notified the European Court of Human Rights that it was considering internment but was advised that internment could not have been sustained before the European Court because there was no real threat to the security of the state, even if police officers were murdered and ministers kidnapped. The state would still survive.

Faulkner wanted to shift the onus for action onto Lynch. He said that his security people in the North had evidence of IRA training camps in the Republic. A man suspected of killing a policeman in Strabane was living in Donegal. More worrying still, the IRA was getting gelignite from the South.

Lynch said that the export of gelignite to the North was legal. There might be a few quarry workers who would pinch a few sticks, but all movements of legal gelignite were supervised by the police. He accepted that 1,000 pounds of gelignite had been stolen but this accounted for a small fraction of the bombing. It would actually have been enough for about twenty large bombs.

Lynch assured the others that the law on possession of firearms had been tightened. Previously, one could be charged with possession of a firearm with the intention of endangering life only if the life so endangered was of someone within the state. Now the law covered people who threatened those outside the state.

They were getting bogged down in detail now.

Lynch raised the question of legally held guns in the North and the potential threat they posed. All licensed guns should be withdrawn, he said, and reissued only in genuine cases. Faulkner replied that there was absolutely no evidence of legally held guns being used for illegal purposes. He said there were slightly more than 99,000 licensed guns of which 80,000 were shotguns or air rifles, and at least a third of those belonged to catholics. He explained that there was no discrimination at all in the issue of gun licences. Over 91,000 of the licensed guns were held in country areas and at least 17,000 shotguns were in mainly catholic areas.

This claim that there was no discrimination in the issue of gun licences seems borne out by the fact that at this time Tony Rosato was a member of a gun club, as were other republicans at Queen's University in Belfast.

It does look as if Faulkner was the commanding presence at these talks, equipped with figures and a coherent if modest proposal, while Lynch could only argue that if the SDLP, which he could not even claim to speak for, had seats in government and internment was ended then the IRA would cease to be a problem. He had no evidence to support this argument.

Tony Rosato says there were some people in the moderate communist/social democratic wing of the Official Republican Movement who did believe that ending internment would have been grounds for a ceasefire but that it would simply have fractured the movement. 'A ceasefire via Lynch would have hastened the arrival of the INLA,' he explains. This was a reference to the Irish National Liberation Army which later broke from the Officials to continue with the armed campaign. 'It would also have led to widespread defections to the provos.'

The idea that the provos had significant numbers in their movement who would have been ready to stand down the campaign in return for an end to internment seems unlikely given that they had already been bombing and killing as energetically as they could before internment was introduced. Indeed, their strategy in that period might have been to wrong-foot the government into introducing internment so that they could claim greater legitimacy for their ongoing campaign.

Those who were ready to shoot at soldiers in the street and risk killing another wee Angela Gallagher felt that they were advancing a revolution that would fully end British rule in Ireland. They weren't asking for a better Stormont or a more liberal security policy. They might reach that position in another twenty-five or thirty years but even then the price for an end to the IRA campaign would be full power sharing and intergovernmental structures. And when they did get to that point, Tommy Gorman, Anthony McIntyre and others would accuse their own IRA leadership of betraying them.

Faulkner then outlined the political changes he was proposing. He would set up parliamentary committees on which nationalists would have seats. He was prepared to ask parliament to consider proportional representation in elections, to enlarge the House of Commons and broaden the senate, the upper house at Stormont, to get more members of the minority community onto it. He would consider bringing into government members of the senate who were not members of the governing party.

After lunch he toned down his enthusiasm a little saying that the ideas were not yet worked out in detail but were only 'an indication of how his mind [was] turning'. He asked that this information be treated as confidential. He didn't want the Irish side leaking his ideas to the media, presumably because he was afraid that he would be in big trouble with his own colleagues if they found out that he was considering nominating catholics to the senate as a route for bringing them into government and giving them ministerial posts.

Heath asked him then to be more specific about the committees he planned. Faulkner said there would be four of them and two would be chaired by representatives of the Opposition. He had already raised the idea with the SDLP and said leading members of the party had given it 'a guarded welcome'. And it could be done quickly, providing salaries for the committee chairs.

As for the senate, when pressed by Heath to be clearer about his plans he said that he would not give members of the Opposition the right to nominate members of the senate but there could, however, be an understanding about the proportion of places.

Suddenly Faulkner's apparent magnanimity was crumbling. Lynch wanted to know if Faulkner would let a member of the SDLP be nominated to the cabinet and he replied this was most unlikely because the SDLP 'differ from the majority on fundamentals'.

Heath said he liked Faulkner's suggestions, even as Faulkner seemed to be backing away from them. He wanted to extract a specific commitment from him.

Faulkner said that he would go for proportional representation but warned that rather than giving more seats to the minority it might in fact give more seats to Rev. Ian Paisley, the firebrand sectarian preacher who was gaining a following for his determined opposition to reform. Paisley was an arch anti-catholic bigot who edited an horrific newspaper called the *Protestant Telegraph* that routinely described the pope as the anti-Christ and 'the whore of Babylon'.

Heath tried to sound out Lynch on whether there was division of opinion within the SDLP on the terms on which they might return to parliament. Lynch said he couldn't speak for the SDLP, though he could report back to them and let them decide for themselves. He had nothing to trade with but the nebulous idea that moderate catholics could shut down the IRA if Faulkner would end internment and agree to restructuring Stormont in such a way as to give ministerial seats to the SDLP.

Heath led the discussion towards the prospect of economic co-operation between North and South. Faulkner said there had been good co-operation between the tourist boards and that it would be good to extend that into other areas.

'Yes, with unification in mind,' said Lynch.

Faulkner's reply to that was, 'You have your ideals and I have mine.'

That night John Hume called the Irish minister for finance, George Colley, with some suggestions for the talks at Chequers which had just ended. This call was reported to Donal O'Sullivan, the Irish ambassador to Great Britain, by one of his officials. Hume said he had two points which he wanted to stress within what he called the 'current negotiations'. He had mistaken a meeting between three leaders, airing their ideas, for an actual negotiation process, and he had assumed that that process was continuing. He appears to have been much more hopeful than was warranted.

First, said Hume, the taoiseach should ask the British to explain what their objections were to a united Ireland. Getting a response to that question 'would enable an offensive position to be adopted' by the Irish government and the SDLP. It would get the objections on the record and then the Irish government and the SDLP would be able to put forward remedies to those objections.

Minister Colley added a further advantage to challenging the British to outline their objection to unification: it would enable the taoiseach to say afterwards that the question had been discussed.

The easy inference from this is that Hume had set his sights on a united Ireland as his ultimate goal and was ready now to push hard for that. This would suggest that the SDLP and the Provisional IRA were working to the same objective and symbiotically too.

Another possibility is that Hume wanted to meet the British objections and find compromises that would lay to rest the question of Irish unification. Colley, I suspect, was thinking more simplistically about placating a republican purist base behind his Fianna Fail party.

Hume also suggested a way to further embarrass the unionists in the North by using a law against them which reserved the right of the sovereign parliament in London to comment on foreign affairs. That would then make it impossible for Faulkner to criticise the Irish government.

What is striking about this strategic intervention is that it came after the Chequers talks. Why hadn't Hume thought of these things a few days earlier and armed Lynch for the talks themselves?

The communiqué issued after the Chequers summit was an embarrassment to the Irish. Brian Faulkner came home and faced the press with a blatant lie:

> I think our statement makes the position of the three Prime Ministers on this [internment] perfectly clear. We said that it was our determination to end violence, internment and other emergency measures as quickly as possible. And you will clearly see from that what our priorities are. The first priority is to bring the violence to an end. Having brought the violence to an end, I don't want to have anyone interned for a day longer than is absolutely necessary, and all three Prime Ministers are agreed on that.[4]

Lynch's insistence that ending internment was the means to ending the violence was ignored and misrepresented.

Faulkner would have been dealt a similar humiliation himself if Hume's tactic of forcing a discussion on Irish unification had been followed. It wasn't, so Faulkner was able to say, 'I went to these talks saying that the constitutional position of Northern Ireland within the United Kingdom was not for negotiation. It wasn't negotiated...'

If he had not been able to say that there had been no discussion on whether, or how, Ireland might be united, he

British soldiers on a side street in the nationalist Falls Road area of Belfast, 7 May 1971. I know how those wee twins feel.

Children playing in the desolation of streets in decay, Belfast, May 1972.

Masked members of the Ulster Defence Association (UDA) manning a barricade on the Shankill Road in Belfast, June 1972.

IRA gunmen checking traffic in the Bogside, Derry, June 1972.

Northern Ireland prime minister Brian Faulkner (*right*) meets British prime minister Edward Heath in London, 1 April 1971.

(*Below left*) Taoiseach Jack Lynch after his first summit with Heath at Chequers, 7 September 1971. (*Below right*) Home secretary Reginald Maudling was one of the few tory ministers with a clear understanding of the problem yet is better remembered for calling Ireland 'a bloody awful country'.

Peter Sellers and Swami Vishnu on a peace mission to Belfast meet Irene Gallagher, mother of wee Angela who was killed by a sniper's ricochet a week earlier.

(*Below left*) Lieutenant General Sir Harry Tuzo, the General Officer Commanding. (*Below right*) Steve Corbett back then patrolled the streets around my home in Riverdale.

In the chaos after British paratroopers killed civil-rights protesters on Bloody Sunday one of those shot is carried away by friends.

Protesters are rounded up at gunpoint by British troops on Bloody Sunday, 30 January 1972. Thirteen have been shot dead in the operation.

Seven IRA men who escaped internment on the prison ship
HMS *Maidstone* give a press conference in Dublin. Tommy Gorman
is second on the left. Also in the picture are Seán MacStíofáin,
Rita O'Hare and Joe Cahill, fourth, fifth and sixth from left. Most
of the escapees billeted in a house across the street from me when
they returned to Belfast to rejoin the IRA campaign.

(*Below left*) A rare picture of Gerry Adams (*centre*), who negotiated
the 1972 ceasefire, marching in formation at an IRA funeral. (*Below
right*) Ruairí Ó Brádaigh, president of Sinn Féin. He said the killing
of Angela Gallagher was 'the sort of thing that happened in war'.

(*Above left*) Bernadette Devlin, Independent Member of Parliament for Mid-Ulster, during an illegal rally organised by the Northern Resistance Movement in Belfast, 13 Feb 1972. The rally was in protest against internment and British troops in Belfast.

(*Above right*) SDLP MP Gerry Fitt talks with constituents on the Falls Road, May 1971.

(*Right*) Ian Paisley addresses a crowd, August 1972.

John Hume (*second from right*) sits by a fire in an early morning demonstration in Derry, February 1972.

Bloody Friday, 21 July 1972. Twenty-two bombs were detonated across Belfast in the space of eighty minutes, killing nine people and injuring 130. At 2.48 p.m. a car bomb exploded outside the Ulsterbus depot, Oxford Street, the busiest bus station in Northern Ireland.

would have alarmed his critics in his own party and exposed himself to attack from rival unionists who would have said that the Union was not safe in his hands.

When Faulkner met the media on his return he provided the 'gentlemen' of the press with a list of thirty-one attacks which had taken place in the period that he was out of Northern Ireland for the talks.

He stuck to his view that people who believed in an Irish republic could not sit at a reformed cabinet. At this stage he believed that he was making a significant concession simply by allowing catholics – members of the minority – to hold office.

Faulkner was asserting that discrimination need not be on religious grounds – and back then that seemed like progress – but on ideological grounds. Absurdly, he cited an appointment to illustrate his argument. David Bleakley of the Northern Ireland Labour Party was the community relations minister, but Bleakley wasn't a roman catholic, he was an anglican. And he had already resigned his post in protest against internment. The appointment had shown, however, that Faulkner could be flexible about people who were not unionists sitting in his government so long as they were not actually demanding a united Ireland.

*

How might things have gone differently in Chequers?

Heath was the host so the first responsibility was his to show that he understood the concerns of his guests and that he was genuinely willing to make an effort to resolve them.

Lynch was at a disadvantage because he did not represent

any party in the North but wanted to stake a claim to his government being part of the solution. The only solution he had in mind was that the British government should commit to an eventual united Ireland and end internment now. Then the catholic community would withdraw support for the IRA. He wanted members of the minority to be given seats on the Northern Ireland government so that they might participate in ruling the region they were committed to merging with the South.

The language that all parties used about the catholics/nationalists dampened down everyone's focus on the problem. Referring to the disgruntled community as the 'minority' enabled Faulkner to suggest that catholics who were not nationalists might be included in government. This would establish that he was not sectarian, but it would do nothing to appease the concerns of those who were nationalists and republicans.

However, Lynch went to Chequers knowing that he was not going to get a united Ireland and probably not actually wanting it yet anyway. So there was little need to alarm Heath with the reminder that his long-term objective was the same as the IRA's.

The big difference between Heath and Lynch was that Heath saw the IRA as the problem and he wasn't amenable to the suggestion that giving them what they wanted was the solution. All Lynch really offered was the idea that delivering the rewards of the IRA campaign to the SDLP would not be a surrender, though he never put it as simply as that.

Faulkner's thinking was much more appealing to Heath.

Faulkner was the leader of a devolved government for which Westminster had responsibility, so Heath was inclined at this stage to be protective towards him. He thought the ideas for incorporating catholics and nationalists into the running of Northern Ireland were good.

As for internment, Faulkner insisted proudly that it was working. The initial violence was only to have been expected, but now things had settled down and 200 hard IRA men were locked up. Did anyone in their right mind really expect him to release them?

Lynch lost a possible advantage in the talks. He could have made more of the British army brutality. The only context in which this arose in the discussions between the three leaders was in relation to internment and Heath said flatly that he thought those complaints were just the sort of propaganda you would expect from a group which had been rounded up like that.

Lynch could have pointed not just to the complaints of ordinary bullying by soldiers but to the interrogation techniques, and he said nothing at all about the disputed killings by soldiers, particularly in the week of internment.

Heath's strength was in his confidence that the army was doing a good job. Lynch did nothing to undermine that.

When Lynch went back to wherever he slept that night of the first talks with Heath, on 6 September, he will surely have received the news that a British soldier in Derry had just shot dead a girl in her school uniform who was standing on a street corner eating ice cream. Lynch did not cite that killing to embarrass the British and Faulkner never showed any sign of anxiety on his part that the behaviour of the army was a vulnerability in his case.

Lynch might have said something like this: There is a reason why catholics are turning so vehemently against the state. It is not just because of unionist rule and internment, it is because of the army. The visible, physical presence, the direct in-your-face manifestation of the problem is the army and the people are afraid. And they are saying, if that is what it takes to defend unionist rule then screw them. Because parents of teenage children worry, of course, that they will get caught up in a riot or that they will be injured in an IRA or loyalist bomb, but they are worried, too, that if they drive through an army checkpoint in the dark they will be shot in the back. They worry that the gruff manner of soldiers at checkpoints will recruit their children into the IRA. If you are completely ignorant of that dynamic then you haven't the slightest grasp on the nature of the problem. And if you are not concerned about the behaviour of your soldiers then either you are not treating people in Northern Ireland as your own citizens or you are not being properly briefed.

But he didn't say that. Children, a mother looking for her children, a priest crawling towards a dying man to give him the last rites, a workman in the back of a car whose driver misreads a signal from a soldier and drives on, these are the innocent people shot dead by soldiers, and the army is not considered in these talks as part of the problem. And presumably that is because the Irish objective was to embarrass the unionists into changing, not to undermine the authority of the British government which could be an ally and force those changes.

Faulkner was too smug altogether. He might at least have said something along the lines of: Yes, I accept there is a problem. I accept that fifty years of continuous rule by a single party will produce abuses of power. I accept that those who regard themselves primarily as Irish in Northern Ireland have a right to full citizenship and to a role in government. I am not sure how that is to be done. Power sharing and mandatory coalition are not the British way. They are not the Irish way either, but neither is dictatorship of the majority, so we have to have to find a new way.

And he would have been endorsed by history because that idea, of power sharing, briefly considered and dismissed, would come back again and again and is the model which, though problematic, has been widely agreed on.

Faulkner pointed to what he saw as a weakness in the idea. He said that if the SDLP was given seats in government then other groups like those around Ian Paisley and William Craig, hardline unionists, would also seek seats. He was right. But that is what was prescribed for in the Good Friday Agreement and by then was viewed as a strength in their arrangement, not a weakness.

Heath, it appears, came to the talks with little ambition. At this stage, he had given no thought to alternative constitutional arrangements. He was simply committed to democratic majority rule. He had delegated the serious thinking about how to deal with Northern Ireland to Reginald Maudling and a committee under him.

What he might have said to Faulkner is: Let us be very clear about a few things – you insist that you are British, but discriminating against minorities in jobs and housing on religious or political grounds is not the British way. And while you say you agree with that now, you have to take responsibility for the fact that your party in local government and your party in government itself has a history of such offensive and unwarranted conduct as besmirches the good name of this great country. So there is an onus on you to make a plain and emphatic break with the past, a gesture for now perhaps, but it had better be a good one.

And if someone had had the initiative to raise the murderous conduct of the army he might have added: And we will achieve nothing against the IRA if the behaviour of our soldiers is little better than theirs.

For a time would come when military excess would be so great that none could ignore it and the political damage would last for decades.

Faced with demands from the Irish government, a boycott of parliament by the SDLP and an IRA campaign, Edward Heath was likely to conclude that all three were on the one road together and he might more clearly have demanded assurance that this was not so. Lynch was adamant that he was taking measures against the IRA.

Heath might have said: But don't you see that when you come in here and demand the same things that the IRA demands you look to me like you are part of the problem? If the IRA sees that you are here talking to me because they have destabilised Northern Ireland, and you are here asking for a united Ireland, then it is in their interests to keep up their campaign.

He might have accused the SDLP and the IRA of playing good cop, bad cop.

He might further have said: If you want any traction with this government, you are going to have to show results against the IRA and you are going to have to go back to the SDLP and tell them that they cannot realistically impose a veto on political change without being adjudged by us here to be part of the same front against us as the IRA.

Heath did more or less take up that position after Chequers. Faulkner went home convinced that he and Heath were 'on the same team' and Heath started to treat Lynch less as a potential partner in peace making and more as a troublesome neighbour who wasn't minding his own fences.

The summit was a wasted opportunity. No party clearly persuaded the others of its own needs and limitations. None foresaw that the death toll would mount into the thousands and that the violence would drag on for decades. None took any responsibility. They spoke as if they thought they were reacting to a storm that would pass. Faulkner had actually said, this is only the second time in fifty years that this has happened so we have stable government. They made no impression on the paramilitaries at all, nor even acknowledged the need to curtail the British army. Faulkner would stay in power, offering minimal reforms that the SDLP would not even consider. The IRA would continue to bomb and kill. The UDA, formed that same month, started to build up death squads that would soon be active, and the army would kill innocents again.

Shooting Women

Many were leaving the city of Belfast to its own horrors. And people leaving was good reason for a party.

Tony Morelli had been a singer with the Witnesses Showband and was famous for the touching, sentimental country songs he had recorded, 'Nobody's Child' and 'Two Little Orphans'. Grief, loneliness, destitution and displacement were big themes for him and went down well in a sentimental culture. He and his wife Kathleen were leaving for England so they were going to be drinking and partying with their friends and neighbours to say goodbye.

This was at a time before redevelopment when the little houses on the tight narrow streets of the Falls Road had outside toilets and fronted directly onto the footpath. But you didn't need a big house for a party when you had the yard and alley at the back and the street at the front for people to spill out into. These houses were in long terraces: two bedrooms, a living room and a scullery and the outside toilet. There were big families, though even with a small one there couldn't be a bed for everyone. At bedtime some of the children might lay themselves down on the living room floor and even be warmer there till the fire died. Many of the streets of the lower Falls Road area, anomalously for a republican stronghold, were named in honour of British imperial battles, Crimea Street, Cawnpore Street, Sevastopol Street. Anomalously too, there was levity and partying in a time of danger. The city was conscious of the continuing violence, but a distinctive feature of life in Belfast at that time was the intermingling of the normal, even the frivolous, and the horrific.

Morelli's friend, another singer called Jim Meehan, joined their leaving party when he had finished his own gig that night as the resident at the Trocadero club.

Jim's wife Maura was already there with her sister Dorothy. Billy Davidson, Jim's driver, came too and Florence O'Riordan. And Dorothy and Maura would nip home to nearby Bantry Street from time to time to check on Maura's four children.

Both Maura and Dorothy were members of Cumann na mBan, a women's support organisation for the IRA, and the Women's Action Committee (WAC). They were of a prestigious republican lineage. Their father Ned Maguire had been part of an IRA jail break in 1943. The story is that a prisoner had discovered an unused trapdoor in the roof of a toilet block in Crumlin Road Gaol. Being a roofer, Maguire had led the escape, followed by Patrick Donnelly, Hugh McAteer and Jimmy Steele. These were top republicans; McAteer had been the most senior IRA man in the country, the chief of staff until his arrest three months earlier. Jimmy Steele had been convicted of leading an ambush to steal guns from Campbell

College in 1935 and was adjutant of the IRA's Northern Command.

News reached the revellers in Balkan Street that British soldiers were in the area in strength, probably to carry out internment raids. As members of the WAC Dorothy and Maura often went out onto the street during raids to wake people up and to alert IRA men in hiding. While the normal routine for this was for women to blow whistles or rattle bin lids, these two had a klaxon.

The plan was simple.

Billy Davidson would drive. Maura Meehan, Dorothy Maguire, Florence O'Riordan and Kathleen Morelli would pile into his Ford Corsair with the klaxon and they would set off around the area making as much noise as they could, to wake people up and let them know there were soldiers on the streets. This was at nearly four o'clock in the morning.

They drove through streets that don't exist any more, Cape Street, Omar Street, and passed army vehicles and patrols. They were about to do a second circuit when Kathleen chose to leave them and got out of the car. Then they went round again.

A corporal in the Royal Green Jackets, Raymond Beadon, says that he saw the car with the rear window broken to enable a gunman to fire out. He says two shots were fired from a pistol, and that he saw their two flashes.

I was about ten to fifteen feet away from the car at this stage. I could see the rear window of the car. There was nothing in the way… I then fired one round rough alignment at the left hand wheelbase of the vehicle with the intention of stopping the vehicle. I then pumped five rounds rapid through the back window of the car. While firing myself I gave an order to fire and saw a rifleman on my left hand side fire one round and a rifleman on my right fire a further two rounds.[1]

As the bullets zipped through the car Billy Davidson lost control and careered into a wall. He managed to get out. Florence O'Riordan beside him suffered cuts all over her body.

Maura Meehan and Dorothy Maguire took bullets through their heads and died.

Billy turned on the soldiers in a fury. He roared at them, called them murderers. He appears not to have feared or cared whether they would shoot him as they had shot the women, but the soldiers did not react to him as if they were afraid he was armed and dangerous. He said later that some of them actually apologised when they realised that they had shot the women. He said also that one of the soldiers did threaten to shoot him but that others intervened.

People were awake now. Locals gathered round to protect Davidson and O'Riordan. They took her to hospital. After her wounds were tended to, the police arrived and arrested her on an attempted murder charge.

Billy Davidson got away through a gathering crowd and evaded arrest long enough to give a press conference later that day. He said no one had fired from the car and that the army had had no legitimate reason to shoot the two women. Then he handed himself over to the police and was also charged with attempted murder.

The army stuck to its story. Major Christopher Dunphie told another press conference that day that terrorists were 'despicable' in using women on their missions. He said: 'One of my men saw a man crawl from the car with what he thought to be a pistol, but before he could open fire on him a crowd appeared.'

So the allegation was that Billy Davidson had spirited away the gun or that there had been a second man in the car who had done so. The army was not apologising for shooting the two women but was keen to claim that the soldiers who opened fire had presumed they were men and, by implication, would not have shot the women if they had looked like women.

Major Dunphie said that even the ambulance men seeing the bodies mistook them for men.

I was on duty at the *Sunday News* that night when the army tried to back up its claim that the women had looked like men by issuing photographs of them to the press. The photos were the most horrific I have ever seen. The faces of the two women were blown out as if sliced from inside and looked like raw meat. The queasiness I felt looking at these was a new sensation for me and I have not often felt it since.

The army statement referred to the checked clothing and belts of the women, though it is unlikely that Corporal Beadon had seen the belts through the rear window.

At the news desk I took a phone call from a man who claimed to have witnessed the shooting. He said that the initial intention of the army had been to stop the car by shooting at a tyre. That is consistent with what Beadon said. But this caller thought that the women were killed because other soldiers had mistaken the corporal's intention and fired directly at the passengers. Beadon's account is that he redirected his own firing from the wheel to the heads of the women and ordered others to join in.

Florence O'Riordan and Billy Davidson were released on bail and tried nearly a year later. Eight soldiers and members of the Royal Military Police and the RUC all gave evidence. O'Riordan and Davidson were acquitted of attempted murder and sentenced for minor offences to the equivalent of the time they had already spent in custody and were set free.

Inquest evidence said that swab tests on the hands of the dead women for lead traces proved positive. Relatives for Justice, an NGO supporting victims of the state and of loyalist groups in Northern Ireland, argues that those tests were unreliable.

Ten years later, Jim Meehan, Maura's husband, received £1,200 in compensation from the army.

Margaret Kennedy, his daughter, continues the campaign for justice for the women, but one of the soldiers, Colin Rudkin, now suffering from post-traumatic stress disorder, told the media years later that the shooting was justified: 'They shot at us and we shot back.'

Relatives for Justice makes a reasonable case that shooting from the car would have been a stupid thing to do, not the behaviour of a trained IRA volunteer. Davidson was driving his own car so even if they had opened fire on the army and made a getaway he would have been quickly traced and arrested. There were other soldiers in front of them at the time of the shooting so they could not have escaped. And why would they have been sounding a klaxon and drawing attention to themselves if their intention had been to shoot soldiers? Surely they would have moved more furtively and quietly.

Colin Rudkin said that a visit from the Historical Enquiries Team (HET) looking into the shootings of Dorothy Maguire and Maura Meehan triggered in him a sudden onset of horrific flashbacks. He has since become a campaigner on behalf of traumatised veterans.

The families of the dead women were traumatised too. Maura's son Jim, who was eight years old at the time, gave a heartrending account of the following days to Roseleen Walsh for a book about the family called *Bridget's Daughters*.[2] He described a family which was better off than the neighbours because of his father's income from singing. Pocket money for him was twelve shillings and sixpence when his friends were getting a shilling.

Maura had won £100 on the pools and this paid for her coffin. Young Jim remembered his brother Eddie at the wake saying, 'Mummy's gone to heaven and she's forgotten to bring her purse.'

He said that in later years he wanted to join the IRA but that his father stopped him. And the family had to move after receiving threatening letters from loyalists. Jim senior had to give up his spot at the Trocadero.

Another contributor to the book, Bridie McMahon, said that she hadn't known that her close friend Dorothy Maguire had been in Cumann na mBan until after the shooting. 'I was not from a republican background so I didn't read the signs.'

But she saw Máire Drumm, vice-president of Sinn Féin, speaking after the killings and urging people to join the IRA, so she did. Just months later she was in Armagh Prison and joined a hunger strike for a time. She went on to become, in the words of Gerry Adams after her death in 2015, 'the total activist'.

The *Tírghrá* tribute to 'Ireland's Patriot Dead' concludes its entry on Maura Meehan with: 'The sacrifice of Maura Meehan and her sister Dorothy was the inspiration for many of the women volunteers who subsequently joined the ranks of Cumann Na mBan and Oglaigh na hEireann [the IRA].'

It certainly sharpened people's fear of the army and illustrated again the readiness of some soldiers to shoot to kill and also the readiness of the army to cover for those soldiers who killed civilians when there was little apparent need to.

On the night that we received the pictures of the women's bodies reports came in of three more killings in Newry, about forty miles south of Belfast.

Soldiers had been stationed on the roof of Woolworths in Hill Street to watch a bank which they believed would be bombed that night. They saw a man from a local pub approach the night-safe to deposit the day's takings and saw three other men gather round him. They were planning to rob him. Soldiers said they assumed these men were the bombers they'd been warned to expect and shouted at them to 'Halt!' The three would-be thieves ran off and the soldiers cut them down with automatic rifle fire.

Witnesses said they had not heard soldiers shout out a warning, though there was noise at the time from a hotel in Marcus Street where there was a dance on.

The dead men were nineteen-year-old Sean Ruddy, twenty-seven-year-old Thomas McLaughlin, who was from the town and married with two children, and twenty-three-year-old Robert Anderson.

McLaughlin's widow sought damages from the army because unnecessary force had been used. Her case was rejected in the House of Lords in 1979 but she took it to the European Court of Human Rights and in 1984 the British government offered her a settlement. *Lost Lives*, a catalogue of all of the dead of the Troubles, says that it believes she was paid £37,000.[3] The three young men are not recorded in *Tírghrá* because they were not members of the IRA.

Forty years after the shootings a report from the Historical Enquiries Team reviewing Troubles killings said that the men had been drinking all day and had 'become involved in an unplanned crime at the very time and place the security forces were expecting a Provisional IRA attack to take place'. The HET had contacted the soldiers who had opened fire but all had declined to make statements. The report said that a Major Wilson who had been in charge of the operation was now living in the United States and did not agree to be interviewed by the HET.

Within twenty hours five unarmed people had been shot dead and no one was to be made answerable.

The Army Gets It Wrong

I felt at that time that if I died as a consequence of the Troubles it was as likely to be by an army bullet as anyone else's, regardless of whether I joined the IRA or not. I could be in a car that backfired or in which the driver failed to see a soldier waving us down in the dark. In those days the streetlights were out because the IRA was stealing the timers from them. And the routine shout from a checkpoint on approach was: 'Put your fucking lights out!'

At that time, the autumn of 1971, the army was killing more catholic civilians than the loyalists were.

The army, however, had a much more positive view of its role in Northern Ireland and even imagined that it was rising in the esteem of the local people. A secret security assessment in November 1971 listed five criteria that had 'regulated operational policy':

1. the need to sustain the credibility of government,
2. the credibility of the security forces,

3. the requirements of the law,

4. the tolerance of the community and

5. the availability of intelligence.[1]

There are some bizarre observations in that document. For instance: 'The need to sustain the credibility of government has necessitated from time to time the committal of the security forces to tasks which offer small prospects of tactical success but assist in the maintenance of public confidence.' Perhaps this refers to the deployment of foot patrols which maintained the profile of the army, assuring sections of the public that they had not been deserted by the government, without making any gains against paramilitaries, indeed providing them with targets.

But that paragraph continues: 'In such cases, however, it has been important to ensure that they have not been drawn into some sterile course or one beyond their capacity simply to satisfy the demands of one or another section of the public. Frequent committal in response to popular clamour will tend to bring the credibility of the forces into question. Moreover, it may well involve them in operations outside the law.'

The impression given here is that the army was so keen to oblige the different communities that it was tempted to break the law simply in order to be seen to be more amenable. One wonders what laws it was tempted to break.

One, certainly, was the legal restraint on lethal force. Much of the army's conduct around internment was indeed in response to a 'clamour' from unionist politicians to crack down on the IRA and did expose it to the charge that soldiers had murdered innocent civilians.

Yet the shooting of civilians provided the army with no obvious tactical advantage while at the same time breaching the core aims listed above, damaging the credibility of a government that endorsed those shootings as well as the credibility of the security forces, breaking the law, stretching the tolerance of the community and jeopardising the availability of intelligence.

If the army's aims were as declared, surely it would have been a lot more careful not to kill people unnecessarily. The document shows that some in authority were anxious that the army should be conspicuously law-abiding. Given the behaviour of some soldiers around the internment operations, the killing of Maura Meehan and Dorothy Maguire and what was yet to follow, it appears that concern did not sufficiently temper the behaviour of men on the ground.

And presumably when soldiers were beating up internees their officers were aware of what they were doing. How was that sustaining the credibility of government?

The contrast between what the army was actually doing and how its behaviour and reputation were described in official reports suggests that senior army officers were oblivious to the effect their men were having on the people they policed.

Many years later I was invited to give a lecture to junior officers of the British army in Germany. While there I attended a lecture given by a general. At the end of the lecture I asked a question. Afterwards some of the junior officers took me aside and said, 'You clearly don't understand army culture. You let the man say what he wants to say, say nothing yourself and then we all get our tea.'

This incident comes back to me when I reflect on this bizarrely ill-informed secret security assessment, which might have been compiled with the intention of leaving senior officers comfortably deluded about how well they were doing.

The officer who thought that the most appalling feature of the killing of the two women was that the IRA had sent them into battle presumably did actually believe that they had been armed and had fired on his men.

The report says: 'Amongst a divided community, it has been particularly necessary to demonstrate that operations are conducted within the requirements of the law. This has sometimes imposed restraints and denied quick, spectacular results.' But there was no shortage of 'spectacular results' when soldiers opened fire without restraint. Those results were the alienation of communities and increased recruitment into the IRA.

The report also suggests that key suspects had escaped because soldiers didn't feel entitled to shoot them, yet some other soldiers had opened fire and killed people with little excuse or justification. So that implies that there was no consistent understanding across the army of when it was legitimate and appropriate to shoot someone.

The author of the security assessment thought soldiers had sacrificed immediate gains against the IRA in order to impress the local population with its respect for the rule of law, the quality of good government and the good sense in providing intelligence to one's protectors.

'However, the credibility of the security forces does not rest on a few ephemeral triumphs but on the general level of

their success in quelling lawlessness over a prolonged period.'
The author was confident that the patience and good sense of
the British soldier would ultimately persuade everyone of his
benign intentions. It would all work out nicely in the end. The
assessment went on to claim that the 'manifestation of scruple
and restraint over a period has increased the tolerance of the
community towards security operations, even in traditionally
Republican areas'.

   This is a wholly opposing view to that which was being
reported to the Irish government. Perhaps the author was
seeking to reinforce morale or give a positive report to ministers
and officials. Perhaps he or she was deceiving superiors about
the real state of relations between the army and the catholic
community, claiming to offer evidence of a softening of catholic
attitudes towards the army.

   The report illustrated this tempering of catholic attitudes
towards the army by comparing reactions to different killings
by soldiers: 'When a petrol bomber [Danny O'Hagan] was shot
by the Army in August 1970, there were 6 days of rioting in
Belfast. When 2 terrorists were shot in the Ardoyne in March
1971, there was no disorderly reaction in any part of the city.'

   This reads like an assurance that the army could shoot
terrorists dead and the catholic community would be content
with that. But I can't work out who the two terrorists in Ardoyne
were. There is no record of deaths meeting that description
in *Lost Lives*. The shooting of Danny O'Hagan was hugely
controversial because he was the first alleged petrol bomber
shot dead and the claim that he was actually throwing petrol
bombs was disputed. And though I can't trace the '2 terrorists

shot in the Ardoyne in March 1971', it is true that some later shootings did not bring huge crowds onto the streets in the way that the shooting of Danny O'Hagan did.

The security assessment I am quoting from concludes from this fact that an 'amplification of public tolerance' of the army has emerged and that this 'has also extended the scope for enterprise in operations and has contributed to the availability of intelligence'.

No serious observer of the Troubles at the time believed that.

Not to comprehend why people would be more enraged by the killing of a teenager wrongly accused – as they believed – of throwing a petrol bomb than by the shooting of '2 terrorists' betrays a failure of any degree of empathy with the community. That community was naturally going to be more concerned about a boy killed at a riot than a volunteer soldier, arming himself to kill others and getting killed in the process. What is difficult to grasp about that?

Another factor the report might have considered was that those tempted to protest were more afraid of the army than before, particularly after the shootings of Maura Meehan and Dorothy Maguire. That wouldn't imply an 'amplification of public tolerance'.

The report claims that the army, until then, had killed 'three dozen' members of the Provisional IRA. By my count, going through various records, it had killed eight, and that's including Meehan and Maguire, who were at that time still claimed by the army as having been killed in return fire. There were four times that number of catholics killed by the army who are listed as civilians in the records of the dead. Some of these, like Danny O'Hagan, were killed in riot situations. The figure of 'three dozen' can only be reached by adding up every killing and treating the most transparently innocent victims as members of the IRA.

It is extraordinary that the army made such a claim for its achievements. This was not a propaganda document but an internal report marked 'Secret', of which only twelve copies were made. It exaggerates army achievements for government and the intelligence services.

Indeed, any public claim, at the time, that the army had killed 'three dozen' members of the Provisional IRA would have been met with outrage and scorn, but the writer of this report trusted its readers to be at a sufficient remove from the action on the street to be impressed.

Worse, an easy inference from this is that all the questionable killings by the army were of value in impressing bosses that it was doing a good job. So, the soldier who killed Fr Hugh Mullan in Ballymurphy while he was trying to give the last rites to a dying man may have disgraced the army in the eyes of Belfast catholics but he had added another number to the list of killings which could be reported to the government as the reduction in the number of Provisional IRA gunmen.

This is appalling.

There may be another explanation of that figure. The army appears to have believed, or at least told its men, that the IRA was hiding its dead.

Gunner Steve Corbett in his book *A Tough Nut to Crack: Andersonstown*[2] says that he was sent on foot patrols through Milltown Cemetery, opposite where he was based. He recalls that he had been instructed to look out for freshly disturbed graves because the IRA hid arms in them and even buried their dead over other people's coffins.

What are we to make of that? Though the IRA admitted in later years that it had killed suspected informers and 'disappeared' their bodies, no admission or even public claim has emerged that IRA members killed by the army were secretly buried. The IRA was proud of its dead and still celebrates them as heroes for the cause. It also owned up to training accidents, such as the death of Tony Henderson. In fact, about half of all IRA deaths in the early years were mishaps with a gun or a premature bomb and there had been no apparent effort to conceal or disguise that fact.

So were soldiers claiming hits they hadn't made? They were often claiming that those innocents they killed were armed at the time and that others spirited away their guns. The claim of 'three dozen' dead provos suggests that many in the army did believe that those killings were justified and that all those it killed were active 'players'.

There were, no doubt, occasions where a gunman would be wounded, seen to fall and his companions would take him away to be treated in a safe house or smuggled over the border to a hospital there rather than take him to a local hospital which would be legally obliged to report him.

If the security services were concerned at this time to preserve the credibility of the army and this assessment was written up to advise on how well the army was doing at winning the support of the catholic community, then you would think that it would have made some reference to those killings of which nationalists were disputing the legitimacy. It had nothing to say about them.

This is the report of an obsequious and timorous jobsworth or of an army officer who simply wants to reassure those above that all is going well. This person is not going to risk a fuss and invite questions from on high about whether the soldiers are murdering people. Or the writer is flattering the army to make readers of the report more amenable to a concern which is more important than the opinion of ordinary citizens.

That concern is intelligence and the need for the different 'staffs' gathering intelligence to share with each other. With the lightest touch and the least criticism the writer returns to that problem several times. But first the reassurance: 'The intelligence product continued to improve over the past six months, a consequence inter alia of the closer working relationship between the intelligence staffs of the security forces. Though detailed tactical intelligence remains far from complete, the flow of reliable material is now fully sufficient to permit regular and substantially accurate assessments of the threat to be made.'

So, they knew the scale of the threat they faced but didn't have the 'tactical intelligence' that would enable them to effectively crush it.

Again, having said the flow of 'reliable material' was fully sufficient, a summary at the end tactfully reminds those for whom the report was written that there is still a problem: 'The security forces must themselves continue to develop joint intelligence, planning and action to make use of their numbers and individual characteristics to the maximum effect.'

The document makes no mention of internment at all, though it was written to cover the period from May to November 1971 during which it was introduced and despite the fact that it triggered the most marked escalation of violence.

Yet the military mind behind it has interesting observations about the various paramilitary groups while dodging any risk of being accused of being unflattering about the British army.

The split between the two wings of the IRA was assessed to be irreconcilable. That proved to be accurate. There had already been armed feuding between the groups in March of that year, temporarily resolved through negotiations conducted by a young republican from Ballymurphy called Gerry Adams.

Adams had had a strong interest in keeping the peace between the Provisionals and the Officials. His sister Margaret and her husband were with the Officials. She was the only member of the Adams family to stay with the socialist wing. Adams's best friend from his youth, Joe McCann, was also a member of the Officials. Adams himself had been a member of the movement and was in good favour with the leadership before the split. The Belfast commander Liam McMillen had seen him as someone who would go far. He was right.

The security assessment is astute in a speculative sort of way. Admitting to weaknesses in the intelligence, these military-minded thinkers behind the report read almost as if they are asking themselves what they would do in the position of the different armed groups, if they were making the key decisions.

The Officials had two courses of action open to them, each presenting problems. One was to continue with political activities backed by terrorism. The weakness in that approach was that the violence would cost the movement electoral support in the future.

This is exactly the dilemma that faced the Provisional movement twenty years later. A choice would have to be made between maintaining an IRA campaign or ending it so that the political party, Sinn Féin, could garner more votes.

But if the Officials were to end their armed campaign to enhance political opportunity, they would lose their hard men to the Provisionals. This is what happened. Anthony McIntyre was one of those who was later dissatisfied with the Officials and defected to the Provisionals for more action.

The report also speculated that the Officials might instead sharpen their political focus but at the same time maintain a level of deniable violence, in order to keep the hard men happy but without letting them taint the name of the movement. The document went on to speculate that bombing would be the preferred activity.

The report sees the Provisional IRA as weakened at this stage and in need of a new rallying cause through which it could demonstrate its power, terrorise its community and recruit new members.

This is a strange analysis and the killing rate of the provos at that time shows that it is simply wrong. In October 1971, the month before the publication of this assessment, the IRA killed fifteen soldiers and police officers. In May, the first month of the period it covers, it killed two.

The report makes no mention of the creation of the Ulster Defence Association out of the vigilante groups and tartan gangs in September. It does mention the Ulster Volunteer

Force, and the 'hooligans' whose attacks on catholics were generating more support for the IRA.

I doubt that is how Eddie Kinner and Tommy Andrews saw things at the time. They thought they were punishing catholics for their support for the IRA, but I can illustrate from my family experience how attacking catholics might lead to greater indulgence of the IRA.

In the early period of the Troubles my brothers and I would often return from town by train to a station in a protestant area and walk home from there. Once my brother Roger was walking from the station with a friend when they were ambushed by a group of boys. The friend got away and ran up to the Riverdale estate where we lived. There was an IRA safe house across the street. Tommy Gorman was one of the IRA men taking shelter there.

Roger's friend told the IRA that Roger was getting a hammering down the road and Tommy Gorman and others ran there and fired over the heads of the young protestants, scaring them off.

So the young hooligans had created a circumstance in which young men who did not support the IRA now had something to be grateful to them for. This was not a productive strategy.

Tommy Andrews gives an account of some of the mischief that he and his friends got up to. After the shootings in Ballymurphy in which Fr Mullan and others were killed (apparently by British paratroopers, though loyalists were firing into Ballymurphy at the time too), local people erected a small shrine to the dead marked by a cross. Neighbours would gather at times and pray there.

Tommy Andrews stole the cross.

'We had seen the cross that sat in Finlay's field in memory of the priest that was shot. I can't remember if someone dared us to go in or if we just wound each other up. We found ourselves climbing over those railings. My mate John and I thought we were the only ones who had climbed over and we got over during a lull in one of the gun battles and got over to where the cross was in the field. But before we got to the cross there was an embankment we had to climb and as we were looking out towards the cross we saw people round it, praying or whatever they were doing.'

John got up and made a dash towards the cross.

'I was running behind him. He grabbed the cross, put it over his shoulder and we ran back into the estate again. Once we got into the estate there were a few women around cheering us. And John took the cross to his house and put it in the attic.'

A day or two later, Tommy was stopped on the street by men in a car. They wanted to know where the cross was and said he wouldn't be harmed.

'I don't know who they were. Then I found out that somebody went to the other boy's house and they got the cross back, and then it was back in that field again.'

What he hadn't known was that a third boy had run after them into the field that day and he got caught.

'They interrogated him in Moyard and apparently he gave the names. Then I don't know if the names were passed to the police or who it was that came to us. But the cross went back to the field.'

The security assessment document says that indulgence of the young hooligans by the police and the army was complicating efforts to tackle the IRA. The army was damaging its credibility when being soft on loyalists but not apparently when killing some catholics who were no threat to it. 'The apparent tolerance of the Loyalist mobs by Army and RUC, the association of these same mobs with Orange and fraternal order processions – even though abhorred by the orders concerned – give credence to the Republican propagandists' allegations of majority licence, minority oppression. Not least, such penalties as these hooligans suffer, however slight, provide the stuff of protest for the demagogues of Protestant extremism.'

But the loyalists are not yet seen as a major threat. The UVF is described as 'small, disorganised and largely unrelated cells' and is not viewed as a paramilitary grouping capable of setting the agenda but one whose 'intervention at some politically sensitive moment may, wittingly or unwittingly, precipitate a crisis'.

Anticipating the moves that the Provisionals might make, the report speculates they would in future concentrate their efforts outside the communities they belonged to but that 'the loss of prestige inherent in abandonment of the enclaves would be insufferable to them'. They would also risk seeing their areas infiltrated by the Officials if they concentrated their attacks outside their areas.

This was naive. There were no other areas the IRA could move to and operate from. They could not have set up units to launch attacks from protestant or wealthier middle-class areas. Some would move to the border areas, but even there they stayed within the shelter of communities of other republicans who would protect them or at least not bother them.

There would be some movement of Provisionals outside the neighbourhoods from which they emerged but very little. Bomb attacks would later be launched in London and Birmingham, and later still in West Germany and attempted in Gibraltar, and there would be some 'sleeper' cells in London years later, but the IRA was not able to load up onto trucks, drive out of west Belfast and set up its structures elsewhere. It was more concerned with strengthening its roots in communities than finding ways of operating outside of them. The whole movement could never have been transplanted.

However, all of this assumes that the Provisionals had been weakened and were regrouping. You might think that, if you really believed that your forces had killed 'three dozen' of their gunmen, but they hadn't. So the army's defence of its absurd killing rate was actually clouding its judgement.

The report says that a more likely course for the Provisionals to take would be 'to attempt yet another campaign'. It anticipates that the future campaign might include kidnapping and assassination. It worries about the Orange parades in the summer providing possible targets for snipers and the prospect of a major escalation of inter-communal violence if a sniper was to kill several people in a single attack on a parade.

One of the final recommendations of the report is that the propaganda of the terrorists must be countered by 'frequent publication of the facts'. To achieve that, the information agencies of the government, the police and the army would have to co-operate more closely.

Viewed in retrospect, this document seems occasionally to demonstrate foresight. It anticipates the Official IRA ceasefire and the contention between intelligence agencies. In other areas it seems naive, failing to see the ascendancy of the loyalist paramilitaries and misreading the strength and momentum of the Provisionals. And it overstates the achievements of the army, most oddly accepting that nearly every killing by a soldier was another IRA gunman taken out of action.

Perhaps the author was deftly flattering the army in order to more easily persuade it to accept that intelligence would have to be shared. Though this was understated within the largely incompetent assessment of events at street level, this may have been the primary concern of the author. Another suggestion not trumpeted is that the Orange parades of the following year be cancelled.

There were twelve copies made of that document so it was intended for a small number of people at the top of government and the security services. If we are to suppose that, for instance, the prime minister took it as sincere and competent, he would have been basing future policy on a significant misreading of the strength of the IRA and the loyalists.

*

Though the security forces in late 1971 saw little threat from loyalists, protestant groups had already killed and used bombs.

The first police officer killed during the Troubles, Victor Arbuckle, was shot dead on the protestant Shankill Road on 12 October 1969 during a riot protesting against, ironically, police reform. But trouble in loyalist areas had mostly been in the form of rioting by young hoodlums like Tommy Andrews and Beano Niblock. The vigilante groups involved older men in more responsible conduct, monitoring strangers in the area, looking out for suspicious activity. That's not to say they weren't scary.

One night I was sent out with another reporter to observe trouble in east Belfast, Niblock's area. This was early in my new job on the *Sunday News* and I hadn't yet been issued with my press card so the paper had given me a letter which read: 'To Whom It May Concern: This is to confirm that Malachi O'Doherty is a bona fides reporter for this newspaper', or words to that effect.

By the time we reached the area the air was filled with gunfire, like a fireworks display without light. Traffic was congested with people trying to get away but loyalist vigilantes were checking drivers. They stopped us.

Now, in Belfast a name like mine screams Irish and catholic, and in future jobs that brought me close to loyalists other reporters at the scene would know not to address me by my name within earshot of touchy men with grim faces, though one has thought it funny to do just that.

One of the vigilantes wanted identification. I showed him the letter. He was civil and quick, pointed to the best street for us to take and waved us on. This was before the UDA and other groups had started picking random catholics off the street and shooting them dead. But that was about to start, that and the bombing of catholic pubs.

Tommy Andrews was in the UDA from the day of its formation. He was told that he and his gang, the Ulster Boot Boys, should attend a community centre meeting one night. The hall was full. Three men in balaclavas sat at a trestle table at the front of the hall. There were guns on the table.

Tommy remembers: 'We would have been all sitting in front of them and it was very simple. They said, "There'll be no more sticks and stones. It's now guns, bombs and bullets. You are either staying here, and if you are willing to kill people you can stay. If you are not willing to do that, leave." Those words were used. I do not remember anybody leaving that room.'

A few days later he was given a combat jacket and told to get his mother to stitch the letters UDA on a sleeve. They were going to train him in how to use a gun but not a sewing needle. The UDA was the newly formed Ulster Defence Association.

Tommy's first acquaintance with guns was accompanying men to battles and gathering up their spent cartridges and dropping them down grates into the sewage drains.

Anthony McIntyre says that he was first allowed to fire a Thompson submachine gun by one of the older IRA men, who was in his twenties at the time.

'This was in the sticky [Official IRA] club in Lagan Street. They had a yard like a barn and they were doing a firing practice one day and he let me fire three shots.'

This use of children by militants was mythologised in the lore of the Troubles to suggest that an Irish mother might be content for a youngster to be out shooting at soldiers so long as he was back home for bedtime. The story is repeated in Patrick Radden Keefe's *Say Nothing*: 'Occasionally a young IRA gunman would go out on a sniper mission, only to round a corner and bump smack into his own mother. Unfazed by the assault rifle in his hands, she would drag him home by the ear.'[3] I don't believe that ever happened. No mother would be indifferent to a child going out to kill. And I wonder how the story originated; perhaps to mythologise the violence as homely and normal, no great strain on the conscience, perhaps also to excuse the use of children as fighters on the pretence that their mothers approved and to illustrate the propaganda that everyone in a community supported the IRA.

More interesting than the stereotyping of the fighting Irish, also implied here, is the survival of the understanding that minors were armed by the paramilitaries, without the teller of the story being appalled or the paramilitaries ashamed. That's what was normal, gunmen sharing their skills with children, not mothers approving murder.

Beano Niblock's gang was invited to join a group called the Red Hand Commando.

'There was a table with a Union Jack and a bible and a gun, and I was sworn in by two officers of the Red Hand Commando. I was taking this seriously, as everybody else was. You knew you were committing yourself to taking orders and doing operations. And that was all explained to you and you knew things were going to change. You were apprehensive, of course you were, but a bit excited. The two guys who came and swore us in were nineteen.'

He says these were the children he had grown up with. They would align themselves with the UVF, the Ulster Volunteer Force, but they would be autonomous. These were youngsters at war and, in fact, they were sometimes more afraid of a parent than a commanding officer.

Eddie Kinner joined the Ulster Volunteer Force: 'My introduction to the UVF would have been gathering intelligence initially. Then armed robberies and then procuring firearms from part-time police, part-time soldiers, going in with a gun and taking them off them. I didn't consider that they would think me an IRA man coming in to shoot them but I accrued quite a lot of weapons for our Young Citizen Volunteers unit doing that.'

So in 1971 people who would become major armed activists were just learning the skills that would make them killers, and the security services were themselves just learning to profile the paramilitary organisations, and to read the changing attitudes within the communities they were supposed to be protecting.

No one had any clear view of how far the violence might escalate or of what measures, political or military, might bring it to an end. The discussions that have been recorded and the interviews with paramilitaries who were so young then reveal a shocking naivety. Political movements and armed groups had coherent objectives, or thought they had, but the energies being unleashed were not under anyone's control. A lot of young people were eager for war and older people were keen to arm and train and lead them.

But no one, not even the government and the British army, was able to stop the slide towards chaos.

Deepening Deadlock

The main question in the air at this stage was whether political progress could be made while the violence continued or if the violence would have to be stopped first.

On 27 October 1971, about the same time that the security assessment in the previous chapter was being made, the Irish ambassador to London wrote home to the Department of Foreign Affairs about a reception he had attended in Downing Street, hosted by Prime Minister Edward Heath. The point of the reception was to honour the national Lions rugby team.

The ambassador, Donal O'Sullivan, wrote, 'There was an attendance of approximately two hundred, made up mainly of prominent people in the rugby world with their ladies.'[1] Heath had come up and chatted with him briefly, said some nice words about the contribution Irish players had made to the team's tour and then spoke more about the 'Common Market matters', concluding with a comment on the Irish referendum on joining the European Economic Community, '"thank God we do not have to have a referendum as in that case we would never get in"'.

He was taken aside for a more direct conversation about Northern Ireland by Sir Harry Jones, 'the Northern Ireland Agent', an official appointed to represent Northern Ireland's interests to the British government. Sir Harry said it would probably be '"a bit embarrassing"' for them to meet at each other's homes. Now that they were both under police protection it would be harder to keep meetings secret. The ambassador said that he had 'stressed the need for an immediate and significant initiative on the political front as the only hope of establishing a basis for peace'.

Sir Harry disagreed. He thought that the two communities in Northern Ireland were now so alienated from each other that there was no point in a political initiative or any attempt at reconciliation 'until violence has been effectively crushed'. This most likely represented the thinking of his employers in Stormont, though some of them would have been appalled to see his other observation reported back to the Irish government: his doubt that the Northern Ireland prime minister Brian Faulkner could survive in office much longer.

At this stage the British government may have thought that crushing the IRA was a feasible prospect, especially if they were relying on security assessments like the one above.

The Irish ambassador, however, got a different message from the Labour Party. One of its leading MPs, James Callaghan, was at the reception. He said that he did want to see 'worthwhile progress towards a solution'.

A month later, Harold Wilson, the leader of the Opposition, sat down in Dublin with the taoiseach Jack Lynch and some of his ministers to suggest a comprehensive conference including all parties and some that were not even represented in a parliament, meaning Sinn Féin. A secret report of that meeting in the National Archives of Ireland says that Wilson believed that the violence in the North 'could only be ended by the production of a new magic formula'.[2] Only a special conference of all parties would produce such a formula.

Wilson didn't seem to grasp that the unionists would simply refuse to attend a conference negotiating the future of Ireland with an Irish government.

He was put right fairly sharply on his unrealistic expectations of the Irish themselves.

The taoiseach and his ministers rejected outright a suggestion from Wilson that Ireland should rejoin the Commonwealth and take an oath of allegiance to the British monarch. He appears to have given ground on the oath. That he raised the idea at all betrays an ignorance of Ireland being a sovereign nation. The Commonwealth is something the Irish are touchy about, yet other countries, like India, that suffered much worse under British imperial rule are happy to be members.

At the end of his meeting with Lynch, and after these sharp rebuttals of his suggestions, Wilson asked if the taoiseach had any objection to accepting an invitation to meet Fianna Fail TD (member of parliament) Kevin Boland. Lynch said he had no objection. Boland was at the harder edge of Irish republicanism within the Fianna Fail party, one of the hawks who thought that Lynch was too soft.

If Lynch expressed any exasperation at this it is not recorded.

Ten days after that big Chequers summit, Edward Heath wrote to Jack Lynch to update him on progress. He said that he had it from Faulkner that an advisory committee was considering the cases of the internees, even those who had not asked for their cases to be examined. The committee 'had considered the first batch'.[3]

He said he had also discussed possible political reform with Faulkner 'in relation to the operation of Parliament, the electoral system and so on'. And having assured him of such progress, Heath delivered a shocker. He informed the taoiseach, the prime minister of a neighbouring state, that he was about to bomb their shared border.

His message read: 'Our intention is, as a first step, to block 84 (eighty-four) of the so-called quote unapproved unquote crossings.' This is probably a literal transcription of a coded message sent by telex.

This plan seemed to the Irish to be more a political insult than a practical security measure, an appeasement of hardline unionists who wanted the Republic punished for what they saw as dilatory measures against the IRA.

The letter continued, 'This will in most cases be achieved by cratering the roads, but care will be taken wherever possible to avoid unreasonable inconvenience, for example to farmers whose land lies on or athwart the Border. The second stage will be to "hump" the quote approved unquote crossing places, so as to slow traffic down and facilitate stopping and searching.'

I suspect the unilateral nature of the decision to bomb border roads, taken after a meeting with Faulkner, put the Irish in a dour mood for dealing with what followed.

British army units had been crossing the border on occasions and the Irish were annoyed about that. Questions in the Dáil, the Irish parliament, on 3 November 1971 revealed that the Irish were aware of forty such crossings by armed soldiers, all of them illegal infringements on the sovereign territory of a supposedly friendly neighbour. Soldiers had also been flown over Irish territory on seventeen occasions.

The British ambassador John Peck then wrote to Jack Lynch on 5 November to assure him that his government had thoroughly investigated claims 'that British armed forces have crossed the border into the Republic'.[4]

He wrote, 'I expect you would prefer it if I did not burden you personally with them [the results of the investigation] at this stage.' So he was sending them to the Department of Foreign Affairs. 'I am therefore writing to assure you most emphatically that British Army units are not crossing the border deliberately, that all units operating in the border area have strict instructions to this effect, and these instructions have been made even more explicit.'

The army had also bombed bridges on the border to inhibit the IRA moving back and forth between the two jurisdictions, smuggling arms or launching attacks and then retreating into territory on which the army could not lawfully pursue them.

Ambassador Peck assured the taoiseach that '[w]here explosions near the border are deemed necessary, they are to be carried out so that no debris falls upon the territory of the Republic'.

There is a smug tone to this. The letter in the archive is crudely typed in a large font with single line spacing, so is probably also a decoder's transcription rather than the original. Peck added a message from the prime minister which reads like an elegant brush-off. At their last meeting at Chequers, Heath and Lynch had agreed that they would meet again in the autumn, with dates yet to be confirmed. 'Mr Heath has asked me to say how welcome you will be at any time; but he fully understands that your many preoccupations could make it hard for you to leave Dublin at present, and he does not want to add to your difficulties by proposing a definite date at this stage.'

So, gently phrased, the point was that there would be no return invitation to Chequers and if Lynch wanted another meeting he would have to ask for it himself.

This reads to me as if the British were punishing Lynch for annoying them with a concern that they probably thought he should have been more flexible about. If Lynch was going to preoccupy himself with trivialities like soldiers stepping over the border while engaged in a war on the IRA, then Heath was going to leave him free to busy himself with the matter and get on with more serious concerns himself.

But a sovereign country is entitled to ask a foreign army to stay out of its territory without being sneered at.

One of the Irish complaints about border intrusions had followed an incident in which a man had been killed.

A Department of Foreign Affairs note on the incursions reads: 'On 29th August, 1971 a border incursion resulted in a fatal shooting within the Six Counties [the official Irish term for Northern Ireland, short for Occupied Six Counties] after a British army patrol had recrossed the border into the North. A strong complaint was conveyed to the British authorities on that occasion about their failure to control movements of their troops in border areas which could be prejudicial to the peace.'[5]

One can be a bit more indulgent of the sniffy tone of the British ambassador's letter and Heath's reduced enthusiasm for another meeting with Lynch when it is clear that the fatality referred to in the note was of a British soldier, Ian Armstrong.

Armstrong and others had crossed the border at Crossmaglen in County Armagh. After going a hundred yards into Irish territory they turned around and found their way blocked by protesters. There was a tense standoff for two hours, the army unable to use force to break through the protesters and the protesters knowing that. This gave the IRA time to organise an ambush in the North when the soldiers eventually returned. The protesters set fire to one of the army vehicles. When the soldiers eventually got back into the North their troubles weren't over. One of the vehicles suffered a puncture, compelling them to stop. The soldiers got out to fix the puncture and exposed themselves to IRA snipers in the hills around them. Those snipers killed Armstrong and wounded another soldier.

So the army had a very good reason not to encroach on Irish territory. Having moved beyond the area in which British soldiers could legally operate, their weapons were useless to them and any Irish civilians might presume the right to detain them.

The most recent incident had occurred when the army faced protesters after bombing a crater in a cross-border road at Castleblaney in County Louth. The Irish complaint said: 'British forces were observed in a firing position inside the 26-Counties.'

An armed Irish army soldier might have felt compelled to shoot a British soldier who appeared to be preparing to fire at an Irish civilian.

Serious indeed.

Confusion about the precise location of the border made life dangerous for the Irish police too. A year later, Garda Samuel Donegan, sixty-one, triggered a roadside booby trap near Newtownbutler, just a few yards inside Northern Ireland, and lost his life.

Here was a dangerous vulnerability in relations between the two countries with the potential to turn the Troubles into an armed conflict between Britain and Ireland, and this on the eve of both of them entering the EEC. The IRA would have loved that to happen.

Years later a member of the Official IRA told me that his organisation had discussed plans to trigger such a crisis. Volunteers would join the Irish army then take armoured vehicles and drive them into Derry. It never happened.

Ireland never had the capability to take on the British army, let alone the desire, but even a brief exchange of fire costing Irish lives would have resonated around the world as validation of the IRA campaign for British withdrawal.

Logically, the Irish Republic, because of its vulnerability, would have to be involved in any long-term political settlement. John Hume's formula in the future, the basis for a long-distant peace process, was that three sets of relationships had to be resolved: between communities in the North, between North and South, and between Britain and Ireland. All three relationships were tetchy at this time.

The Irish Department of Foreign Affairs received a secret
report in November 1971 from a diplomat who had been
sounding out senior members of the Social Democratic and
Labour Party on their opinions. He found that John Hume,
who was the de facto leader of the SDLP though Gerry Fitt
nominally held that role, wanted all efforts of his party directed
towards bringing down Stormont, the parliament with the
fixed unionist majority. Then, he believed, political progress
towards peace might be possible.

Strangely, Paddy Devlin, an old die-hard socialist who had
been in the IRA in the forties, and Gerry Fitt believed that the
IRA could be defeated militarily. So the same question that
divided the British and Irish governments also divided the
main party of Irish nationalism in the North.

John Hume disclosed to the emissary that his objective
was simply to bring about Irish unity. The emissary reported
to the Department of Foreign Affairs in Dublin: 'I asked
him to consider his tactics on this – for example it might be
preferable to let the conference [to be set up following the
suspension of Stormont] to continue for a time to talk about
radical reform structures in the North plus a connection
with Dublin and when, as is reasonably certain, the Unionist
conferees prove intransigent about this the ultimate question
could be thrown in.'[6]

This is interesting. Hume is not remembered as a champion
of Irish unity but as a deft compromiser. He was, naturally
enough, a nationalist, but while Irish unity seemed unattainable
in that generation he was more concerned that those who
aspired to it should have a place in the governing of the North.

Yet here was an Irish diplomat suggesting tactics to him on how to manage future talks towards considering unification by testing to destruction any unionist interest in compromise short of that.

Hume's prediction that Stormont would fall would prove correct. So also would his prediction that unionism would refuse a compromise, though it would split on it. This was still two years away but Brian Faulkner would eventually compromise and settle for power sharing and then be brought down by popular rejection of the idea among unionists.

At that point Hume would not choose to focus on unity as the only remaining option, as the emissary suggested he ought, but would work for more than twenty years to restore that power-sharing model.

The diplomat's letter also reported that the SDLP had a plan to bring down Stormont by persuading most catholic public servants to resign, including Maurice Hayes, the chair of the Community Relations Commission: 'All these are indicators that Mr Faulkner's credibility has completely disappeared. If he is to remain in office he can only do so supported by guns.'

It is hard to know what sense to make of that last remark. Every government in the world is supported by guns.

Maurice Hayes was interesting because he was an Irish-speaking catholic in the Northern Irish civil service. He told me in an interview many years later that he had thought it more appropriate for nationalists in the North to settle terms with the unionists and try to make the place work. He had reached this conclusion after the South declared itself a republic, reasoning that it was now more concerned with itself as a sovereign state than with trying to incorporate the North. It was therefore time for northern nationalists to look after themselves and to make the best of partition.

There were structures in place to try to ameliorate stresses between the two jurisdictions on the island of Ireland but reports from them read bizarrely now.

The Irish government had set up an Inter-departmental Unit on the North of Ireland. This unit met to discuss ways of seeking increased co-operation with Northern Ireland, a region whose name the unit was averse to actually using.

The October '71 meeting heard about a plan to set up an Assembly of the Northern Irish people, a project by the SDLP to establish an alternative forum to Stormont. The unit had itself provided draft rules for the assembly and discussed minor digressions from these in published documents. This was of little significance. The assembly would meet once and die.

They discussed also a proposal by Tyrone and Monaghan councils to rebuild 'the cross-border bridge at Moy'[7] and the refusal by the Northern Ireland minister of development to allow this. It's hard to be clear what this refers to since Moy is not on the border or anywhere near it.

Then the members got down to discussing a proposed North/South joint study group. This was a favourite project of the taoiseach, who wanted closer co-operation with Northern Ireland. The unionists in the North weren't keen. They thought that the idea of joint industrial ventures in border areas 'might be of doubtful value at this time because, due to the unrest, there is now no new foreign investment in Northern Ireland'.

The counter-suggestion from the North was that departments in both jurisdictions concerned with development should set up a Standing Joint Study Group, including the Industrial Development Authority. Some members thought the Standing Joint Study Group should have a wider remit than the economy. They thought 'the idea of a Standing Joint Study Group might be an attempt by Mr Brian Faulkner to avoid the creation of an Economic Council of Ireland'.

Then they discussed a proposal for joint co-operation from the Public Record Office of Northern Ireland (PRONI). The Irish were as sniffy about this as the North had been about economic co-operation. They detected 'excessive zeal' from PRONI.

This Inter-departmental Unit on the North of Ireland reported to the Irish government that a 'business records committee of archivists' studying counties was split over how to proceed. 'The Northern side had suggested that Monaghan be dealt with next and had offered to provide a full team for the studies there but our own Public Record Office had a strong preference for Meath because the County Librarian there was known to be more cooperative.'

It was a reminder that while armed groups were advancing their agendas, or trying to, through murder and sabotage, and while governments laboured to find a balance between political initiative and armed force, sometimes the prospects of co-operation between North and South hung, not on high-wire diplomacy and military strategy, but on the genial nature of the county librarian. Division was real and trust was low. That was the problem.

Living in the Middle of It

There was a little river running past our house when I was small. Hence the name for the estate, Riverdale. It was a sluggish little brook where we caught tiny fish we called spricks and muddied ourselves jumping across it. That was a good place for children then. Later the river was filled in, probably redirected through pipes to integrate with the sewage system.

When I was young there were protestant neighbours, most of them families of police constables serving the Dunmurry RUC station. They went to work on bicycles. By 1971 most of the protestants had left and catholics from other parts of Belfast had moved in. Some of them were members of the IRA. Two sisters living on our corner allowed their homes to be used by the IRA as billets.

Tommy Gorman says, 'The real heroes were the people who were sleeping with weapons below their beds. There were women getting up at three o'clock in the morning to make people fries and stuff like that.'

As a young man of twenty I was living in a barricaded ghetto.

Other young men I didn't know would eye me with suspicion, even stop me, in imitation of the British army, when I returned home at night after being dropped off by a friend. Who are you? Where are you going? This was my direct contact with the IRA, the people who were bringing bombs into the city centre, calling in the bomb hoaxes, organising riots on the main road, shooting at passing army patrols.

I saw one of them firing at a helicopter on a summer morning. The rifle made two blunt reports for each shot. If he had hit the helicopter he would have brought it down on someone's house and garden, or into the middle of a road filled with traffic. I had been walking along Finaghy Road North and saw a young woman call children into her doorway for shelter. Being older I was embarrassed to be joining them but she invited me too and we stood and smiled uneasily until the shooting stopped and the helicopter moved away.

Another time I was walking down Slievegallion Drive. Movement at a window caught my eye. I looked up and saw two rifle barrels and young men behind them. They started shooting. I looked left and saw an army Pig with rifles poking out from the slats at the back and the wisps of smoke as they returned fire. I turned again to the window and saw ricochets below the window ledge. A group of small boys were beside me. I told them to lie flat on the ground, feeling awkward, doing something you don't do. When the shooting stopped and I got up to cross the road, my friend Philip was standing in front of me, waving his arms in a panic. He had not had the advantage of seeing the whole thing and knowing that the danger had passed.

This was why riots always had audiences, why even mature adults came out to watch. It was because you feel safer when you see what is happening and can assess the risk to yourself. People got arrested when riots were broken up, and sometimes they had only been watching, posing no threat, but the perception of others was often that they should not have been there, even that they were encouraging the riot by providing attention.

In the evenings at home, as darkness descended, usually when *Coronation Street* was starting, I would hear the gunshots and explosions out on the main road, when my neighbour's guests went looking for an opportunity to kill a soldier. My mother, if she wasn't working that night, would respond with simple exasperation, 'They've started. We'll get no peace tonight.'

I did not want to be part of that, but that did not make me exceptional. I had some friends who, like Tony Henderson, had joined the IRA. Some others were in the Official IRA, the stickies, and a former classmate had joined the Catholic Ex-Servicemen's Association and was getting arms training. But there was nothing weird or geeky about not wanting to join the IRA. I had more friends working in the civil service, administering Northern Ireland, than urging on the revolution. But soldiers were a menace to me too, particularly the paratroopers who had already shown a greater willingness to kill the innocent bystander.

One soldier who served there for a time told me that the paratroopers sent to Belfast were a problem for other regiments: 'Some infantry regiments looked upon themselves as being some kind of "elite", and they would go in hard when carrying out lift operations or searches. The paras were absolute bastards for doing this, and on several occasions they came into our area, caused trouble and then left, with us having to deal with the consequences.'

Those consequences would be the deepened anger in the neighbourhood and greater determination of the IRA locally to kill a soldier in revenge for para brutality.

This man says that a senior officer within his regiment complained to Brigade HQ and demanded that the paras be kept out of his area.

Riverdale features in some of the army memoirs of the period, like Steve Corbett's *A Tough Nut to Crack: Andersonstown* or Harry Beaves's *Down Among the Weeds*. I was a weed! Beaves wasn't inclined to feign any regard for us.

Steve Corbett was a descendant of Irish catholics. His mother was a Fitzsimmons. He says that friends of his family shunned him after he joined the army. He was posted to Andersonstown in November 1971 and stationed at the bus depot which was beside the fortified police station and facing Milltown Cemetery.

Steve wants to be thought of as a decent chap who did his best and not as a brutal invader. He says, 'Our battery commander was of the old school, and we were all expected to act within the law and be polite at all times. Even the Provisional IRA had to admit to the way that we conducted ourselves.'

He has kept a cutting from an IRA newsheet, *The Volunteer*, which acknowledges the civility of his men:

NOTHING PERSONAL

It is not very often we commend British military personnel for their attitude towards any of our people. Truth, however, is the best weapon we have and we must comment favourably on the units who were engaged on the raids in the Riverdale Estate on Wednesday night.

From what we hear they were almost apologetic and were certainly much better behaved than we have become accustomed to expect from 'our protectors'. Could this be that at least some of them are beginning to realise just how they are being used and for what reason?

Unfortunately we will probably find that they will be injured in the next engagement or the one after that. If they read this we would like to thank them for their concern and to assure them that if they are injured or killed there is nothing personal in it.[1]

Steve was nineteen years old, in uniform and armed with a self-loading rifle, often driving in an armoured vehicle that was stoned and fired on. He had no human contact for months other than with people in the same position as himself. He had not gone there to be anyone's enemy. One might say he should have read the newspapers and known his history, but like most of those attacking him, he was only a kid.

He says, 'It was a bit of an eye opener to me when I was sent to Belfast... so much hatred directed towards us, and I really couldn't understand why. Those first few days we spent there were quite frightening, and I have to be honest and say that I cannot remember one single act of kindness directed towards us from the Catholic community. It was not until my second tour at New Lodge in 1974 that I managed to engage in proper conversation with some members of the community, and to see a different side to the people we saw on the streets when we engaged in conversation with them in the comfort of their own home.'

I didn't throw stones at soldiers or wish them killed but when a foot patrol passed me on the street I usually ignored them. My brother once joked that he had nearly struck a match on a soldier to light a cigarette, meaning that he was as indifferent to him as to a lamp post.

Steve says, 'Generally speaking, our battery commander kept us on a very tight rein, and I can only think of two occasions when things threatened to spiral out of control. Both incidents happened in the immediate aftermath of two separate shooting incidents when we had men gravely injured. The first incident was on Wednesday December 15th 1971, and involved a young gunner by the name of Fred Jeffries. He was shot in the lower back while sat in the back of a Pig which was ambushed at the junction of Ramoan Gardens/Glen Road and he ended up paralysed for life. Bombardier Kingsnorth was shot in the back of the head in the same incident, but his injuries were not as severe as Fred's. In the follow-up operation the soldiers went in a bit heavy handed… feelings amongst our lads were running fairly high. The soldiers responsible were put before the battery commander and received a very strong verbal warning for their actions.'

I wonder what 'heavy handed' means in this context and

if it entailed criminal violence, in which case perhaps 'a very strong verbal warning' was letting them off lightly.

'The second incident involved the shooting of Lance Bombardier Johnny Sutton on Thursday February 24th 1972. He was out with the RUC delivering court summonses, and their Pig was ambushed as it drove up Bingnian Drive. He was shot above the right eye, the bullet lodging in the back of his brain and he was paralysed down the right side of his body. The *Belfast Telegraph* published his name in their report of the incident, and this led to some of the residents in Andersonstown shouting abuse at passing patrols… "Sutton's going to die". Feelings amongst us were already running high, and this further inflamed tensions and thoughts of seeking revenge. In his wisdom, the battery commander stood the whole battery down and units from Brigade Reserve were drafted in to take over for twenty-four hours while we had a chance to cool down.'

Steve Corbett describes the life of a soldier in Northern Ireland then with an emphasis on his vulnerability and uncertainty. He was young. He was under intense pressure and he was in a job in which mistakes were potentially lethal: 'I can only speak for myself, but I was more frightened of the consequences of shooting an innocent person than anything else. When caught up in riots and other situations, where you would see someone peeking from behind a parked vehicle – or perhaps around a corner – if they were holding a stick – or something else in their hand, in the heat of the moment it could quite easily be mistaken for a weapon. You only have moments to react to the situation which is developing in front of you… you are thinking, "Have they got a gun, and are they about to shoot at me?" The provos were very adept at using rioters as cover while they engaged the soldiers. I have been in that situation where I have wondered whether those poles being deliberately stuck out of bedroom windows in failing light were indeed rifles being pointed my way. I was always hesitant in such situations, and that same hesitation cost some soldiers their life. It is all so easy to judge the actions of others, but unless you have been a soldier and have experienced such situations, you could never understand how it felt to face such a dreadful dilemma.'

In his book Steve describes a stake-out around the Green Briar, a pub popular with provos then, on the lower slope of Black Mountain. He says he saw two men crawling through bushes away from him and thought they might be armed. He chose not to open fire on them. Reflecting on it now, he thinks that was probably a mistake.

My dealings with the army were limited. In my work I phoned those supercilious army press officers and when covering a story I occasionally got talking to a soldier on the street, for instance, standing by a security barrier waiting for a bomb to blow out the front of a shop. When the same soldier would say hello to me closer to home I would pretend not to know him and remind him that he should have more sense than to embarrass me like that.

I was often stopped at checkpoints and searched, sometimes by soldiers who were civil or at least efficient and brisk, sometimes by surly thugs, once by surly thugs who were drunk.

I was drunk myself at times, quite often in fact.

There was so little comfort in living in a dangerous city and going home to a dangerous street. The first time I heard shooting close to the house I was lying in bed, wondering if I should hide under it. The sounds of the shots were cleaner and rounder than the shooting you heard in films or on television. The bullets were not impacting nearby. There was no whizz or ping. In fact they were about half a mile away and it turned out that one of those carrying out the shooting was a woman I knew. I had been in her house. Rita O'Hare was small and politically passionate but I had never expected her to pick up a rifle and take her chances against an army foot patrol that would shoot back.

She was tried a few days later by a special court convened in her hospital ward but she managed to escape to the South. She would become one of those contentious cases that the British regarded as evidence that the Irish government was not doing enough in the war against the IRA.

But it wasn't politics that I dwelt on. It was the incongruity of a young mother trying to kill young men with a rifle almost the size of herself. It was imagining the bullets from army rifles cutting through her little body and her somehow surviving. More, it was imagining the bullets cutting through my own body.

With two safe houses on our corner the IRA had set up a warning system to alert them when the army was spotted in the area. Women would come out onto the street and rattle metal bin lids on the tarmac, or blow whistles.

I never took part in that. It was drama on the street, celebratory, uncouth, livid, fun.

But I bought a little whistle in the Athletic Stores thinking

that I might join in, just once. Not that I cared to protect the
IRA men but perhaps I felt it would be a way to be part of the
community, doing the least it would take to be involved in
something rowdy and rebellious, marvelling at the way the
people who led this were the ones who would normally have
told you to behave yourself if you were raucous on the street.
I don't know why I bought the whistle. Who can explain in
later life the silly things they did when young?

Then one night, when I had been drinking with a friend
and had about three pints of beer in me, I was getting ready
for bed in a bedroom I shared with three brothers when my
father came into the room and told us that we should put out
the light. There were soldiers in the back garden.

I took my new whistle from a drawer and opened the window
to test a shrill blast from it and blew hard into the cold night;
the stupidest thing I have ever done.

First there was silence.

Then the loud thuds and the moments it took to realise
that this was our back door being kicked in. We all went out
onto the stairs to watch and the door, which was never used
and had a little ornate serving trolley parked in front of it,
was open, the trolley flung aside, and a very large soldier
with blackened face and a rifle was standing looking up at us.

Perhaps he recognised me, had seen me at the window. The
worst that he could have done was arrest one of my brothers
or my father for an action of mine, so I went downstairs to
give myself over to him. His uniform up close smelt of oil
and sweat. He clutched my shirt front and lifted me right
off the floor.

My mother was standing in a pink nightie shrieking at him to let me down, perhaps afraid that he would choke me.

My emotional responses had cut out by then. I was only watching this with curiosity.

The soldier took me out into our back garden where other soldiers stood around. He ordered me to stand against a wall and said, 'I am going to shoot you, Paddy.' He levelled his rifle at my chest.

I understood that a bullet fired from a few feet away would go through me and into the house. 'Could we not do it over there?' I suggested, indicating to another part of the garden.

It was almost as if this soldier and I were negotiating deep intimacy, like first sex. I knew that I was at least going to get a hammering and I had resigned myself to it and he seemed as gauchely ill-prepared for it as I was.

He pulled me away from the wall and dragged me by the hair round to the front of the house and through the front garden. When he lost hold of me pulling me through a hedge he kicked me hard in the middle of my forehead. My shirt was in shreds.

Their Pig was parked at Riverdale Park South, just at the end of our garden. We had a long front garden because we were a corner house and the corner was acute. Now he got me to stand against the Pig with my hands on it. One of my fingers went into a little viewing slat that was levered shut from inside. The soldier drew the shutter closed over my finger and opened it again to see my reaction. 'Must you?' I said, and he smiled and let it go.

The soldier who had brought me there bent down and

released a chain from the chassis of the Pig and when it touched the tarmac it flared with a pink and blue flame. Then I felt the first tingle through my fingers and body.

He started barking questions at me, stupid, ill-considered questions: 'Are you in the IRA? Who is in the IRA?'

And I felt more tingles but nothing more from the electric shocks they were trying to give me. I was as impervious to them in that state as I had been to the threats and kicks. I told them that I was a journalist. I named the soldiers I knew in the army press office. I don't know if they took that into account when they eventually let me go.

I walked back across our next-door neighbour's garden towards the hedge the soldier had pulled me through. I moved slowly for I considered that if I ran he might shoot me and say I had tried to escape. When I reached the hedge I could find no way in. I'd assumed there would be a gap where I had just minutes earlier been dragged through. I couldn't find it, so I walked the length of the hedge to the corner of the street and back to the house from there.

My parents were relieved to have me home. I had expected them to be angry but then I understood that my mother didn't know about me blowing the whistle. Two men came to the back door, members of the IRA. They asked what had happened and I told them. I was bragging now about how I would get my revenge as a journalist and tell the story and make a complaint.

I would do nothing.

I first made contact with Steve Corbett to ask if he might have been posted to Andersonstown at that time and he thinks not. I'm not sure of the actual date. He arrived on 25 November 1971. I think my beating was probably before that.

He says, 'I can fully understand why you would be dragged out of your house for blowing the whistle, but there was certainly no excuse for roughing you up. I'm quite confident that you do remember why whistles were blown, though, they were a highly effective means of warning IRA units of the presence of security forces being in the area. As for the electric shocks from the Pig, I have heard rumours in the past that this was done by some units, but I can categorically deny that we ever used such tactics... and I never saw any devices fitted to the Pigs that would enable this to be done.'

A few days after the incident, one of the IRA men who had come to our house after that incident stopped me on the street and said, 'Some people aren't pulling their weight around here.'

Routines of Murder

People in Belfast were getting used to the IRA's routines. It tried to bomb targets in ways that spared civilian casualties, but was not so moved by the suffering it caused despite these efforts that it considered stopping the bombing altogether. There were three different approaches taken in the early days.

One was to deliver a bomb to a target and warn people that they had a limited time in which to escape. The bomber would set the bomb down in a pub or hotel, shout out, 'You have two minutes to get out,' and people would scramble to safety.

Another approach, safer for the bomber, was to leave the bomb at the target discreetly then phone in a warning that the place had to be evacuated.

The IRA quickly found that it could cause enormous disruption by calling in warnings even when there was no bomb. All of commercial life in Belfast was destabilised by these hoaxes. But then people stopped believing the warnings and started getting careless.

The third approach developed at this time was the bomb with an anti-handling device. Instead of using a timer they would fit the device with a trigger that would only work when it was moved. That, theoretically, kept everyone safe, except for the army bomb-disposal officers whose job was to disarm the bomb.

Terry McDermott, who was only nineteen, was blown up by a cat, according to the IRA's own catalogue of the dead, *Tírghrá*. His intention was to bomb an electricity substation at Harmony Height, Lisburn. He and another IRA member had put the bomb in place, having primed the anti-handling device, 'when a cat ran out and triggered the bomb'.

My brother went to school with Terry McDermott. He says he was 'a nice bloke' and 'nobody knew' that he was in the IRA.

Despite trying to address the problem of civilian deaths by these various methods the IRA continued to kill civilians when its declared objective was to protect people – or at least to protect catholics – and to wage war on Britain by damaging the economy.

Usually those sent out to plant bombs were not the people who had made the bomb or prepared the timer. Nor did they have access to the timer when the unit was encased. The bomb team would be told that the device would go off at a specific time, and their job was to get it to the target before that time and not get blown up, which did happen on occasions.

What also happened was that the bombers arrived with too little time to give a viable warning, which was the case with the bombing of the popular Red Lion pub on the Ormeau Road, then a mostly protestant area. It was close to the Ballynafeigh

Leabharlann Ráth Maonais
Rathmines Library
01-2228466

RUC station and the Curzon cinema. A drapery shop was bombed at the same time.

Three IRA men went into the bar at half-past four on a Tuesday afternoon, not a time when it would have been expected to be busy, by which point there were only seconds left before detonation. One of them stood guard with a pistol while the others placed the bomb and shouted that everyone had ten seconds to get out.

Some rushed to a side door and found it locked, a precaution against someone coming in and leaving a bomb in the toilets.

Molly Gemmell, a woman in her fifties, died sitting in an upstairs lounge alone and would not have heard the warning. John Cochrane, sixty-seven, and William Jordan, thirty-one, were killed in the blast, failing to get out in time. All three were protestants.

The bombs in the bar and the drapery shop had been set against walls adjoining an RUC station that was between them, so it may be that the timing was short to deny the police the chance to hear of the warning and evacuate.

Years later a similar short-timer bomb was used in an attempt to kill the leadership of the Ulster Defence Association. This was at Frizzell's fish shop on the Shankill Road. On that occasion, nothing having been learnt from the Red Lion experience, nine civilians and one of the bombers died. The intended target, a meeting of loyalists upstairs, had already finished.

In December 1971 three bombers blew themselves up in a car. Jim Sheridan and John Bateson were twenty years old, Martin Lee was only eighteen. They were travelling in Bateson's car, which does not suggest they were experienced operators.

Sheridan was in the back seat with the bomb in his lap. They had one pistol between them. The police have since said that they believe they were going out to bomb another electricity substation. This was in the town of Magherafelt, in South Derry, near where the poet Seamus Heaney grew up.

Though the blast took the roof off the car leaving only the engine and two front wheels, Martin Lee survived for a short while after. A police sergeant took him to the Mid Ulster Hospital but he was dead before they got there.

Accidents or 'own goals' were routine in the IRA and many who died in them were very young and inexperienced.

While killings and blunders continued to disrupt and bereave, and the rancour between and within communities was growing harsher as fear intensified, relations between Britain and the Irish Republic were worsening too.

The British believed that the Irish government was soft on the IRA and British ambassador John Peck came back at the taoiseach with an angry letter after murders close to the border.

Kenneth Smyth was twenty-eight years old and a part-time soldier in the Ulster Defence Regiment. He was off duty. His catholic friend Daniel McCormick had also been in the regiment but had left. Smyth had recently got married. McCormick was twenty-nine years old and had five children and lived in Strabane. They were planning to do a day's work together, sitting in a civilian Land Rover waiting for another workmate to join them. It was nine o'clock in the morning, a couple of weeks before Christmas, near the village of Clady, right on the border.

It is a beautiful area, more verdant than the rugged north of County Donegal, but still you could feel when you crossed the border there that you had entered into a more placid agricultural region. The predominant smell in the air at that time of year would have been turf smoke from domestic fires.

Strabane on the northern, British side had a strong IRA presence. Nearby in the Republic, Castlefin was also a base for activists and they were out to prove that day that they had free access to the border and could cross it as they pleased.

A casual assassin shot Kenneth Smyth and Daniel McCormick dead. Ambassador Peck's letter says the killer was joined by another man, and 'then walked across the Border about 200 metres away'.[1]

This was the second attempt to kill Kenneth Smyth, who had only been married for three months. In August '71, while he lived with his parents, gunmen called at the house looking for him when he was out.

The British were livid about the ease with which the killers had been able to walk to safety, out of the reach of the army.

Then two days later, in the same area, about 400 metres from the border, members of the Official IRA shot and killed Senator Jack Barnhill. They said afterwards that they had not set out to kill him. They had only wanted to burn down his house but the man had had the temerity to try to obstruct them. The account in *Lost Lives* says that Jack Barnhill answered the door to his killers and they shot him and laid his body beside their bomb, telling his wife she had two minutes to get out of the house.

The ambassador said, 'HMG regard it as intolerable that the Republic should provide a refuge from which the murderers can operate with impunity, whether the men are from the south or the north.' He set out details of the action that the British wanted the taoiseach to take, which was to instruct the army and the Irish police, the Garda Síochána, to 'take more vigorous action against the gangs operating across the Border, particularly near Strabane'.

The hope was that 'this could provide the basis for close cooperation between security forces on both sides of the Border and for follow-up action should the RUC or Gardai obtain leads to perpetrators of these crimes'.

Perhaps he was hoping that 'follow-up action' would entail the right for forces on either side of the border to cross it in pursuit of suspects. That would never be agreed to.

Peck also demanded more effective extradition procedures. Lynch had already said he preferred to see suspects tried rather than interned. Peck said he found it hard to accept 'that those against whom charges have been brought, and who will be brought to trial if caught, can enjoy a safe haven from which they can perpetrate further crimes'.

This was a low point in British–Irish relations, with the British effectively accusing the Irish government of making life easy for the IRA. The Irish, however, rejected the claim that they were soft on terrorism and denied that the ease with which gunmen could cross the border was part of the problem.

Even so, the taoiseach Jack Lynch suggested that the two governments should jointly ask the United Nations Security

Council to provide an observer group on both sides of the border 'to expose or prevent activities prejudicial to the peace'.

This was in a speech in the Dáil on 16 December, just four days after the killing of Senator Barnhill. He claimed that the whole question of border security was being raised to shift attention away from a failure of British policy: 'Every objective observer is well aware that the causes of violence in the North lie in the refusal of civil and human rights to 40 per cent of the population in the area for half a century – a deprivation which current policies are not correcting.'

The blame, as he saw it, lay with the unionist government in Stormont.

The Irish may also have been miffed about the British ambassador concerning himself more about the murders of a UDR man and a senator than with a much more significant act of violence just days earlier.

*

The greatest single atrocity of 1971 took place on 4 December. It was a loyalist bomb attack on a catholic bar, McGurk's in North Queen Street.

On Saturdays at the *Sunday News* we functioned like a daily paper, following the news up to the time of going to press, which on those busy weekends might be the early hours of the morning.

I heard the bomb just before nine o'clock that evening.

One of my jobs was to phone the army press office every hour to ask if anything was happening. The soldier on the other end would be civil and helpful within the limits of professional courtesy. He told me that there had been an explosion in North Queen Street. We had two reporters out of the office at the time on another job, Steve and Paddy, and, when they phoned in, the news editor Jim asked them to go and see what had happened.

In Belfast at that time some bars were associated with one of the IRA factions or a loyalist group but McGurk's wasn't that kind of place. It was a family-run pub with the children in bed upstairs. A team from the UVF had gone out that night to attack a different bar but couldn't muster the resolve to approach it and settled for an easier target, apparently thinking, why waste a bomb?

I took calls from Paddy and Steve but I wasn't allowed to go out there myself. My job was to type up the notes that they phoned through, keeping in touch with the army press office and nipping out to buy fags for Jim.

We knew this was serious but not yet how serious. Direct sectarian attacks on pubs with the naked purpose of killing people were not yet a routine practice for any paramilitary group. An exception before this had been an IRA attack on a bar, the Four Step Inn, on the protestant Shankill Road. That attack was on 29 September, a Friday night, when the bar was full of supporters of the Linfield football team. Someone had placed a bomb in the hallway. When it exploded it killed Alexander Andrews, sixty, and Ernie Bates, thirty-eight, two popular characters on the road.

It was one of those bombs that the IRA did not claim, probably because it didn't fit with the organisation's presentation of itself as non-sectarian. A rumour went round that it had been made by loyalists and had gone off prematurely. One English journalist told us at the *Sunday News* that the army had actually briefed him that that is what had happened.

The nationalist leaders at the time, however, condemned the bomb as sectarian, the work of madmen.

But that same story was told about the bomb at McGurk's, that it was an own goal. This may have been an army strategy for reducing tension. One army source actually claimed that those killed in McGurk's had been gathering round, getting a lesson in how to make a bomb. And there had indeed been several accidents of that kind and would be more.

Maybe the British ambassador believed that story at the time he was writing to the Irish government and didn't feel called upon by courtesy or compassion to express his sorrow that fourteen people, including thirteen-year-old James Cromie and fourteen-year-old Marie McGurk, were among those murdered. A married couple were also among the dead, Eddie and Sarah Keenan. The oldest victim was Philip Garry, seventy-three, a school-crossing patrol man.

William Rutherford was a surgeon at the Royal Victoria Hospital on duty that night. He was in charge of Casualty. When news came in about the scale of the carnage he decided not to wait for ambulances to bring in the injured but to move facilities from the hospital to the scene.

He was there when people were digging the dead and injured out of the rubble, when IRA men were firing on the army nearby. He told me that he had brought morphine to treat the injured and that they stood in front of him with horrific injuries and told him that they were not in pain.

The IRA had no connection with McGurk's Bar, and the family who owned it urged that there be no retaliation for the attack, but the IRA chose to avenge the murder of catholic innocents a week later with the murder of protestant innocents.

On the following Saturday, early in the afternoon, when the Shankill Road was always dense with shoppers, two IRA members stopped in a car outside the Moffat's Balmoral Furniture Showrooms. One of them carried a parcel to the front of the shop.

Moffat's was a Victorian building and when the bomb exploded moments later the entire structure collapsed on the people inside.

One of the children to die was two-year-old Tracy Munn. Her twenty-two-year-old mother was pushing her in a pram past the shop when the bomb went off. The explosion fractured the young woman's skull and her pelvis. She came to consciousness to find an ambulance man putting a mask on her face while others lifted bricks off her body.

People rallying to help clear the rubble from the injured and the dead saw an ambulance man carry a baby's body wrapped in sheets but dripping blood like meat from a butcher's slab. That was seventeen-month-old Colin Nicholl. He had been adopted by Ann and Jackie Nicholl because they had not had a child of their own after seven years of marriage.

Jackie said, 'Through all the tragedies you don't really realise how much it is going to hurt.'

Two adult men were killed in the blast, one a catholic, twenty-year-old Harold King, the other a protestant, thirty-year-old Hugh Bruce, who had two children.

Eddie Kinner was there. He told me, 'I think you were pretty much more in shock and anger. It gave me the determination that if that's happening on the Shankill, I would want to do the same, twice as much, on the Falls. That was my mentality at that stage.'

Republicans frequently insist that the campaign of the IRA was not sectarian. This was a revenge attack against a protestant community from which the UVF – which had bombed McGurk's – had come. It did nothing to damage or curtail the UVF but actually fired up Eddie Kinner and others to get involved and retaliate. It confirmed them in a view that the IRA was a sectarian enemy whose prime objection to them was simply that they were protestant.

The conviction nurtured in both communities was that they were hated and targeted for their religious roots, regardless of their politics or whether they supported paramilitaries. What politics had Tracy Munn?

There was now no force in play – not the army, the loyalists or the republicans – that had not been carelessly murderous, that had not lashed out against bystanders. For me and any other person living in Northern Ireland, but especially, so far, in Belfast, there was no way in which I could live my life free of the danger of being shot by a soldier, bombed by a loyalist or bombed by the IRA. And there was no power I could turn to that would offer me security. Life was now anarchic. Only luck or the ordinary laws of averages and a degree of informed caution would get me through the coming years without being killed or injured. The IRA and the army both said they were there to defend me but the price of their supposed protection was actually greater jeopardy.

The loyalists would have relished the opportunity to kill me, not because they had anything personal against me or cared what I believed but because I was a fenian, a taig. (These were their derisive terms for someone from an Irish catholic background.) Even they would rationalise my murder or they would disclaim it, understanding that pure naked sectarian hatred is something decent people don't own up to.

And that is why the IRA didn't own up to the bombing of Moffat's furniture shop on the Shankill when Christmas shoppers thronged the road.

The ruination of Northern Ireland, the horror of it all, was to be measured not just in the death toll or in the deaths of children and the deployment of mere teenagers as bombers and killers, the callousness and the incompetence of the IRA, but also in the burden it imposed on ordinary people, those who wanted to go to work, those who had businesses to run.

*

Diljit Rana had been a refugee from Pakistan after the partition of India in 1947. He came to Belfast in 1966 and took over a chip shop. He claims to have invented the curried chip. He tried to expand his business as the city was shutting down in the face of violence.

He says, 'I spotted a restaurant, the Burlington, in a good position for sale on Dublin Road and made a bid to take it over. The owner had lost interest because of the violence and was easy to deal with. I paid him £5,000 for the lease, took possession of the restaurant at the beginning of November

1971 and opened for business within a few days. Although the Burlington's evening trade had collapsed, I reckoned the large number of offices in the area could provide good lunchtime custom to make the business viable. Things went well for about a month… until just before lunchtime on Monday, 6th December 1971 when bombers entered a neighbouring carpet and linoleum warehouse and planted several incendiary devices. The alarm was raised and the warehouse was quickly evacuated with hundreds of female workers pouring out of the shirt factory on the floors above and all nearby premises including my new restaurant. As we watched, horrified, the bombs exploded causing a fierce fire to spread uncontrollably throughout the five-storey Victorian building, consuming everything in its path.'

Today Lord Rana counts up the number of times his businesses were bombed: twenty-seven.

The worst year was to come, but 1971 still had some venom to expend. Loyalists would kill sixteen-year-old Jim McCallum in a bomb attack on Murtagh's pub on the Springfield Road.

Two IRA snipers firing at soldiers from a house on the Crumlin Road would injure one and kill twenty-year-old Margaret McCorry.

Sixty-year-old John Lavery would be killed by the IRA bomb he carried out of his pub.

The British army would shoot dead Gerard McDade, whom the IRA would describe as 'an extremely active freedom fighter'. The republican cause had further grief to bring to that family. Three years later, Gerard's older brother James would blow himself up with his own bomb in Coventry.

And the IRA would kill another soldier, Richard Ham, in Derry.

The last death of the year was another own goal. IRA man Jack McCabe's bomb would explode in a garage in Dublin. McCabe at fifty-five was a long-standing republican who had served time in jail in England.

By the end of 1971, 210 people had died since the start of the Troubles in August 1969. About two-thirds of them, 136, had died in the previous four months since the introduction of internment.

It's Normal Now

I had come of age to the realisation not just that I was vulnerable but that the whole society in which I lived could crack and split apart, that the buses could stop running, there would be smoke on the breeze, news coming through about the dead, and those who might have been dependable supports were instead threatening and dangerous.

I was so young that the men of the neighbourhood remembered me as a child and I remembered them as strong and admirable; now they were crazy, building barricades, unloading rifles from a van across the street.

And though I had regarded the police as distant I had not thought of them as troublesome. But what would have happened had I called them and said I know where guns are hidden? An army raid might have left bodies on the street and I would have been responsible. I was in a society in which I had no reliable bearings, no authority to turn to or even to obey.

And routinely on the news, after reports of further madness, there would be statements by politicians about the courage and dependability of 'our forces', ignoring the role they played as irritants.

But still the sun came out.

When the film makers and novelists try to recreate that time they often get it wrong. Yes, there were times when the very air was tense and you seemed to know as soon as you stepped out the front door that the sky was leaden with worry.

But still there was the pub and the walk to the shops, the laughter about other things, the day you walked up the mountain paths you'd used as a child and saw Scotland in the blue haze. There were still other things on television apart from the news.

And when Northern Ireland's violence featured, even in 1972, very early in the Troubles, the newsreader would drop tone, almost sigh, expecting the national audience to be bored.

The pathetic fallacy, the device in Shakespeare in which even the heavens respond to the madness below, is richly deployed in historic documentaries about Northern Ireland. The brief cuts and the managed pace and the dramatic delivery of the presentation tell you that events you already knew about, had lived through, had a potent significance you didn't quite catch at the time.

But the failure is in the recall of the programme makers. They miss the point that most of life was not absorbed in the background drone of tension.

Yet, I think now that we who lived through it fail to admit to ourselves how bad it was, as we allowed ourselves to forget it at the time. There was always an early recovery from shock. Was this resilience or self-delusion or just the momentum of the new normal?

People are conditioned to play down their own suffering by fear of seeming to upstage those who have suffered worse. No one wants to be thought an attention seeker by proclaiming how shaken they were by a bomb exploding nearby when someone else was killed or crippled by that bomb. Nor would people then talk of the fear they felt being evacuated from an office building during a bomb scare because the important part of that story is that there was no bomb, that nothing of consequence happened. The appropriate response is relief.

But even if you only had your sleep disturbed by distant bombs and no one you knew or cared for was killed or injured, that was sufficient burden to make life wearisome, but how could you complain about that when it was the minimal experience of everyone who lived in the city? It was the common part of daily life that was worth mentioning, like the weather, but hardly worth dwelling on.

One thing that was different was the way in which people responded to the news. Back then, I recall that we were obsessed with it. For some people there wasn't enough and they monitored police radio on shortwave and bulletins from foreign stations.

Why was that?

During the Troubles the deaths were small enough in number for each to be dwelt on and the city was small enough for it to be likely that you would know personally some of those killed. The bomb in a bar might have caught you or your brother on a different night because you had been in that bar.

The car that was shot at by soldiers after passing through a checkpoint might have been your car. The driver who had mistaken a signal to stop for a signal to proceed – for it was only a dim lamp waved in the air – might as easily have been you.

And while the trouble confined us to our homes on nights when it was too dangerous to go out, when we did go out we saw the architecture of war, the barricades, the security screens on police stations, the burnt buildings, the soldiers in uniform, the helicopter overhead.

*

The IRA called a three-day ceasefire for Christmas 1971, probably as much to give its own members a rest as to allow the people to go shopping without fear of being caught in a bomb attack or trapped in traffic jams caused by bomb scares in the early darkness of midwinter. But a ceasefire is a military operation and calls for total control of an organisation. When the IRA showed that a ceasefire order was obeyed throughout the whole organisation it demonstrated its coherence and discipline.

I had now been a working journalist for four months. The *Sunday News* was not thought by professionals to be a good place to start on a paper. The older journalists I knew had started out on provincial weeklics, getting their experience covering courts and councils and then moving to dailies in the city. Other journalists from around the world were coming to Belfast because the violence was a big story but I was too young and inexperienced to join in at their level. I met a lot of these journalists but did not feel I could easily identify with them because they had an easy distance from the story that I did not have.

One evening I was on the Antrim Road at a bomb alert. The press were being held back by soldiers, waiting for something to happen. Standing beside me was a familiar broadcast reporter from London. He was joking with one of the soldiers. This was a legitimate way for him to try to ingratiate himself and tease out a bit of detail that would enrich his story. But I was confused by this on a couple of levels.

I saw that the soldier was a lot more relaxed with this reporter than he would have been with me or another local journalist. That English accent got the reporter a degree of access that I was not going to get. But did it also put the reporter on the same side as the soldier? It felt to me that it did and it made me wary of the reporter. But why shouldn't an English reporter feel affinity with an English soldier, both of them away from home, perhaps sharing the same perception of the trouble as alien?

Might he be signalling to the soldier that he is not with me, that he is not like these others with their Belfast accents, who you could never be sure weren't sympathisers or sneaking regarders of the bombers and snipers? I felt revulsion and a wariness of him.

And maybe what appalled me was journalism itself, its pretence of being above the story.

He annoyed me both as a brit being matey with another brit, but also as someone who regarded himself as an outsider looking in. His affinity with the soldier was that they would both go back to England, hopefully untouched by their experience beyond having a few yarns to share.

This reporter was never going to come under suspicion of being a bomber. He was never going to be slammed up against a wall and frisked by a soldier. It wasn't his fault that I suffered these vulnerabilities by virtue of being local but it still established a difference between us that would make empathy difficult.

In a sense it was impossible for me really to be a journalist there, at least not the kind of journalist who stands back from a story, reports it to people who are also removed from it, and goes home to bed to give it no further thought.

The press pack in Belfast was mostly based at the Europa Hotel in the centre of the city. I went home to my parents' house in Riverdale. The bomber who had made the story of the day might be staying in a safe house across the street from me. Soldiers who came into the estate came ready to be attacked, sometimes in the big whining Saracen armoured carriers that gave them more protection than the standard Pigs. The reporters would have filed their copy and met up in the bar to unwind after a long and stressful day.

My problem was that my position was ambiguous. I would have loved to have been outside the story but by then I could never have approached a British soldier without arousing suspicion among those who saw us talking. Even at work, hearing protestant journalists express their contempt for the IRA I was inclined to bridle and feel implicated, for part of me would want to argue back. I would never have defended the IRA but I could not indulge the easy superficial contempt for them that assumed no one else was in the wrong.

From a unionist or security perception – indeed it was government policy – the IRA was the whole problem and security was the answer. There was little allowance for how

huge numbers had lost respect for the army and saw it as
part of the problem. People had come to accept that having
an army in the city would lead to civilian deaths. Though the
phrase 'collateral damage' had not yet been coined and the
principle was not being as bluntly asserted as to be given a
name, there was still as much a feeling among those supporting
the army as those supporting the IRA that innocents would
die, and that's what I was, an innocent. As Ruairí Ó Brádaigh
had said, these things happen in war.

One day I took a phone call at the office from Major Barry
Brooking of the Green Howards regiment which had men
billeted in north Belfast. After giving me some details about
an incident he invited me up to the base for a drink, said he
would give me a lift home. 'Riverdale? No problem.'

A real reporter would have been happy to go but asked to
be dropped off at the Europa and perhaps got a taxi home
from there. I didn't give it even a moment's consideration.
Nothing would have induced me to get drunk and matey
with soldiers. And what if neighbours in the IRA had seen me
brought home in an army vehicle? I might have been shot as
an informer. More likely our house would have been attacked
and daubed and we would all have had to leave. Did Major
Brooking not understand that?

*

Looking towards the new year, our paper, the *Sunday News*,
carried predictions from the 'world renowned clairvoyant'
Maurice Woodruff. Weirdly, his predictions did match unfolding
reality, though not as he expected. He said that by March

Brian Faulkner would be able to relax. Indeed he would, but not because the pressure of the violence would ease up but because the British government would relieve him of his job.

He also predicted that Ted Heath would announce his engagement – Woodruff had failed to recognise a confirmed bachelor – and Ian Paisley the firebrand would 'start to think of the people and the country as a whole'. That's not bad. After direct rule was introduced by Westminster in March 1972 Paisley would split unionism by arguing for the integration of Northern Ireland into Great Britain and an end to devolution.

Woodruff suspected that it would take a lot to please John Hume and that he would not have a satisfactory year ahead 'because he will allow himself to be overruled by fanatical people'. Indeed, Hume would attempt to mediate a peace with the IRA and, after a ceasefire, the provos would escalate their war.

A New Year

1972 began as bloodily and sloppily as the previous year had ended, with killings by the army, the IRA and loyalists and with fatal accidents.

A sniper shot dead soldier Keith Bryan of the Gloucestershire Regiment on the Falls Road on 5 January. He was eighteen years old. Next day a soldier shot Danny O'Neill. He was twenty-one and he died two days later. The army had been following up a gun attack and opened fire on a car.

Peter Woods was a twenty-nine-year-old publican. Gunmen burst into his house to steal the takings from his bar, the Gibraltar in York Street, and shot him dead. Having scooped up the cash one of the gunmen turned to another and said, 'We have got the money, Seamus. Come on.' The authors of *Lost Lives* believe that this was a sectarian assassination by loyalists pretending to be catholics.

And the first own goal of the year was the shooting in a training exercise of Michael Sloan. He was a boy of fifteen and a member of the junior wing of the IRA, the Fianna. An ambulance crew found his body in a house in New Barnsley Park after a neighbour waved them down while they were on another call. Michael had a pistol in his pocket and there were several other guns in the room, left behind by those who had been with him and had panicked and fled.

Tírghrá says that he had joined up to 'play his part in the struggle for national independence'.

The new year quickly provided examples of bombings, land mine attacks, snipings, close-quarter assassination, ambushes and accidents, the whole range. For instance, Sydney Agnew was a forty-year-old bus driver. His bus had been hijacked and he had agreed to give evidence in court against the suspected hijackers. Two teenagers called at his home in the Mount, asked a child who answered the door if her daddy was a bus driver and opened fire on him when he came out.

There was another accidental death of a terrorist when Peter McNulty's bomb exploded prematurely. His intended target had been Crossmaglen RUC station.

Tommy Gorman was now interned on the *Maidstone* prison ship moored in Belfast Lough, along with other members of the company he had been operating with: Tucker Kane and Sean Convery, his Officer Commanding, whom he and Kane had previously tried to spring out of Crumlin Road Gaol.

Gorman says that when the internees he was among were joined on the *Maidstone* by James Bryson and Tommy 'Todler' Tolan an escape from the ship became possible: 'They were two fucking hard men and I thought, there's the sort of people we need behind an escape.'

Bryson and Tolan were IRA men from Ballymurphy. Bryson would later be shot dead by an army sniper and Tolan would be killed in a feud with the Official IRA. They worked out how to get off the boat avoiding security alarms by watching the movement of seals through a porthole.

There was a plan which, if it had gone ahead, would have got them out one afternoon, to be met by a lorry with dry clothes and hot soup. But they had to postpone until later that evening.

They climbed down a hawser with socks over their hands to ease the friction. The water was cold. Convery nearly drowned because he couldn't swim. Tommy Gorman heard him screaming to God but did not go back for him. The men had agreed that if one went down the others would carry on without him.

Gorman recalls, 'I was first out and I was hunkered beside a wee jetty. I got up and started to walk around the street and a parked bus was sitting outside one of the gates. The driver was hunkered down just reading a magazine. He said, what's wrong? I said, I fell into the water and I need to get to the hospital. He put his hand on me and he was saying, come on, come on. I said, give us your coat. He took off his coat and I was walking round and he was saying, come on, and he grabbed me, so I fucking hooked him.'

As the others appeared near naked and wet, walking out of the water like weird creatures, the wet socks extending their arms, they accepted for a time that Convery had been lost.

'We got into a wee yellow car – talking and talking about what to do. We were only about a hundred yards from where people were working. It was like being off stage by the light. So Convery appears. So I says, there's a bus parked round the corner so that's where we're going to go.

'I had the driver's coat on. Jim Bryson had nothing on. He was naked. Others lifted covers from the car and we went back to the bus. There was a wee minivan parked behind the bus. That was apparently the security for the shipyard. Peter Rogers had been a bus driver so he jumped on.'

The bus driver turned up then and tried to recover his vehicle but they hit him again. They drove out into the Markets area. They ran to the nearest pub and kids jumped onto the bus and started vandalising it.

'And people started taking their clothes off and giving us clothes. We were out of the place in five minutes and away on up into billets in Lenadoon.'

For the next few months the men were billeted at two safe houses in Riverdale, both of them within view of my own front door. They carried out bombings and shootings from there.

*

In Derry, on 27 January, the IRA shot and killed two policemen in a patrol car, the first police officers to be killed in the city since the start of the Troubles. It was a sophisticated ambush with several gunmen spaced along the road firing on their car with a variety of weapons including a Thompson submachine gun.

One of the dead policemen, Peter Gilgunn, was a catholic who had joined the RUC six years earlier, before the Troubles.

He was twenty-six years old and married with one child. The other, David Montgomery, was a single man of twenty and a protestant. He had joined two years earlier and was engaged to marry a local girl.

We were now approaching one of the great calamities of the whole Troubles period, Bloody Sunday in Derry.

The Civil Rights Association was trying to present an alternative to violence, to revive the protest march and make a case against the state for the ending of internment and the withdrawal of the army from catholic areas. But the government had banned all marches.

A week earlier, a march along Magilligan Strand to the prison there, to protest against internment, ended in chaos as soldiers beat the marchers with batons and fired rubber bullets at them. John Hume had confronted the officer in charge. The officer defended his actions on behalf of the government and Hume said plainly that he didn't recognise that government. He accused the soldiers of opening fire with CS gas grenades and rubber bullets before the protesters reached the army barrier. But Hume was so shocked by the intensity of the army's violence, even though no one had been killed, that he advised against the march on 30 January and declined to take part in it himself.

The report on this to the Joint Security Committee the following Thursday gives it only one line: 'No trouble until marchers infringed Army territory and had to be repulsed.'[1]

Anticipating the following Sunday's march in Derry, the report said, 'The basic plan will be to block all routes into

William Street and to stop the march there. The operation might well develop into rioting and even a shooting war.'

British paratroopers would shoot dead thirteen people on that march.

Bloody Sunday

I wasn't there. I was at home that Sunday afternoon watching television with my father and mother. My father grew up in Derry and the street names on news reports coming through from the city meant more to him. They were reminders of his youth, prompts perhaps to memories of antics and friendships.

I hadn't been at recent protest marches though I agreed with their objectives, to end internment and get the army out of residential areas. I understood that people like John Hume wanted to show that non-violent protest could work and that in doing so they could build an argument against the IRA campaign, but even he had decided to stay out of this one, having seen how his efforts at peaceful protest the previous week had been swept aside by soldiers who didn't hesitate to fire rubber bullets and CS gas.

I suspect that Derry was still in the giddy phase of the early Troubles, when one might still think of it as exciting. Belfast was a darker place where more people had been killed and where the protestant and catholic communities were butted against each other.

Two wings of the IRA had sealed off the Bogside and Creggan areas as 'Free Derry', controlled movement in and out and even kept the army at bay. There had been army recognition of 'Free Derry' at times, and a sense that if they were ever to move against it, to crash through the barricades and confront the two IRAs, hundreds might die.

So, some in Derry felt that they had reclaimed and secured territory, started a revolution.

That would not have been the thinking of all the people who joined the march behind a lorry leading them and the Civil Rights banner, and wound their way from the hillside of the Creggan estate towards the river and the city. There were teachers and civil servants, doctors and accountants, nurses and taxi drivers, and barmen and mechanics. Most were young men. Some chatting and smoking, but all walking at a steady determined pace set by the lorry.

Even when they passed an army barricade most carried on. And when some broke away to confront the soldiers at the barbed wire coils, the soldiers reacted calmly, spoke to them and urged them to stay back, as did march stewards. And press photographers inched round the crowd to capture the event. There was no sign of great anxiety or of anger at that stage.

The first news we heard at home was that two were dead. Through the afternoon there were updates on the figure until it was higher than any we had heard before in reports of a single day's trouble. I felt myself, sitting with my father, aware of nothing else, almost contracting inside myself, growing heavier, shrinking appalled from the world, understanding now that things were worse than ever and would stay that way.

That was a brisk and cold winter afternoon when 15,000 people descended the hill on a winding road towards the Bogside and the more level ground they would follow towards the city centre and the Guildhall. They knew they were walking towards obstruction and danger but there was comfort in huge numbers. When the march stopped at a barrier the main body turned to gather round a lorry to hear speeches from Bernadette Devlin, Lord Brockway, the eighty-three-year-old Labour peer and peace activist, and others. Those who were keen on a riot carried on ahead to face the soldiers. Things got hot and heavy with rioters throwing stones and, in one case, a CS gas canister. The soldiers used rubber bullets and gas at first and brought up a water cannon.

This was familiar stuff to the soldiers and the rioters. Lord Saville, reporting on the shootings nearly forty years later, would commend those soldiers of the Royal Green Jackets who 'acted with restraint in the face of rioting... and deployed no more than properly proportionate force in seeking to deal with it'.

Then two soldiers fired five shots and hit fifteen-year-old Damien Donaghy in the leg and fifty-five-year-old John Johnson who was standing behind him. These were the first shots of the day.

The next shots were fired by a gunman of the Official IRA, aiming at soldiers on a wall beside the presbyterian church. He missed and hit a drainpipe.

Two Pigs roared into the Bogside and stopped at the car park under Rossville Flats. Dismounting soldiers fired baton rounds at a fleeing crowd. Lieutenant N (as he is named in the report) fired rifle shots over the heads of some of them.

He said that he was trying to prevent the crowd from attacking him. Saville didn't accept that: 'In our view this use of his weapon cannot be justified.'

Lord Saville's inquiry suggested that the sound of Lieutenant N's firing had alarmed other soldiers and enhanced the impression of the danger they were in.

Then other soldiers in the car park started firing. They killed a seventeen-year-old boy, Jackie Duddy, and wounded six others.

Several other army vehicles now rushed to the car park, an anti-tank platoon and a mortar platoon. Neither would face tanks or need mortars. Soldiers took up positions by a block of flats called Kells Walk and opened fire on the crowd. They killed seventeen-year-old Michael Kelly. Several people rushed to move Michael's body from near a rubble barricade and after that soldiers at Rossville Street shot and killed five more people near the barricade.

These were seventeen-year-old Hugh Gilmour, nineteen-year-old William Nash, seventeen-year-old John Young, twenty-year-old Michael McDaid and seventeen-year-old Kevin McElhinney. Alexander Nash rushed over to help his son and he was shot too, though not killed.

Now four soldiers pursued people fleeing them into Glenfada Park North, a housing complex. Saville says that within seconds of the soldiers entering the complex they started shooting. They killed twenty-six-year-old William McKinney and twenty-two-year-old Jim Wray. They shot Wray twice, the second shot when he was on the ground wounded. They wounded four, possibly five others.

In Abbey Park another soldier shot and killed two people with one bullet. These were thirty-five-year-old Gerard McKinney and seventeen-year-old Gerald Donaghey.

After clearing Glenfada Park North, the soldiers there returned and fired across Rossville Street at the flats. There they killed two more and wounded two more. The dead were forty-one-year-old Bernard McGuigan and thirty-two-year-old Patrick Doherty.

The whole business had taken just ten minutes and one hundred rounds.

We know more now about Bloody Sunday than about any other major incident of the Troubles period. There have been two judicial inquiries and several books have been written about it. There is a museum to the event in Derry and there have been a number of television documentaries that attempted to get to the heart of it.

The first inquiry was chaired by Lord Chief Justice Widgery just weeks after the killings. Widgery believed the soldiers gave honest accounts of their experience but he also concluded that 'none of the deceased or wounded is proved to have been shot whilst handling a firearm or bomb'. He said that some of the dead were 'wholly acquitted' but that there was a strong suspicion that others had been armed at some stage during that afternoon.

He said that some of the firing had 'bordered on the reckless' and that 'the hazard to civilians' of an arrest operation carried out in battalion strength, in a situation in which soldiers were likely to come under fire, 'may have been under-estimated'.

He concluded also that there was no general breakdown in discipline. 'For the most part the soldiers acted as they did because they thought their orders required it. No order and no training can ensure that a soldier will always act wisely, as well as bravely and with initiative. The individual soldier ought not to have to bear the burden of deciding whether to open fire in confusion such as prevailed on 30 January. In the conditions prevailing in Northern Ireland, however, this is often inescapable.'

That excused everybody, the innocent dead, the soldiers who killed them and the people who had ordered the soldiers in.

He even said that 'in view of the experience of this unit in operations of this kind', it was not necessary for them to have been given more precise orders than they were given.

The experience of this unit had included the killing of civilians in Ballymurphy in the week of the first internment raids the previous August.

Widgery's was an 'accidents will happen' type of conclusion and this one would not have happened if an illegal march had not been staged in the city.

At the time the Widgery Report was dismissed as a whitewash, though it clearly contradicted the army accounts immediately after the shootings, which claimed that all of the dead had been gunmen or bombers.

One of those who saw merit in it was Henry Kelly of the *Irish Times*: 'He clearly supported the contention that all killed were innocent. All he could do was cast suspicion on some of them, while completely exonerating most.'[1]

Once the inquiry by Lord Widgery was announced, discussion of the killings was curtailed in the media, which treated the matter as *sub judice*.

British cabinet records show that ministers discussed possible queries about the viability of a single judge sitting on the inquiry. Heath suggested that it should be 'more widely known' that Widgery had personally chosen to sit alone. This might help allay speculation that the government was trying to avoid a split judgment. He was content, however, that 'it could not be convincingly argued that the Lord Chief Justice of England lacked impartiality'.

Twenty-six years later Prime Minister Tony Blair commissioned another inquiry, this time by Lord Saville. This was at the height of the peace process and carried significance as a signal that the government hoped to facilitate progress by acknowledging army excesses. That inquiry would last ten years.

Saville contradicted Widgery in his main conclusions. He said that the army had lost control and that the Parachute Regiment's Commanding Officer, Lieutenant Colonel Derek Wilford, had exceeded his orders. He agreed with Widgery, however, on a point that had been much denied by justice campaigners and others down the years, that the soldiers had been fired on before they had opened fire themselves. Soldiers had not, however, faced the 200 shots that the army claimed had been fired at them.

Saville had little difficulty doubting the evidence of some of the soldiers:

As will be seen from other parts of this report, we have been unable to accept much of what Private U said he did and saw after disembarking from the APC [armoured personnel carrier]. In our view his evidence is unreliable in so many respects that in the absence of any supporting evidence from those in the APC with him, we can place no reliance on his account of hearing automatic gunfire while in the APC. Had he heard such gunfire, we are sure that other soldiers in the vehicle would also have heard and commented on it. Indeed, Private U agreed in his evidence to the Widgery Inquiry that he could see no reason why the soldiers in the leading APC would not have been able to hear automatic fire.

The Saville report is long and impressively meticulous in its interrogation of the credibility of witnesses. But the division of opinion over its conclusions turns on the question of competence and intent. Did the soldiers blunder into a shambles in which civilians were killed who would not have died if the army had had more control of its men or if the men had had more concern to spare the innocent? Or was there a plan in advance to punish the people of the Bogside who, since the start of the Troubles, had preserved barricades against the army entering 'Free Derry'?

There was much scepticism at the time of the theory that the soldiers had lost control or run amok.

Bernadette Devlin, the independent MP for Mid Ulster, was there and lay face down on the ground during the shooting. In her contribution to a parliamentary debate a few days later she said, 'Whatever the reasons may be – and the permutations may be endless – I personally do not believe that the paratroops went berserk. I do not believe that a regiment like the British Parachute Regiment is trained and then goes berserk. It was a normal ordinary exercise to those men. I do not think they lost any night's sleep over it, but they fired into a crowd of unarmed civilians and thousands lay there.'[2]

The Saville Report acknowledges the evidence that the army wanted to hit hard. Earlier that month Major General Robert Ford, the Commander of Land Forces in Northern Ireland, had visited Derry and complained to the General Officer Commanding (GOC), Sir Harry Tuzo, that the army was 'virtually incapable' of dealing with the 'Derry Young Hooligans' who were destroying the city. His prescription was to give clear warnings then shoot some of the ringleaders dead.

But Saville says this proposal was not 'put forward as a means of dealing with the forthcoming civil rights march or any rioting that might accompany it'.

Yet it was Ford who decided to send the First Battalion of the Parachute Regiment to the city, though they were instructed that they would be under the command of Brigadier Patrick MacLellan, the Commander of the Eighth Infantry Brigade, and would be required to carry out an arrest operation that he had devised.

Colonel Wilford, the commander of the paras, was expected to defer to Brigadier MacLellan and follow his plan. But he didn't. MacLellan's priority was to move in and arrest rioters only after they had clearly been separated from the main body of protesters.

Wilford suggested a change to the plan he had been told to follow. He wanted to send paratroopers through some of the barriers to tackle the rioters and make arrests. He could not get an immediate reply to this suggestion from MacLellan.

Twelve minutes after Wilford's request for permission to launch an arrest operation MacLellan got back to him with clearance, but with strict instructions to avoid getting 'mixed up' with the peaceful protesters.

Saville says, 'Colonel Wilford did not comply with Brigadier MacLellan's order... There was thus no separation between peaceful marchers and those who had been rioting and no means whereby soldiers could identify and arrest only the latter.' Saville concludes that Wilford either 'deliberately disobeyed Brigadier MacLellan's order or failed for no good reason to appreciate the clear limits on what he had been authorised to do'.

Wilford had been exasperated by MacLellan's delay in getting back to him, perhaps feared that the opportunity to make arrests would be lost, but Saville says that, in those circumstances, MacLellan 'might well have called off the arrest operation altogether, on the grounds that this deployment would not have provided sufficient separation between rioters and civil rights marchers'.

And Wilford didn't even tell his men, as they moved into the Bogside, that there were limits to how far they could go. Saville says he should have understood 'that he was being ordered not to chase rioters any distance' into the Bogside.

Clearly there were divisions of opinion within the army about how much care should be taken to avoid jeopardising peaceful civilians.

Saville found that all the killings were unjustified and that all the victims were unarmed, 'with the probable exception of

Gerald Donaghey'. The army claimed he had four nail bombs in his possession when he was shot. Even so, Saville concluded that Donaghey was not preparing to throw a grenade at the time he was shot and that his killing was unjustified.

The suggestion was raised by the army that some of these killings were accidental, that soldiers had been aiming at actual gunmen but missed and hit innocents. Saville conceded that some of those wounded may not have been the intended targets but said those at whom the shots were aimed were also unarmed and that those shots therefore could not be justified.

And again the army claimed that gunmen they had killed had been secretly buried.

'It was also submitted that soldiers fired at and killed or injured other people who were posing such a threat, but that the existence of these casualties had been kept secret by those civilians who knew that this had happened, in order to deprive the soldiers of evidence that their firing was justified.' Saville found 'no substance' in that. 'Had there been such casualties, we have no doubt that this would have come to light many years ago.'

Saville accepted that the soldiers on that day had had reason to be frightened or at least apprehensive. They were sent into an area that had been secured by the IRA and had reason to expect that they might be fired on. They stopped in front of the Rossville flats, in open space overseen by several possible firing positions. He allowed for what he called 'the Derry sound', an echo created by the geography of the city and the high walls which might have amplified the shooting and the firing of baton rounds.

With that in mind, he criticised the first shots fired by Lieutenant N as having been likely to give other soldiers the impression that a gun battle was under way.

One soldier has been charged with murder out of the several who opened fire on civilians that day, Soldier F. At the time of writing his trial has been postponed because of Covid-19 restrictions.

Saville said, 'We are sure that he fired either in the belief that no-one in the area into which he fired was posing a threat of causing death or serious injury, or not caring whether or not anyone there was posing such a threat.' In fact, he regarded that to be true of almost all of the shooting that day. He also rejected the theories that the shootings were a pre-planned punitive measure or that it could have been foreseen that the paras would fire recklessly at unarmed civilians.

Here he seems naive, especially where he says:

So far as the United Kingdom Government was concerned, what the evidence did establish was that in the months before Bloody Sunday, genuine and serious attempts were being made at the highest level to work towards a peaceful political settlement in Northern Ireland. Any action involving the use or likely use of unwarranted lethal force against nationalists on the occasion of the march (or otherwise) would have been entirely counterproductive to the plans for a peaceful settlement; and was neither contemplated nor foreseen by the United Kingdom Government. So far as the Northern Ireland Government was concerned,

although it had been pressing the United Kingdom
Government and the Army to step up their efforts to
counter republican paramilitaries and to deal with
banned marches, we found no evidence that suggested
to us that it advocated the use of unwarranted lethal
force or was indifferent to its use on the occasion of
the march.

But the Irish government had already expressed the view that
the British were taking no meaningful measures to reach a
political solution and accused them of seeking a military defeat
of the IRA. Lynch complained of this after the five killings in
one day in October of Maura Meehan and Dorothy Maguire
and the three men attempting a robbery in Newry, Sean Ruddy,
Thomas McLaughlin and Robert Anderson.

It was in fact clear that Heath and Faulkner both believed
at this stage that a security solution was possible, alongside
political moves towards reform that would fall short of the
civil-rights protesters' demands let alone those of the IRA.
And the government had not demonstrated that it understood
that violence against the nationalist community would be
'entirely counterproductive'. Indeed, experience at that stage
had shown that internment had exacerbated the problem but
Faulkner and Heath accepted that as a cost to be borne. The
army – the same units, in fact – had recklessly killed civilians
and no apparent additional political damage had resulted
from that. Those killings had not even featured in the summit
talks between the prime ministers.

And the secret security assessment from November 1971

discussed in an earlier chapter shows that the army was deluding itself that relations with the 'minority' community were actually improving.

It would not have been naive of Heath to suppose that the paras would do a good job of curtailing the IRA if he believed the briefings he was getting that told him innocent civilian deaths were actual hits scored against terrorists. And until then no one was telling him any different. He was being informed that everyone shot by a soldier was a terrorist, that the terrorists were therefore being weakened and that the people were easing up in their protests against the army because hearts and minds were being won over.

Saville said, 'It was also submitted that in dealing with the security situation in Northern Ireland generally, the authorities (the United Kingdom and Northern Ireland Governments and the Army) tolerated if not encouraged the use of unjustified lethal force; and that this was the cause or a contributory cause of what happened on Bloody Sunday. We found no evidence of such toleration or encouragement.'

The evidence he failed to see was in the numbers of innocent people who had already been shot dead by the army but whose killings had been misrepresented as legitimate hits against gunmen and bombers.

Bernadette Devlin made the point in the parliamentary debate. 'Thirteen people died and 17 people were injured all in the space of 10 minutes, but they were not the first 13 people. We remember Barney Watt, Annette McGavigan and Eamonn McDavitt. The list goes on forever of people who have been accused after their death. After accusations have been blazoned in the newspapers they have been found innocent but never cleared.'[3]

But then even she had failed to make the connection to the killings around Belfast on internment week.

One might ask why the army would send a regiment like the paratroopers into Derry given their record in Ballymurphy and the number of innocent civilians they killed there. But we have seen from the security assessment in November 1971 that the army did not face internal criticism for killing civilians, that all killings were regarded as legitimate hits against gunmen. In that context, those soldiers who had killed civilians on internment week were likely to conclude that they would be covered for again when they opened fire on civilians in Derry. With such an opinion of the paras, that they only killed terrorists and killed a lot of them, why wouldn't they have been the perfect choice for an arrest operation in Derry in which they might come under fire? And we saw after Bloody Sunday that that understanding was retained and defended at the highest level of government and the army.

Saville wondered about General Ford's decision to deploy the paras in Derry given that they had a reputation for 'excessive physical violence'. He concluded, 'General Ford had no reason to believe and did not believe that the risk of soldiers of 1 PARA firing unjustifiably during the course of the arrest operation was such that it was inappropriate for that reason for him to use them for such an operation.'

And he accepted Ford's denial that there was any plan to coax the IRA out into a firefight in which top gunmen might be killed. Saville was, however, 'surprised that an officer of his seniority should seriously consider' shooting dead ringleaders of the Derry Young Hooligans, as he had done in correspondence with the GOC earlier that month.

For Saville to say that no one could have anticipated the soldiers would have shot civilians was to overlook the controversial killings by the army up to that point or to accept the army's accounts of them. So while he had absolved those killed in Derry of any guilt, he had, by implication, accepted that all previous killings had been justified and that no rational grounds had existed till then for fearing that soldiers would commit murder.

Much of the journalism and the eye-witness reports from Derry said simply that the British army had opened fire without cause or warning. The country was appalled.

That night there was rioting on the main Andersonstown Road near my family home. On the following day there was patchy frozen snow on the ground and I saw children who had hijacked a lorry that had been transporting convector heaters. Some were tobogganing on heaters and others were calling at houses and giving them away.

On the Monday morning the IRA took over a house in Durham Street and, from there, shot and killed a soldier who had stepped onto the road to open a barrier, as they had presumably watched him do before. The soldier was twenty-three-year-old Ian Bramley of the Gloucestershire Regiment. He had two children.

My brother Roger was, at that time, a student at St Joseph's, a catholic teacher training college in Belfast. He says, 'Bloody Sunday hit us like a lightning bolt. On the Monday morning, by the time I arrived at the college most of the students had gathered in the main lecture hall and were hearing the eye-witness accounts from colleagues who had witnessed the massacre. The anger and hurt were palpable.'

On the day after Bloody Sunday the home secretary Reginald Maudling announced that there would be an inquiry but made clear that he had already made up his own mind to stand by the army. 'The Army returned the fire directed at them with aimed shots and inflicted a number of casualties on those who were attacking them with firearms and with bombs.'[4]

A Ministry of Defence statement said, 'Throughout the fighting that ensued, the Army fired only at identified targets – at attacking gunmen and bombers. At all times the soldiers obeyed their standing instructions to fire only in self-defence or in defence of others threatened.'

The Irish government had had its own observers there and rejected this entirely.

Seamus Heaney wrote a song about the day of the funerals, intended for Luke Kelly. Kelly didn't like it. He thought the tune that Heaney suggested for it was too slow. There are three surviving stanzas. The song ends:

> And in the dirt, lay justice like an acorn in
>   the winter
> Till its oak would sprout in Derry where
>   the thirteen men lay dead.

There were huge protests around the British Embassy in Dublin. British and Irish diplomats were already arguing over what had happened. We have the record of a conversation between Kelvin White, head of the Ireland division at the

Foreign and Commonwealth Office, and C. V. Whelan, who was minister plenipotentiary at the Irish Embassy in London, in which White accused the Irish of prejudging an inquiry.[5] Transposing the indirect speech of Whelan's account back into dialogue gives a clear sense of how angry the men were. Whelan said the problem was that British army spokesmen had already contradicted impartial and unprejudiced observers.

White then read to Whelan the report of the shooting in that morning's *Times* and asked him, 'Are you not prepared to accept that the army returned fire on gunmen and nail bombers? You are accusing the British army of telling lies. In which case there is little point in us discussing this further.'

Whelan said that people didn't believe the army and had previously disputed army reports of why they had killed one person or another. 'I'm not saying the army are liars but that you have to take into account that the Irish people and neutral observers alike have rejected the army's efforts to rid itself of blame.'

White was furious. 'The army record has to be accepted. You should withdraw those remarks.'

Whelan didn't withdraw his remarks. Instead he pressed on to say that the Irish government demanded that British troops be withdrawn from 'Derry and Catholic ghettos elsewhere and cease its harassment of the minority population'.

White said, 'You presume to lecture the British government on how it should carry out policy within the United Kingdom. This is hardly acceptable. And you should recognise that the measures which have been taken by the British army in the

North have met with considerable success in reducing terrorism and in substantial arms finds.'

'Perhaps,' said Whelan, 'but at the cost of alienating the catholic minority.'

Whelan's report of the meeting says, 'We had a considerable argument on this point, Mr White maintaining that the troops were highly disciplined and well controlled under extreme provocation, while I reminded him of several individual incidents in which members of the army had behaved in either a reckless or a brutal fashion.'

In the end White conceded, 'we had both lost and the only people to have gained were the IRA'. He was right about that and perhaps this was the earliest acknowledgement by the British that the killings in Derry had left them with a major problem.

The two men agreed to keep in close personal contact.

*

My brother Roger says that students occupied St Joseph's in order to plan a response: 'Many of us stayed overnight in the college fearing that our activities might attract an army raid. I would sit up into the early hours talking and sharing experiences. No guns came into the college though people on the run did. We also had a radio transmitter but failed to get it working.

'There was a residential block in the college which was overlooked by houses in a nearby protestant area. One afternoon a sniper took a shot at one of the windows though no one was hurt.

'We were a small part of a larger picture of open revolt against the state.'

The British ambassador John Peck notified the Irish government that London was putting at his disposal a large aircraft to evacuate most of his staff. He had come to the conclusion that there had been a breakdown of law and order in Dublin. Hooligans had gone so far as to throw a petrol bomb at a maternity hospital and the landlord of one of his staff had been ordered to evict him or face 'dire consequences'.

The Civil Rights Association now organised a march in Newry for the following Saturday and tension would build towards that event with fears that Bloody Sunday would be repeated.

Bernadette Devlin had announced the plans for that march to shouts of 'Shame' in the House of Commons.

> But we will be in Newry on Saturday and we will be marching. We have been kicked and batoned by the police, we have been imprisoned and interned and finally we have been slaughtered by the British Army. But we have yet to be defeated. I would say, not so much to the British Government on the benches opposite, but to the people who strengthen their nerve and stiffen their resolve at home and to their friends in this country, that the paratroopers may have had their day on our bloody Sunday, but we have a saying in Ireland that there is another day coming.[6]

Gerry Fitt in the same debate said, 'If I condemn the violence of anyone in Northern Ireland I must condemn the violence of the British Army that was meted out to the Irish people in the City of Derry last Sunday.'[7] The Conservative MP for Macclesfield, Nicholas Winterton, shouted, 'Nonsense.'

When the cabinet discussed the need to try to get the Newry march called off, Heath reported that he had personally written to the Roman Catholic archbishop of Westminster and to the Roman Catholic primate of All Ireland and that he had sent a message through the ambassador to Lynch asking him to urge citizens of the Republic not to take part.

The British ambassador then phoned the Department of the Taoiseach to say that the Civil Rights Association would not be interfered with if they had a rally but that legally they could not 'proceed to and from it in formation'.

The Irish wanted to know if the Parachute Regiment would be in Newry. Ambassador Peck said there would be some paratroops in reserve but that they would not be visible unless required.

My brother Roger says, 'It was anticipated that the Newry march would be bigger than any previous as the strength of feeling about Derry was so strong. We at the college were doing what we could to assist in the organisation of transport and accommodation. I travelled to Newry on the Saturday with a friend, Patrick. We went to a building where people were being given the addresses of people in Newry who would put people up. Bernadette Devlin herself was behind a desk and sent Patrick and me off to a housing estate. It seemed that every house in Newry was putting someone up. The hope was that strength of feeling and numbers would make interfering with this march unthinkable.

'I had never seen such a crowd. I don't think I have seen one since though, except the anti-Iraq War march in London in 2003. Most towns and villages in Ireland must have been represented. Many people came from England and further afield. I got nowhere near the speakers' platform or even heard any speeches the crowd was so big. But I was delighted to see people carrying placards that I had screenprinted at the college during the week.'

The poets Michael Longley and Seamus Heaney travelled together to Newry.

Huge numbers came into the town. In the poem 'The Sunday After Bloody Sunday', Jean Bleakney described the fears of a protestant family witnessing the arrivals. She was tuning into the police radio and hearing 'their anxiety':

> We stood, my father and I, beside the fire
>   extinguisher,
> roll of chicken wire, lathes, hammer and nails
> and watched the steady stream of outsiders:
>   their beards,
> sheepskin jackets and duffle coats, their
>   Southern accents.

That anxiety was shared at the highest level of government in Belfast and Dublin. The record of a meeting between Faulkner and Heath, and key members of the cabinet, shows that they considered the prospect of a civil war engulfing all of Ireland and which would result in 'tremendous military demands' on Britain.[8]

Faulkner argued that the Newry march should be stopped

because the Orange marches could not be expected to respect the ban on parades if it wasn't. Ministers also feared that if there was trouble in Newry the public and backbench MPs would start demanding the withdrawal of the army from Northern Ireland.

Then the ministers had an extraordinary discussion of possible options for a settlement, including redrawing the border, which Faulkner opposed, and exchanges of population across the border proposed by Sir Alec Douglas-Home, the foreign and commonwealth secretary. Faulkner asked 'what relevance that would have to the core of the whole problem, the attitude of Belfast Catholics'.

They discussed a plebiscite on the border which might disprove Lynch's claim that all catholics in Northern Ireland wanted a united Ireland. In the context of that discussion Heath said that while Irish unity might be Lynch's ultimate aim 'he did not really seek for it at present. He must realise that, on financial and economic grounds alone, the thing was not feasible.'

Mr Faulkner reminded them that the GOC expected to be 'on top of the Belfast situation by March' with 'the hard-core IRA virtually inactive in the city'.

Then, Heath said, they would have to confront the IRA in Derry. This would be a major task requiring 3,000 soldiers. Lord Carrington, the defence minister, said this suggested a military operation on a scale that public opinion could not tolerate.

Faulkner said this wouldn't be necessary. Forces could infiltrate the area by dead of night.

These reports show the ferment of ideas that were in play, most of them unrealistic. They suggest a panic at the highest levels of government in Belfast and London after Bloody Sunday. Only after Saville's report in 2010 would the British apologise. That apology would be delivered by Prime Minister David Cameron to whom no blame could be attributed since he was only five years old at the time of the killings. Back then no British official could say plainly that the army had disgraced itself and exacerbated the problem of Northern Ireland but all were applying their minds now to managing the damage done. They would have to come up with something.

Britain Is Now
the Problem

Recruitment to the Provisional IRA increased sharply after Bloody Sunday. The feeling of many, including myself, was that the whole mess had become unresolvable; the British had let themselves down so badly that they could not be trusted as enablers for justice and peace. Nobody could be relied on. Some in the army were just as bad as the IRA. For me personally this was confusing and frightening. The routine statements of politicians and columnists on our paper were calling for thoughtful members of the 'minority' to disown the IRA and, in effect, put their trust in the state.

I had no power to disown the IRA and had little enough space in which to keep myself at a distance.

Murders by loyalists had not built a similar momentum yet, but the McGurk's Bar bomb demonstrated that they were a threat too. I lived in danger, working in the city centre, and I felt that I had no secure foundation to my life.

On the Tuesday after Bloody Sunday, Faulkner made a hopeless appeal to the 'minority', the people to whom he could not even attribute a coherent politics. He was more conciliatory than the politicians in Westminster who stood by the soldiers. He said, in a speech in a Belfast hotel, 'The events in Londonderry at the weekend were a tragedy. They were tragic in themselves, in that there was considerable loss of human life.'[1]

So he was expressing some compassion but then claiming that others were now manipulating the trauma.

'What is also tragic is that those events are being used as a lever to prise the two sections of the Ulster community further apart. Yet one must hope that when people have had time to reflect on what has happened that they will be drawn up short before this situation and forced to rethink their attitudes.'

This approach separated the machinations of the politically minded from the hurt felt by the bereaved communities and betrayed a sense that ordinary catholic families were not reacting rationally but were too easily controlled. I was thinking rationally. I was thinking that the state offered me no protection that I could rely on. Worse, if I were to seek the protection of the state, soldiers might come into my street and murder people. Faulkner thought the 'good sense' of people like me was 'numbed by shock'. Indeed, something in me was numbed by shock but good sense said plainly that the army was now a threat to me and to the stability of the region I lived in. It could not assuage fear and bring peace, but was now exacerbating the violence.

Faulkner continued: 'These propaganda vultures who feed on a people whose suffering they have brought about bear a grave responsibility. For there is no getting round this fact: if there had been no marching in defiance of the law in Londonderry on Sunday, there would have been no confrontations and there would have been no deaths.'

So the blame lay with the civil-rights movement, the people who were trying to provide an alternative form of agitation to that offered by the IRA. And now they were to be invalidated.

Faulkner thought that the alternative to violence and street protest was inter-party talks and a reliance on the democratic state. He dismissed talk of a united Ireland and the taoiseach Jack Lynch's assertion that that was the ultimate solution. 'Their only contribution in terms of policy is to pretend that they could swallow the Ulster problem by absorbing Northern Ireland into the republic, when anyone with any sense of economics, politics or military strategy knows that what Mr Lynch proposes would be not only a disaster for the citizens of Northern Ireland but would cripple the whole island in almost every sense of the word.'

Which was right, but that reality only compounded the disheartening impact of that moment in our history. He might as well have said, 'You are stuck with us; get used to it.' Faulkner wanted talks that would include 'responsible Ulstermen of both religious persuasions'. As if it were theological differences that needed sorting out.

He was afraid now that London would move against him and strip his government of control of security, even as London was proclaiming that the army had done a good job when confronted by gunmen and bombers. Control was slipping away from everybody.

He recognised that his government 'may be slandered

every day of the week as a fascist junta anxious only to beat
the Catholics into the ground', but his reality was that he had
no more power to influence events and would have warmly
embraced any Catholics in politics who would have stepped
forward to save him, and none would.

Two days later, Faulkner chaired a meeting of the Joint
Security Committee. The committee received a report from
Special Branch that 'the Brady IRA', that is the Provisionals,
had received a supply of guns through Dublin 'from the
continent'. The report said also that 'recent detentions
included 3 explosives officers, one of them a top man, and
that intelligence gleaned suggested that the tighter controls
over explosives on both sides of the Border had bitten into
the terrorists' supply lines'.[2]

That second part will have assuaged a fear that the IRA
was getting gelignite from the South, but the real security
story of the day that was missed was that young people were
now queuing up to join the IRA in the hopes of hitting back
at the army.

The army GOC, Sir Harry Tuzo, was at the meeting and
'expressed gratification for the support the Army had received
from the Government and indeed from members of the public'.

*

Bloody Sunday changed the frame in which many people in
Northern Ireland thought about the political problems of
the time. I have puzzled over why the numerous killings of
innocents by the army had not become central to the arguments
of nationalists like the SDLP and I think it is perhaps because

they were focused at the time on the Stormont government being the problem and on the prospect of Britain providing the solution. From the beginning, the civil-rights campaign had been an appeal to Britain to curtail unionist excesses. The SDLP and others directed their energies into protesting against internment, which they blamed on Brian Faulkner, the Northern Ireland prime minister. Perhaps they didn't want to split their attention. They had protested vehemently about the killings of Seamus Cusack and Desmond Beattie in Derry, yet at Chequers the entire strategy of Jack Lynch, the taoiseach, had been to argue against internment and for radical reform in Northern Ireland with the prospect being opened up for a united Ireland. What he really meant was that he wanted nationalism to have a voice in government.

Bloody Sunday diverted attention directly to the British government. This is telling. What it reveals is that Irish nationalism, up to that point, had a more relaxed view of the British. Few believed that uniting Ireland was possible or that it was the core challenge of the time. The Provisional and Official IRA organisations did want a united Ireland but they had not succeeded in getting the majority of nationalists to assert that demand alongside them.

After the killings, John Hume said that for many people in Derry the bottom line was now that Ireland must be united and Britain removed.

Ian Paisley, the Democratic Unionist Party MP, took that as exposing the civil-rights campaign and the SDLP as sharing the same goals as the IRA. He said in that parliamentary debate, 'When we hear the leader of the SDLP in Londonderry,

Mr John Hume, say that it is a United Ireland or nothing, we learn the real objective behind this present state of agitation and riot and revolution in Northern Ireland. The vast majority of people in Northern Ireland cannot accept that the only political solution to the problem is a United Ireland.'[3]

Paisley himself was conceding that this was new language from Hume and assumed that it betrayed a hidden agenda, rather than that Hume was pointing to a radical change in thinking among others around him.

Bernadette Devlin, the independent MP for Mid Ulster, speaking in the same debate said, 'All through the whole of the North of Ireland, throughout the 32 counties, people are outraged and indignant, and the Conservative Government by their activities on Sunday may well have lit a fire in Ireland the flames of which may not die out until the last vestige of British rule has ended in that country, until the last trace of British domination has gone.'[4]

And Gerry Fitt, the MP for West Belfast, said, 'The political solution that would have been acceptable last Saturday is not acceptable today. I tell the Home Secretary with all the seriousness at my command, so that he and the Government will know, the British Army and those on the Conservative benches will know, and my honourable friends will know, what is happening in Ireland. There is a national fervour throughout the 32 counties of Ireland that has not existed since the years 1916 and 1921.'[5]

Bloody Sunday was shocking for the deaths but also for the sense it generated that Britain simply did not understand Ireland, had treated the people there as if they did not actually have full citizenship and entitlement to the state's protection.

That sense that Britain had devalued them is what put the Union in question in the minds of many, not just the atrocity itself, but the defence of it. If they had felt that it was their own army that had killed thirteen people and that their own government had either ordered it or disowned it, then no question would have arisen from the shootings about the nature of the state itself. But the failure of the British to respond with any empathy at all disqualified them in the minds of many as a legitimate government.

If the army had shot dead thirteen striking miners in Lancashire, this would have been just as outrageous, of course, but it would not have called into question whether or not the miners were British. The reaction to the shooting plainly demonstrated that the Union was not organic, that people in Derry did not feel British and Britain did not regard them as such.

But there was no way the Parachute Regiment would ever have done that in England.

The response would have been, you are our government, you cannot treat us like this.

The response in Ireland was, you are not our government, and you cannot treat us like this.

There had been some identification with Britain among Irish nationalists. There always has been. But it is not rock solid.

Britain had failed to understand that the dilute Britishness of the Northern Irish catholics had to be managed carefully, yet they had been placed lower in the regard of the government than a clutch of psychopathic soldiers who had disgraced that government.

Scoffed at by Nicholas Winterton MP for condemning the army's action in phrasing that compared it to the violence of the IRA, Gerry Fitt said, 'Never did I realise more in my life, in the debate today and yesterday, but particularly during this afternoon's debate, that I am an Irishman and the honourable gentleman is an Englishman. That is where the difference lies. The honourable gentleman has no sympathy, no understanding, no conscience for the people who live in Derry who are Irish.'

The original crisis in Northern Ireland had been the estrangement of northern catholics from the Northern Ireland government, and the civil-rights protests had been directed at Stormont while soliciting the help of Britain. The interim solution to the violence had been the intervention of the British army, initially welcomed in catholic areas. But Bloody Sunday represented the estrangement of the catholics from the British and seemed to confirm the republican analysis, until then widely thought to be extreme and naive, that the British were the real problem.

That parliamentary debate, in which English MPs seemed impervious to Irish anger at British soldiers murdering Irish civilians, ended when Bernadette Devlin crossed the floor and walloped the home secretary Reginald Maudling.

That sense that people were disillusioned by Bloody Sunday, after feeling that a recourse to the British government over the heads of Stormont might bring change, was summed up by the late radio DJ Gerry Anderson in an interview he gave me: 'You know what the shock of Bloody Sunday was – we had

imagined that the brits would come in and recognise that
we were just the same as themselves. We assumed that they
wouldn't shoot us, that they would behave better here than
they had in Aden. But we were just mad paddies to the paras.
They didn't give a fuck about us. Seeing that was scary.'

Many on the British left were interested in what was
happening in Northern Ireland. Julie Cockburn was a member
of the Claimants Union and travelled to Belfast occasionally as
the girlfriend of IRA Belfast Brigade press officer Gerry O'Hare.
She went once when Rita, his wife, was in prison on a charge of
shooting a soldier. Dolours Price, later famous for bombings in
London and a long hunger strike, was minding the kids.

She went to Derry to join the protest on Bloody Sunday but
the coach bringing people from Belfast was stopped so many
times by the army that it arrived late.

She says, 'We heard gunfire. The driver got us back on
the bus and drove down towards the Bogside and we went
in on foot. As we were going in, towards the demonstration,
people were coming down shouting, don't go up there, they're
shooting. Someone heard my English accent and said, what's a
brit doing here? And other people said, they're not all against
us. It was a sticky moment.'

The coach party was taken to a community hall and then
people were sent to houses in the neighbourhood that had
volunteered to take in protesters, and in one of the houses,
over tea, Julie heard the news coming in about the dead and
the wounded.

Returning to Belfast and fearing further army searches,
the coach crossed into Donegal and took a protracted route

back into the North well away from Derry. Even then the bus was stopped and searched again and soldiers confiscated their placards.

'We stopped at a pub at some point and that's where we found out what had happened, the numbers killed.'

She arrived back in Belfast when the city was in turmoil. 'There were fires on the road. Gerry met me off the bus. It was very scary. We could hear gunfire all night.'

She had to go back to England for a court hearing in London on a charge of spray painting a social security office. She laughs about it now. 'I asked the court for a minute's silence to honour the Bloody Sunday dead and they bloody did.'

Rita O'Hare had jumped bail and gone south.

'I was staying with Gerry and we got the kids together and packed the car and drove down to meet her in Dublin. Which was a bit weird. Must have been weird for the kids. And nerve wracking.

'At the Sinn Féin offices Rita was there with a lot of big guys. They brought us to some big old mansion. There were refugee families from the North there. We stayed there. And that was the only time I met Rita. We all slept in a room and the army [IRA] men slept on the other side.

'I was in a relationship with Gerry. Rita was fine. I slept with Rita that night and she said, feel the hole. I remember feeling the bullet hole in the back of her head. So we got on fine.'

Julie knew that Gerry was in the IRA. Once he brought her to Long Kesh to visit a prisoner. She recalls, 'He got me to give him some dope, to wrap it up, put it in my mouth. I can't remember who it was. I kissed him to pass the dope across. As you do when you are young and silly.'

'Young and silly' might describe actions that were much more irresponsible than Julie's while most people were still trying to live normal lives.

Dennis Patton and Tina Kelly had just got married. They were holding their reception party in the Woodleigh Hotel on Asylum Road in Derry. Dennis was from Creggan and Tina from the Bogside. Phonsie Patton was the best man and found that one of his duties in that role was to intercept the IRA bombers who arrived to spoil the party.

The bomb gang told the party they had three minutes to get out and Phonsie thought that ought to be negotiable. He pleaded with the IRA to go away and let them enjoy their day. The IRA's response to that was to register the full seriousness of the situation by shooting him in the face.

The IRA claimed that they had bombed the hotel because it was 'a haven for RUC Special Branch men and British intelligence'.

Shane Paul O'Doherty, who turned seventeen that month, says, 'I remember standing outside the Woodleigh with a girl and a gun hoping to shoot any off-duty soldier who came out.'

The bombing triggered a row with the Official IRA who described the attack as 'crass stupidity'.

The IRA was a burden on the community it presumed to defend and you can see indications of this even in the death notices of some of those republicans who died: while many honoured them as fallen heroes, others in the same family made no reference to their role in the movement.

On 10 February 1972, twenty-six-year-old Joseph Cunningham was killed when out with others on a mission to murder a factory boss who served as a major in the UDR. He had parked in Church Road, Newtownabbey, but two police Land Rovers turned up and closed off their exit routes. The IRA's own account in *Tírghrá* says that the police opened fire first and that Cunningham returned fire with a Thompson submachine gun to enable the others in the gang to escape across fields. The Thompson jammed after a short burst and the police shot him.

Cunningham had lived at the time in Rathcoole, which, after population shifts, had become predominantly protestant. Two other catholics who had left the area and joined the IRA were Bobby Sands and Bobby Storey.

The family's memoriam notice for Joseph Cunningham on the twenty-fifth anniversary of his death made no mention of his having been in the IRA: 'Sadly missed by his mother Rosaleen Cunningham, his sisters and brother, sister in law and brother in law and large family circle.'

Yet his sisters Rosemary and Marian, in a separate notice, wrote, 'In proud and loving memory of my brother Vol. Joseph Cunningham, Belfast Brigade, Oglaigh na hEireann [IRA], killed on active service…' Their brother Gerry used similar phrasing, though he left out the reference to 'active service'.

Joseph Cunningham's wife's notice says he was killed but makes no mention of his membership of the IRA. Nor does a notice on behalf of 'aunts, uncles, cousins and the wider family circle'.

This shows that even families within the catholic communities were divided in their regard for the IRA and is a reminder that many of those shown on television newscasts marching behind a coffin at an IRA funeral did not share the violent intentions of the deceased.

The IRA was busy in February 1972, in the immediate aftermath of Bloody Sunday. It killed fourteen people in the first three weeks. Three of them were catholic civilians. Eight were bombers blowing themselves up, though two are not listed as members in *Tírghrá*.

The British army killed one that month, Thomas McIlroy, who was working on his car in Ballymurphy when a soldier shot him from the Henry Taggart army base.

The Official IRA bombed Parachute Regiment headquarters in Aldershot, Hampshire, on 22 February, killing seven people, including the catholic chaplain Fr Gerry Weston and five members of the domestic staff. The Official IRA claimed that its bomb had killed at least twelve officers and that these deaths had been covered up.

Three days later, an Official IRA gunman tried to kill the Stormont minister of home affairs, John Taylor, shooting him in the face as he sat in a car in Armagh.

Then the IRA killed two members of the UDR in their homes. They shot Henry Dickson in Lurgan in the hallway and injured his eleven-year-old daughter. They took John Fletcher from his home at gunpoint and told his wife they were taking him hostage then fired fourteen bullets into his body.

Fletcher was the two hundred and seventy-eighth person killed in the Troubles. The bloodiest year had still not brought the tally to a tenth of the number that would be killed in the whole Troubles period.

Many of the IRA activists of that time were minors like Shane Paul O'Doherty, Anthony McIntyre and Bobby Storey, so the army wanted to arrest and interrogate people who were too young to be interned.

Anthony McIntyre was fourteen years old when he was arrested for the first time.

'They came round at six o'clock in the morning and raided our house, took me out, threw me into a Saracen, really really heavy handed, trying to be frightening, and I was just determined to put the head down, say nothing to them, give them not a snippet of information. I was really proud of myself. I didn't know why they were picking on me but the next thing they threw my friend Frankie on top of me – Frankie Rea. They held us in the barracks and I remember thinking – they had me standing over a radiator, beating me, and I was thinking, everything that has ever been said about these bastards is true. I expect them to beat me and I'll pay them back in spades whenever I have the opportunity. This was an older guy, looked ancient to me, a grey-haired guy, beating me over a radiator. Slaps, rabbit punches. It wasn't hard but it made a lasting impression on me.'

His school organised a protest against the arrests of children. He was held for six hours and then released.

As the violence increased, the prospects of Faulkner's survival as prime minister of Northern Ireland declined. Two major forces within unionism were moving against him. One was the Democratic Unionist Party led by Rev. Ian Paisley. His objection to Irish nationalism was that it was catholic. Northern Ireland, which he called Ulster, was protestant and would remain protestant. That is now an obsolete viewpoint but it had a substantial following at the time. Paisley also believed that internment had been a mistake, Faulkner's mistake.

The other force opening within unionism was Ulster Vanguard. This was set up by the former minister of home affairs at Stormont, William Craig, who had banned the first civil-rights parades and ordered the police to break them up. He, like Paisley, was pitching for the leadership of unionism. When he was sober he was a soft-spoken man with a minor speech impediment; he would pronounce 'accept' as 'assept'. When he was drunk he was luridly threatening.

Vanguard staged mass rallies around Northern Ireland, with Craig arriving in an old limousine with motorbike outriders to inspect ranks of his followers. Craig had seen the rise of the loyalist paramilitary groups and he appears to have wanted to bring them under his direction. The movement grew out of the Unionist Party and sought to take control of it. The steering committee had been formed from most of the constituency associations of the Unionist Party coming together, forty-three of the fifty-two.

When Craig launched the movement in February 1972 he was flanked by Rev. Martin Smyth, the country grand master of the Orange Order in Belfast, Billy Hull of the Loyalist Association of Workers (LAW), and a representative of the Young Unionists, Brian Smyth. Other senior unionists were there too, all of them known for their opposition to political reform that might give nationalists more influence.

Journalist Henry Kelly, who witnessed the first Vanguard rally in Lisburn, wrote that it 'was a sickening sight'.[6] Craig

(*Top left*) Anthony McIntyre. He joined the Official IRA junior wing at fourteen. He moved to the Provisionals and served a life sentence for murder, got a university education while in prison and completed a PhD after his release.
(*Top right*) Tommy Gorman was an active IRA bomber and gunman. He was one of the seven who escaped from internment on the prison ship HMS *Maidstone*.

Bobby 'Beano' Niblock was a member of the loyalist Red Hand Commando. He is now a writer and seeks to discourage young people from getting involved in violence.

A fading wall mural in Ballymurphy links Sinn Féin political hopes
to reverence for the IRA campaign.

A Falls Road mural. Today parts of Belfast are like theme parks to
glorify paramilitary campaigns.

A mural on the Shankill Road, to mark the scene of the IRA bombing of the Balmoral furniture shop.

Joe McCann, who was shot dead by British soldiers, is revered as a martyr by socialist republicans.

(*Top left*) Eddie Kinner, formerly a bomber for the UVF. (*Top right*) Tony Rosato had been a friend and comrade of Joe McCann and lectured young Official IRA volunteers on socialism.

Tommy Andrews was a 'deep end' member of the UDA and now regrets it.

(*Right*) Jennifer McNern lost both her legs to an IRA bomb left under a table in the Abercorn Restaurant.

(*Bottom left*) Angelina Fusco and her family fled their home on the Springfield Road in Belfast during the tumultuous violence of the week of the first internment raids.

(*Bottom right*) Julie Cockburn, a Claimants Union activist in London, befriended IRA Belfast Brigade press officer Gerry O'Hare and witnessed much of the early violence.

McGurk's bar on North Queen Street and those who died in the bomb there are now memorialized in a mural.

Flowers are still placed at the scene where wee Angela Gallagher was shot.

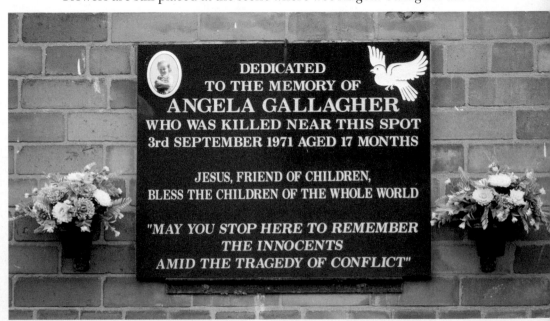

Peace line gates on the Springfield Road, scarred by recent rioting.

The Sunflower bar retains the old security gate erected to keep drinkers safe in more violent times.

A memorial to the IRA dead of Riverdale and the surrounding area, modelled on the ancient Irish dolmen.

The centenary of Northern Ireland marked by a flag erected by the East Belfast Protestant Boys.

had read out a covenant pledging opposition to reform and called on a thousand men marshalled in ranks before him to pledge themselves to it with 'I do.' The crowd cheered when Craig said, 'We are determined, ladies and gentlemen, to preserve our British traditions and way of life, and God help those who get in our way.'

Kelly says that it was 'disheartening' that the Unionist Party leadership remained silent about this, but it is likely that Craig was hoping to engineer a confrontation with Faulkner, or at least to demonstrate that Faulkner was too weak to stand up to him at this stage.

Kelly described Faulkner's silence as 'criminally irresponsible'.

It was the Democratic Unionist Party that attacked Vanguard for its threatening language. Desmond Boal, who was Paisley's partner in setting up the party, described it as 'very dangerous and irresponsible'. He feared that people would turn their anger on innocent catholics. 'And if that happens it brings this community not one step but a dozen steps closer to civil war.'[7]

Innocent catholics were being murdered already but in the following months loyalists would make a routine of picking up individuals, often men walking alone at night, and shooting them dead.

Vanguard grew and the rallies got bigger and bigger through February and into March.

Craig wanted the restoration of the old disbanded constabularies, the B and C Specials, all-protestant militias which had been raised to augment the RUC and defend the country against the IRA. He said, 'If the government do not mobilise the people, the people will mobilise themselves.'[8]

Asked by a journalist, Liam Hourican, if violent action against 'the enemies of Ulster' would mean killing 'all the catholics in Belfast', Craig said, 'It might not go as far as that but it could go as far as killing. It could be similar to the situation in the 1920s where Roman Catholics identified in Republican rebellion could find themselves unwelcome in their places of work and under pressure to leave their homes.'[9]

Extreme as this was, Craig had built up a support base within the Ulster Unionist Party, the Orange Order and the loyalist groups like LAW and the tartan gangs. He had been humiliated in 1968 after triggering the violence around the civil-rights campaign and getting sacked by the then prime minister Terence O'Neill. Since that time he had been garnering support by visiting Orange lodges and party constituencies to find allies in the cause of reversing the reforms that had followed.

He had checked Faulkner, who now could not move against him without splitting his party.

When Faulkner struck back it was in Killinchy, near his family retreat, a cabin on an island in Strangford Lough. Even then he could not name Vanguard as the target of his criticism, but he spoke of rallies being 'alien' and 'sinister', a 'comic opera' that would not succeed in coercing unionists.

However, Faulkner was losing relevance now. The SDLP would not take him up on his offer of talks and party support was bleeding to Paisley and Craig. Heath was sketching out a plan to take over the running of Northern Ireland and perhaps wondering for now if he was in danger of triggering the feared 'protestant backlash' if he did.

Faulkner was not a bullish extremist like Craig or a theologically motivated fanatic like Paisley. He was a deal maker without the substance of a deal or a partner to make that deal with.

I have asked his son Michael, who wrote a book, *The Blue Cabin*, about the family's weekend and holiday hideaway on Strangford Lough, what sort of man he was. He described to me a man wholly unlike the stiff and mannered figure we saw on television back then. I wondered if Faulkner had feigned his accent, much as Heath was accused of doing. He says, '… it's certainly true he was a good mimic and often had the family in stitches. He used to do a Columbo routine on his way out the door, patting the pockets of his raincoat, scratching his head and saying, "Just one more thing…"'

Faulkner had a police security team around him that must have been aware that he would have been an easy target if the IRA ever found out about the cabin on the island.

Michael says, 'The rest of us had crossed to the island and my mother sent me back in the rubber dinghy to hurry him up. The security team were standing on the stone pier looking a bit restless – the sergeant in charge, who was with the Da through all his ministerial posts and until he retired, always hated it when my father stopped to chat "in the open" for any length of time – and Da was on the foreshore down below, sitting on a rock with his trousers rolled up and his feet in the water, swapping stories with a local shipwright called Bob Scott, a decent, old-fashioned type, the sort of guy my father had a lot of time for. If I hadn't gone to get him he would have been there all day.'

It is an endearing portrait of a man who was reviled at the time for interning republican suspects without charge, but who would later try again to make a deal with nationalists and concede more and was about to discover that Heath regarded him as expendable.

Henry Kelly theorised in *How Stormont Fell* that Heath had watched the growth of Vanguard to assess from it whether a major protestant backlash was likely if he suspended Stormont. He had concluded that the risk was worth taking.

The Abercorn

Some people were still managing to live normal lives in the torn city and to disregard the danger and stay out of the political arguments. Jennifer McNern and her sister Rosie enjoyed life. Their mother and father were from south-west Donegal and they spent all their school holidays there. Their father died in 1965, before the trouble started, and they lived with their mother and two brothers in Manor Street.

They went to convent schools, 'first the Convent of Mercy and then up to Our Lady of Mercy'.

Jennifer says, 'You were aware of difference then, the different buses. But I never got involved.' Sectarianism was beneath her interest. 'I was into knee-high boots and miniskirts.'

She was friendly with the soldiers when they first came.

'They were billeted across the road from us in the Boys' Club. If you were making a cup of tea, whoever was on duty you brought them over a cup. And it was all very amicable. And then something happened. Word went round that you weren't allowed to bring them over tea. It just came through the grapevine. And you didn't. So if you were going out to work in the morning and you saw somebody you had brought tea to the morning before, you just gave them a look and went on. They knew, I think.'

Jennifer trained in catering and started work in catering management and liked going to dances in the Starlite, Romanos and the other clubs, though nightlife was draining out of Belfast in 1972.

'We always went to somebody's house to get ready to go out. And off to the dance. In the Starlite if you had more than three dances with somebody you went down and had a cup of coffee and an apple tart. I knew friends who went to the jazz clubs. I was more into country and western. They were obviously more sophisticated than I was.'

She was approaching twenty-one years old. She says that when there was rioting in Ardoyne she would sometimes go with her mother in a wee Morris 1100 to watch.

'People used to listen in to the police radio to see what was going on.'

The girls would walk to the Starlite when the buses were off and even when there was gunfire nearby.

'People were shooting at the army or the army at the people. You didn't really care.' I wonder if she is a bit more blithe about those experiences now because they didn't compare with the horror that followed.

'One night I came home from the dance and all our windows were out, and the neighbours' as well. Somebody had bombed a hall down Roe Street. That was the first time it hit home.' She says her mother was 'a coper, thank goodness'. 'We slept in the house that night, of course. You didn't have central heating at that time. It wasn't as if you were coming home to a warm house anyway. You were used to the cold.'

On 4 March 1972 Jennifer was working in Holy Rosary school and had a Saturday job in a launderette.

'Rosie wanted to go into town so I said OK. Whether I was in the launderette or not didn't matter. I could come back for closing up. We went into town. We went to Wallis's, a clothes shop in High Street. We decided then we would go round to the Abercorn and have a coffee. We deliberated over it because I was thinking we should really be getting back. That's where you went for a cup of coffee when you went into town. There was a queue.'

While they were waiting their turn to be served at the counter, two girls came in behind them and jumped the queue and took a table that came vacant.

'They were two young girls. It's a wonder somebody didn't say to them, excuse me there's a queue. Then the two girls left. They didn't order anything. And then two girls who were in front of us in the queue took their seats. Then two other seats in that corner came available and Rosaleen and I moved up and took them. We had our coffee. We were just getting our stuff together and about to leave and that's all I remember.'

The two girls who had jumped the queue had left a bomb under their table. The girls who had taken that table after them were killed outright. They were Janet Bereen and Ann Owens. Janet was twenty-one. Anne was twenty-two. For what it's worth, both were catholics, members of the community the IRA had pledged to defend.

*

Tommy Andrews was outside the bar when the bomb went off.

'We were in Corn Market doing fenian bashing as part of the tartan gang. I was fifteen. It was a muffled explosion, not a loud one. We were in Woolworths and we were told to leave. I came out of there and went into the market and the first thing I saw was a man running out of the cloud of smoke and directly towards me.

'His clothes were ripped to shreds. His hair was full of dust. There was a lump of wood sticking out of the right side of his head. He started banging his head with his arm, saying, "Talk to me, talk to me."

'And some woman pulled the wood out of his head and the blood just spurted out like a fountain. And my feet never touched the ground till I got to the bottom of the Shankill Road. I just ran as fast as I could.'

The IRA never took responsibility for the Abercorn bomb but Tommy Gorman who was now making bombs for them said it was 'fucking terrible'.

He says, 'There's things that happen that make you say to yourself, fuck me pink. And all the time you're saying to yourself, no, it wasn't us. But you have to face the facts. At the time you rationalise.'

Jennifer McNern would dance again but on prosthetic legs. In fact, many years later she danced with me and fell over – and laughed. But there wasn't much to laugh about that day.

*

Brian Faulkner summarised the scale of the carnage in a statement:

At 4.28 pm an anonymous person called the operator at Telephone House and stated that a bomb, due to go off in five minutes, had been planted in Castle Lane. One minute later, before its whereabouts was known and before the security forces could move into the area, a bomb of approximately 5 lbs exploded on the ground floor of the Abercorn restaurant. As a result two young women were killed and 136 other people were injured… many of them maimed for life.[1]

He said, 'Any illusion that we were not at war with the enemies of society must by now have been dispelled, and we may as well face the facts.'

These facts, for him, included his continuing claim that large quantities of gelignite were being stolen in the Republic and that the government there was not doing enough to curtail terrorism.

He went on to state that in the previous three months there had been 148 explosions in Belfast and 218 explosions in the rest of Northern Ireland, this despite 136 other bombs having been 'neutralised'. However, he claimed some success against the bombers: since the beginning of the year thirty-nine people had been sentenced for firearms and explosive offences and the police had made sixty-two detections in Belfast 'involving the planting or possession of explosives'.

'In other cases the bombers have been caught red-handed, and only last Saturday morning two were shot, one fatally, as they were igniting a bomb at a telephone exchange in Apollo Road, Belfast.'

This referred to the killing by the police of eighteen-year-old Albert Kavanagh from Cavendish Street who had joined the IRA when he was sixteen. The IRA's account of his death in *Tírghrá* says that one of the policemen emptied a revolver into him as he lay wounded on the ground.

Faulkner was exasperated that despite all this murdering and sabotage people made excuses for the bombers and would not report them. It seemed plain to him that beyond a certain level of horror, well surpassed by now, no excuse could be made for those who would leave a bomb in a crowded restaurant and no failing of his government could justify such a response.

To report these people, he said, 'is not to take political "sides" in any way – the menace to the public which we are facing is something completely outside the realm of politics'.

That is not how the eventual peace agreement twenty-six years later would view the bombings. It would draw a clear link between political causes and violent effects and make political changes for the express purpose of ending the violence.

What Faulkner did not mention, though it would have reinforced his argument, was that the bombing campaign was a huge risk to the young people who were preparing and delivering the bombs. He might have asked why the IRA was using kids who were too young to vote to make and deliver their bombs. Some teenagers, like Albert Kavanagh, got killed by the army or police but many more killed themselves through the carelessness and ineptitude that are intrinsic to youth.

Five days after the Abercorn bomb another four young people died in an accidental explosion, this time at a house in Clonard Street. They had been preparing a thirty-pound bomb. The blast demolished the house they were in and buried a mother and child under rubble in a house next door. They survived. The dead bombers were nineteen-year-old Gerard Crossan, seventeen-year-old Tony Lewis, nineteen-year-old Sean Johnston and twenty-year-old Tom McCann.

Gerry Adams, now the most famous of the leaders of the Provisionals, said in his autobiography, *Before the Dawn*, that he had joined in a search for Tom McCann in the hope that he had not been killed in the blast but that he was finally identified as one of the dead by his scalp: 'dark hair with a very distinctive white patch'.[2]

Johnston was described by the IRA as a lieutenant, an explosives expert and a devout catholic who had been to confession that morning. His family asked that there be no paramilitary trappings at the funeral.

At this stage the loyalist paramilitary project of killing random catholics had not yet taken off. The loyalist paramilitary threat should have been obvious, especially after the McGurk's Bar bomb, but even that had not fully registered in media discussion of the violence as loyalist. The army had said the deaths were another own goal, the premature explosion of an IRA bomb, and these were frequent enough for that to be plausible.

On the afternoon of the Abercorn bomb we had discussed in the office how we should report it and the big question was whether the UDA was behind it. The IRA had not claimed the bomb and we naively believed that the IRA owned up to its mistakes. And the dead had been catholics.

Still, the threat from loyalism was building.

Vanguard was staging vast rallies of a military character and the tartan gangs were attacking catholics on the street, but the hallmark loyalist tactic of shooting individual catholics dead on their doorsteps or in back alleys – the protestant backlash – was emerging slowly enough for many to easily kid themselves that it was not happening at all.

Patrick McCrory was a nineteen-year-old engineering worker. He lived in a protestant area and the family fitted in well and had good relations with neighbours in the lower Ravenhill Road. Patrick had twice in previous months been attacked by tartan gangs. Then a man shot him dead at his front door.

The family made a strong statement denying suggestions that he had been killed by one or other wing of the IRA. The authors of *Lost Lives* say their sources confirmed that the UDA was responsible.

In the coming weeks and months a growing number of loyalist killings would eventually penetrate the resistance to believing that a new murder campaign was under way. Two loyalist murders in March, three in April, nine in May.

Ulster Vanguard was hardening the mood in loyalist areas and political figures were speculating that the British government was on the brink of dissolving Stormont. If there was rational thought behind the killing, it was perhaps to warn Britain that it would have the added challenge of loyalist violence to deal with if it sought to make a deal with the IRA to get the republican campaign stopped.

And there were signs that the government was moving towards a deal with the IRA and that the IRA was listening.

On 14 March the IRA called a three-day ceasefire to facilitate a meeting with the leader of the Opposition and former Labour prime minister Harold Wilson. Wilson, accompanied by Merlyn Rees (a future secretary of state for Northern Ireland) and two others, met Dáithí Ó Conaill, Joe Cahill and John Kelly. Nothing ostensible emerged from the meeting but the IRA had demonstrated again the tight control of its organisation, that it could order a halt to all bombings and shootings and that the leadership would be obeyed.

That must have been some assurance to the British that when the time came to negotiate they would be dealing with a coherent organisation and not an unmanageable rabble.

John Kelly later said in an interview that Wilson had not specifically asked to meet the IRA leaders but 'friends of the Republican movement' who might be able to advise him on how a ceasefire could be achieved. The conceit was maintained throughout the meeting, he said, that this was not the actual IRA leadership but he believed that Wilson understood clearly that it was.

Kelly also believed that Wilson was acting as a messenger from the government. At this time Stormont was still in control of security so an actual government official meeting the IRA, and securing a ceasefire for that meeting, would have been an untenable embarrassment for Faulkner.

The more naive media speculated that the IRA had called the ceasefire simply to get a rest. The Vanguard leader William Craig dismissed it as a gimmick. He staged a mass rally in the Ormeau Park on 18 March and said he needed a 'fighting fund', claiming, 'We are going to do more than just talk.'[3]

But the triteness of the analysis some loyalists were offering was plain in the speech of the Rev. Martin Smyth who said, 'We would have peace in our time if the Bishop of Rome [the Pope] would put his house in order.'[4]

Beano Niblock was able to attend the rally and line up for inspection because he had been released on bail after being caught making nail bombs. It was his birthday. He was now seventeen years old, one of the many teenagers twitching for war. We would all have been better off if Beano Niblock, Tommy Andrews, Gerard Crossan, Tony Lewis, Sean Johnston, Tom McCann, Albert Kavanagh and the girls who left a bomb under a table in the Abercorn had all, like Jennifer and Rosie, preferred dancing to killing. And they would be better off themselves.

But there were already hundreds of people dead and thousands injured for whom the damage was already done. No grandiose speeches nor bombings nor shootings would enthuse them with the idea that a better day was coming after just a bit more killing.

If the stupid girls who had left the bomb in the Abercorn could have seen the damage they had caused, it might have woken them up to the horror they were responsible for.

Jennifer McNern woke up in Ward 17 of the Royal Victoria Hospital. Her broken arm was in traction. There was a hazy period during which she noticed the Mass cards and get well cards, and exchanged a few words with a nurse who observed that she was briefly conscious.

'Mummy and my younger sister Bernie were in. Whatever way I turned in the bed, I lifted the blankets and I noticed that my right leg was missing.

'I remember just screaming. I'll never forget. I don't even know where the scream came from.

'And Mummy was walking away down the old corridor. And she came running back in and I was all over the place and the nurse injected me.

'Next day the doctor came in and pulled the curtains round and started to explain the extent of my injuries and he said, Jennifer you haven't just lost your right leg, you've lost your left leg as well.

'And how could I have been sitting up talking to people and not even… because you can still feel your legs and all the rest of it. It's the weirdest thing. I was sitting up and cracking jokes and all the rest of it. High as a kite on whatever painkillers they were giving me. It must have been weird for them, me not mentioning anything or saying anything.'

Rosie's injuries were even worse.

'Mummy said that when she went to see her she was double the size. She was all puffed, blown up. When my younger sister was eventually brought in to see her she didn't even recognise her. I wasn't even asking about Rosaleen. That's weird as well. Just shows you where your head goes to.

'A nurse said to me, your sister's photograph is in the paper. I thought, God, that's strange. It still didn't dawn on me. I said, why would Rosaleen's photograph be in the paper? Mummy came in then and I said, Nurse says Rosaleen's photograph is in the paper. Mummy just looked at me. I said, I want to see it.

'She brought it in. Even people writing letters to me, I wasn't getting any letters in case they said what the injuries were. Mummy brought it in and there was a photograph of her and her fiancé at the time. Mummy thought I would just look at the photograph but I read underneath what her injuries were. I went berserk. I wanted to see her.'

But Rosie was in intensive care still and it wasn't yet possible to bring the sisters together.

'So poor Mummy was running between us. If I get angry about anything now it is about my mum and what she had to go through.'

Then they met.

'And it was weird to see your sister being pushed towards you. She hadn't got any legs and minus an arm.'

Their first meeting was about make-up and who owned what.

'She was as high as a kite. She just looked at my bedside cabinet and said, "That's mine." "That's mine. That's mine, and that's mine." Everything was new. You know the way if you go into hospital you say, go and get me a nightdress or something. So Mummy just lifted all her stuff and brought it down to me. All the staff were standing round waiting to see this big reunion. "That's mine. That's mine."

'And she went off holding this stuff. And that was the meeting. It was hilarious. We laugh about it now. She doesn't remember.'

London Takes Control

A paradoxical consequence of Bloody Sunday was that the British government, having overseen and defended the worst army atrocity, would take over full responsibility for security. It had hopes now of stabilising Northern Ireland quickly and wanted the Stormont government out of its way. This was a complete reversal of the approach Heath had adopted after the Chequers summit in September '71 when he had resolved to support Faulkner and even bombed border roads at his instigation.

Faulkner would refuse to agree to this and would go down, making way for full direct rule.

On 3 February 1972, Heath's cabinet had a wide-ranging discussion about the problems the government now faced. It needed to lower political tension in the Republic since it seemed that Lynch was now in a weakened position and that if he fell he would be replaced by someone who would be more difficult to deal with.

The ministers acknowledged a growing demand for the army to be withdrawn but the point was raised that a threat of withdrawal might signal weakness, while actually carrying it out would only result in extensive bloodshed in Northern Ireland, in which the Roman Catholic element of the population might well be the main sufferers'.[1]

The army could not be withdrawn until there was an acceptable state of law and order and a satisfactory political settlement. Moreover, support for the army staying would require that 'movement towards some political solution of the conflict should be seen to be in prospect'.

Ministers also expected increased international pressure on them for a political initiative.

This was bad news for Faulkner. He was not going to be left in place as the chief driver of political reform when so much now depended on success.

Lynch's weakness at Chequers had played to Faulkner's advantage. Now it signalled to the British the need to support him by showing results that would endorse him. Direct rule was inevitable and there had been leaks and intimations months before this.

One ardent opponent of it in the Conservative Party was the former prime minister SirAlec Douglas-Home (ironically pronounced Hume). He wrote to Heath but copied his letter to the home secretary, the defence secretary, the chancellor of the exchequer, the lord president of the council and the secretary of the cabinet, so he wasn't coy about his idea.

Douglas-Home's letter, dated 13 March 1972 and marked 'Personal and Secret', argued that the people of Northern Ireland are not like the Scots or the Welsh. 'The real British interest would I think be served best by pushing them towards a United Ireland rather than tying them closer to the United Kingdom. Our own parliamentary history is one of long trouble with the Irish.'

Douglas-Home had been a foreign secretary during the Cuba crisis and supported President Kennedy. He had briefly been prime minister, after Harold Macmillan, and gave up a seat in the Lords to enable him to take that position; he was Heath's foreign and commonwealth secretary at the time that he wrote that letter.

At this stage, on the brink of direct rule, Douglas-Home's understanding was that Heath would appoint a secretary of state for security, removing those powers from Stormont, but he anticipated correctly that this would go down so badly with Faulkner that Stormont would have to be prorogued. He suggested that prorogation be time limited to six months and after that Britain should impose its own solution and call a general election. 'I think the odds are that the Northern Irish would not boycott such an election and that a different political pattern in Northern Ireland would emerge… If that plan failed, it would be easier than it is now to accept the inevitable.'

Heath phoned Faulkner two days later. The call was recorded and provides a beautiful illustration of Heath's deadly tact. His tone suggests throughout that he is doing Faulkner a favour.

'The situation is that we have now reached the stage where we have carefully considered everything you have said to us and we have done a complete review of our position and now we would like to go over it all with you again.'

Faulkner said, 'It would help me a lot – I don't know if it is possible – if you can give me anything in writing before that so that I can prepare for what I am going to talk about.'

Heath replied, 'Well, we did consider that, because of the note in your own letter to me. And we really felt that there was so much from the point of view of the general points that is really very difficult to put down on a piece of paper.'

'I understand that,' said Faulkner, though it is hard to see how he could have done.

Before Faulkner got to London both militant loyalism and militant republicanism declared themselves. Craig staged his massive rally at the Ormeau Park, which Henry Kelly interpreted as some reassurance to Heath that Vanguard would not erupt on the streets when direct rule was announced. The IRA murdered seven people with a car bomb just yards from the newspaper office where I worked. The dead included two policemen and an off-duty UDR man.

So minds were focused on the urgency of finding a solution when Heath and Faulkner met.

Heath laid it out for Faulkner. There could be no military solution: 'Londonderry would require a major military operation if it was to be cleared. The casualties that had occurred on 30 January [Bloody Sunday] would be minute compared with what would happen if there were to be an attempt at a military pacification.'

The army could deal with the IRA 'up to a point' but not with the 'individual bomber'.

The military presence in Northern Ireland had caused 'massive interference with the British Government's international commitments'. He specifically blamed internment, Faulkner's plan, for exacerbating divisions. And it wasn't just a Northern Ireland matter 'because it affected the United Kingdom and had bad repercussions on its international relationships'. And while Britain was taking flak from all round because of internment, it had no real power over security policy. This was no longer acceptable.

Faulkner now knew that he had not been invited over to discuss his proposals but to hear Heath's decision, which was to take over control of security in Northern Ireland and to do this in the full expectation that Faulkner would reject the plan and resign, forcing Britain to prorogue Stormont and govern directly.

William Whitelaw was appointed secretary of state for Northern Ireland with a brief to wind down internment and enter into talks with the IRA.

Meanwhile, the killing continued. Soldiers shot the youngest paramilitary to die in the Troubles, thirteen-year-old Sean O'Riordain. *Tírghrá* says, 'like many of the young men of his generation he was politicised at a young age...'

The circumstances of his killing are not clear. He was close to an exchange of fire between IRA members and the army but the coroner accepted that there was no firm evidence to link him to violence and his family insisted he had been playing on the street.

Sixteen-year-old Patrick Campbell died in a shooting incident of some kind. *Tírghrá* says he was 'shot while on active service', not specifying who shot him, while *Lost Lives* reports that he was killed accidentally by another member of the IRA. Gerry Kelly in his book *Playing My Part* says Campbell had lied about his age to get into the IRA, which, he claims, normally didn't accept recruits under the age of seventeen. Kelly wrote: 'The whole staff was made up of teenagers.'[2] This was because older members, like their OC James Bryson, had been interned.

On the following day the UDA also killed one of its own, Ingram Beckett, who was thirty-seven. This killing was deliberate. Beckett had visited members of the organisation on the Shankill Road to take the side of a relative who had been beaten up after a quarrel. A fight developed there and one of the UDA men shot him dead.

The death toll by 30 March 1972, when direct rule was introduced, was 325.

Killing number 324 was politically significant. Martha Crawford, a thirty-nine-year-old catholic mother of ten, was shot dead by teenage gunmen of the IRA. They had been exchanging fire with soldiers in Rossnareen Avenue, on a housing estate near a school. The shooting had continued throughout the afternoon. The shot that killed Mrs Crawford was one of the last of the day.

It clarified for many the burden that the IRA imposed on the community it presumed to defend.

New Strategies

April was a month in which the Provisional IRA killed relatively few people, apart from accidents. Their first carnage of the month was yet another bunch of kids blowing themselves up. These were Sammy Hughes, Charles McCrystal and John McErlean, all of them just seventeen years old. April ended with them shooting dead an eight-year-old girl, Rosaleen Gavin, as another sniper missed the target.

The three boys had been building a bomb in a lockup garage on Bawnmore Grove. Sammy Hughes's family had thought he was in town shopping when they heard the blast, so it did not occur to them that their youngest child might have died in it. He had only recently joined the IRA. The boys got a joint funeral with no republican trappings.

On the same day an IRA sniper killed a British soldier, twenty-two-year-old Peter Sime, on the Springfield Road.

I was sent with Stephen, another reporter, to the home of Rosaleen Gavin and saw distress such as I had never seen before or perhaps never since. Her mother's eyes seemed swollen with tears. The women brought us in, sat us down and treated us in their delirious grief as if we needed attention. One actually said to me, 'You poor boy.'

The provos killed eight people that month. Four killings were accidental, two were soldiers, one was a protestant woman caught in a bomb blast with an inadequate warning, and one was a catholic man taken from his home and shot at close range.

They carried out a massive bombing campaign on 14 April, presumably to affirm that they were determined to continue but perhaps also to demonstrate that they could bomb numerous targets in one day without killing too many civilians. They had killed sixty-three-year-old Elizabeth McAuley in the main street of Ballymoney the previous day. The police had managed to evacuate her husband in time but the building was set on fire by the blast and she was incinerated inside.

A situation report on 14 April listed twenty-four explosions, with a further five bombs being defused. Most of the bombs were in rural areas:

> The Smithfield bus station was extensively damaged by a 50-100 lb bomb; and a car hire firm in Grosvenor Road was also seriously damaged by a 100 lb bomb; and a 15 lb bomb caused minor damage to the Beechlawn Hotel, Dunmurry. A malicious fire at the University Air Squadron, caused four civilian casualties, a fourth bomb, in a car in Corporation Street, was dealt with by a trained soldier firing a Carl Gustav anti-tank rocket with an inert warhead at the car under the supervision of a bomb disposal expert: the first operational use of this technique and a considerable success.

(The idiosyncratic punctuation is the work of the author of the report.)

In addition there were fourteen shooting incidents. In Derry the army returned fire and claimed a hit.

On the same day 500 protestant women demonstrated on the Crumlin Road against the release of internees.

The report adds: 'Two wanted arrests were made in Belfast. There was the usual hooligan activity in both Belfast and Londonderry. There were three armed robberies in the rural areas.'

The Official IRA was busier than usual that month, killing five soldiers, no civilians and with none of their members blowing themselves up.

Loyalists were busy too, and killed two young catholics in separate attacks, Sean McConville, seventeen, and Gerard Donnelly, twenty-two. Stephen and I went out to the scene of the McConville shooting on a bright Saturday evening. There was no sign that anything had happened. It was the quiet time between coming home from work and going out to the pub.

The army was also killing in familiar disputed circumstances. Patrick Magee, who was twenty, and Patrick Donaghy, who was eighty-six, were both shot dead by soldiers. Magee and his friend were student teachers fired on as they were leaving St Comgall's school where they were on training placements. They were going for their lunch. On the next day, Patrick Donaghy had been standing at the window of his eighth-floor flat in Divis Tower. Soldiers who had fired at him claimed they had seen gun smoke.

Two young men were shot and wounded on the Whiterock

Road by undercover soldiers of the Military Reaction Force, and a child, eleven-year-old Francis Rowntree, died after being hit by a rubber bullet, or baton round.

However, the biggest story of the month was the killing of Official IRA leader Joe McCann.

McCann was regarded as a hero. He had joined the IRA as a teenager before the violence of the late sixties and the split that produced the breakaway Provisionals. That is to say that he had been a committed armed republican when there was no campaign and the cause was not a popular one. He stayed with the Official IRA when others, like his friend Gerry Adams, were leaving, objecting to its alleged failure to defend catholic areas during the rioting of August 1969. McCann stayed with the more socialist wing, though he was an ardently religious catholic and part-time lay Franciscan, something his comrades teased him about.

The Provisionals at that time were regarded as more conservative catholics. The often cited illustration of this was their refusal to use condoms filled with acid as triggers for incendiary bombs because they were banned by the Catholic Church.

Tony Rosato was a close associate of Joe McCann's. He remembers McCann experimenting with disguises because he knew that he was high on the army's wanted list: 'I was in the Old House on Saturday night where there was good music and I arrived. It was packed as usual and I went up to the bar to get a drink and next thing this guy comes up and he is standing beside me. I didn't look. He says, Hi mite, get me a drink, eh? – in an English accent.

'I looked round. I didn't know the guy. I thought he was a journalist. Big coat, little glasses.

'He says, for fuck's sake, Tony, it's me.

'That was Joe. He was thinking of times like the early Troubles. It was almost like Michael Collins. Joe thought he could fool them.'

A split was developing in the Official movement at the time. The army's security assessment that the Officials would opt for a ceasefire was one of its few insights but there was strong division of opinion.

Some of those worried about the moves towards a ceasefire asked Rosato to meet them. He was a member of the Ard Chomhairle, the high council of the movement, and therefore in a position to relay their concerns to the army council of the Officials.

'And people were saying,' he recalls, 'Dublin [the leadership] doesn't know how we think, can you go down and take the message?

'The first thing I said was, "You guys are here speaking on military matters. Have you got permission of your OC?" Every one of them could have been either executed or kneecapped for being at that meeting. There was Ardoyne, New Lodge, Oldpark, everywhere. They wanted the message conveyed to Dublin that it was time to supply short arms [pistols]. We knew that there was an awful lot of stuff coming into Dublin that was not moved north.'

These men wanted to kill loyalists but the leadership in Dublin was wary of getting embroiled in a sectarian civil war.

'But the boys that were actually on the job in Belfast said

you don't need submachine guns, you don't need rifles if you are going out to take out loyalists who are involved in killing people. You need shorts.'

In April the Officials had excelled their previous record in hits against the British army but the drift of the trouble was towards greater sectarian warfare, confronting loyalists rather than the army. Some of the Officials wanted that. Others wanted to confine attacks to the army and targets that could be rationalised as part of a war for a socialist united Ireland. Either that or a ceasefire. Killing protestant workers was the last thing that made sense for a republican socialist.

Joe McCann was with those who opposed a ceasefire while knowing that there was no prospect of fighting a war that would not bring republicans into conflict with loyalists.

Tony Rosato told me how the Officials tried to use guns to frighten off loyalists without killing any. 'Catholics coming up on a Saturday night from the Mass in St Malachy's were getting stoned by people from Donegall Pass. The Officials decided to deal with this. I went over, by chance, and I was asked to get my car. When I think back to the stupidity, they had no other means of moving the guys. There were four carbines put into the car and the guys. The OC's brother was one of the people being sent with us. And we were told by the OC, if any of you fire into the protestant crowd, my orders are to put a bullet in you. You fire over their heads. And these were people who were attacking catholics. I would say some of the boys if they had had a free hand in it would have shot into the crowd. But no, the weapons were discharged, one round each and over the mob.'

McCann was up for a war with the loyalists. 'Joe passionately believed that if you were interested in protecting the working-class position, the socialist position, you had to deal with loyalist fascists who were content to kill catholics.'

Anthony McIntyre was a scout for Joe McCann. His job was to go ahead of him and look out for police or army patrols.

He recalls, 'Joe stayed in Mornington Street on the last day of his life. That was a Friday. On the following day I called round to my mate Frankie and Frankie says, Joe's here and we are going to have to get him out. We went up ahead of him and we got to the corner of Essex Street on the Ormeau Road and there was a cop, so I turned back and says to Joe, there's a fucking peeler standing up there. Then he went into Farrell's bar.

'That afternoon we were playing football on an all-weather pitch at the bottom of River Terrace. We heard the shots. SLR [self-loading rifle] shots, pretty heavy duty. Didn't think anything of it. I went down the Ormeau Road later and meeting Frankie's mother, Dolores, outside Allen's shoe shop at the corner of Donegall Pass and her telling me that Joe had been shot.'

Rosato says, 'It was Grand National day. Joe came out of the Markets, was spotted by two branchmen, got away from them, ran round into Joy Street. Paratroops were sitting there, got him in two.'

Tony Rosato had been waiting to meet McCann in Kelly's Cellars, one of the oldest pubs in Belfast. It is linked in folk memory with the revolution of 1798 because the United Irishmen leader Henry Joy McCracken took refuge there.

Rosato went from the wake in the Turf Lodge estate. 'I saw more gear that day. The brits didn't go into Turf Lodge. I saw lines of fellas with self-loading rifles behind walls. There was gear but half the time it was hidden.'

Anthony McIntyre went too. 'I went over to Turf Lodge to see him in his coffin. I was involved in the rioting on the night of his death on the Ormeau Road. Petrol bombing. I remember after it the brits surrounding the whole place.'

But McCann should not have been in Belfast that day. He was under orders to stay out of Belfast because he was viewed by the leadership as a threat to the ceasefire plan.

At this time the HMS *Maidstone* escapees, Tommy Gorman and the other six, were back in Belfast and operating mostly from Riverdale, where I lived. The prison ship had been closed by then as well. The prisoners had staged a hunger strike against the quality of the food for two weeks and then they were taken out and flown by helicopter to the main camp for internees at Long Kesh near Lisburn. Gerry Adams was one of the prisoners moved.

But it suited the government's new agenda to close the prison ship and start releasing internees. Whether by calculation or accident, McCann's death suited that agenda too, for it made an Official IRA ceasefire more likely. This in turn would make it easier for the Provisionals to have their own ceasefire.

Dublin's Pitch for Unity

The Irish government was elated by the collapse of Stormont and now turned its immediate attention to working on the British to persuade them to set a united Ireland as the goal of their policy. An advisory paper compiled for the Department of Foreign Affairs in Dublin set out the reasoning behind this. The paper was called 'Towards a general settlement?' and was marked 'Secret'.

The paper contests the British claim that Ireland could not be united without the consent of a majority in the North: 'The Taoiseach has said that the unionist population in Northern Ireland do not form a majority in UK or in Irish terms. Nevertheless Faulkner, Craig and others are spokesmen for the idea that Unionists, because they are a majority in Northern Ireland, are entitled to a determinant voice on British policy in regard to Northern Ireland.'[1]

The paper argued that the British parliament, at which unionists were represented, had the authority to end the Union. It then went on to argue that though, in principle, the unionists should not have a veto, it made sense to win some of them over to the idea of a united Ireland. 'But there are many kinds of persuasion, besides intellectual argument, without running close to "persuasion" by bomb and bullet.'

Cardinal Conway, the primate of All Ireland, had said that the IRA was wrong to think it could 'bomb a million Protestants into a united Ireland'. The paper viewed that statement as 'unfortunate' because 'it assumes that all Protestants in Northern Ireland are against the idea of a united Ireland'. However, at this stage the Irish were working on the parallel assumption that all northern catholics did want a united Ireland.

The taoiseach should now assert that Irish policy was 'to change the constitutional status of Northern Ireland altogether'. The paper said, 'That is not conquest, not assimilation, not victory. It is a constitutional reform which history imposes on the country as a whole.'

So how was it to be done?

'The first requirement of a successful beginning of the disengagement of Britain from Ireland is that Britain should decide, in her own interest, that she should encourage Irish unity.' The paper advised that unionists themselves in the North had no incentive to change their thinking other than 'the refusal of the minority to behave, a potential demographic change in the future and the possibility that Britain will get fed up carrying the Northern state on its back'.

Government policy now should be to work on the British to help them see it as in their own interest to tell the unionists that partition could not endure forever.

The advisory paper emphasised that Irish unity was an objective of Irish government policy already. '... not unity eventually nor unity ultimately... If unity were to become available immediately the Government would be bound to take it with whatever stresses might result.'

The first application of that strategy came when the minister for foreign affairs Patrick Hillery, a future Irish president, met with the new Northern Ireland secretary of state William Whitelaw at the end of April. He practically badgered Whitelaw into accepting that the ultimate goal of his new political initiative must be a united Ireland.[2]

Heath in cabinet had emphasised the need to protect the position of the taoiseach Jack Lynch but the British were now facing as emphatic a thrust for a united Ireland as they might have expected from republican hardliners who would replace Lynch if he fell.

The two men chatted about what a lovely city Derry was. Whitelaw had made a visit there.

Getting down to business, Whitelaw said an immediate priority was to assuage the wrath of extreme unionism. Massive protests had turned out against direct rule. He told Hillery that he believed that William Craig's Vanguard movement was armed, though he believed that Craig would not order violence.

Whitelaw said that he would lift the ban on marches retroactively to the previous December. Those who had taken part in the Bloody Sunday and Newry marches would no longer be regarded as having broken the law. And he would continue with the release of internees. He had already closed the *Maidstone* prison ship and moved the internees to Long

Kesh. He anticipated that releasing internees would get more difficult when he reached the 'hard core' cases which caused him considerable anxiety.

He had released one senior IRA man, Sean Keenan from Derry. One month before this meeting Sean Keenan's nineteen-year-old son Colm had been shot dead by soldiers in Derry alongside nineteen-year-old Eugene McGillan. *Tírghrá* says Colm Keenan was 'one of the most active, effective and daring volunteers in the Derry Brigade'. Evidence that the men had been armed on the night they were shot was disputed by Keenan's family and by the IRA. Whitelaw said he had released Keenan senior on the assurance from John Hume that he 'is likely to give a lead against violence'. The man was a senior provo. He had travelled to the US in 1970 to help set up Noraid, the New York-based organisation that for years would provide the IRA with money and weapons. He would break away from the provos in 1986 to join Ruairí Ó Brádaigh in the more purist republican Sinn Féin, suspicious that Gerry Adams was leading the IRA into constitutional politics. He was to be an ardent opponent of the peace process that Hume developed with Adams in the 1990s.

But the IRA was coming under pressure from Hume and the other SDLP leaders to call a ceasefire and give political negotiation a chance. Did Hume see Keenan as one who would advance the argument for a ceasefire? The SDLP had not yet announced its own intention to enter negotiations.

At one point in the discussions with Hillery, Whitelaw admitted that protestant reaction and police morale were considerations that restrained him from moving too quickly.

So he wasn't just thinking about the best balance of political forces and the most broadly acceptable compromise; he was trying to prevent all-out civil war. He was acknowledging that the threat of violence works and can constrain a British government.

Hillery said he wanted the taoiseach to be able to say in a speech that he viewed the initiative of direct rule as 'part of the road forward to a final and peaceful resolution'.

'In this statement,' says the Department of Foreign Affairs' report of the meeting, 'the Taoiseach could talk about the arrangements which he is making for the study of possible changes in the Constitution in an effort to influence Protestant thinking on the question of a United Ireland. A statement of this nature would have a useful appeal to moderate Protestants. The Minister also indicated that he thought it might be useful to get down to North/South cooperation, possibly at official level.'

Whitelaw said that even moderate unionists were fearful of a united Ireland.

Then, said Hillery, surely the taoiseach could express a 'personal view' that we were now on our way to a united Ireland, without attributing that perspective to Whitelaw.

Whitelaw softened a bit and admitted that he could not see Stormont coming back, at any rate in its previous form. He was probably thinking that a reform of the Irish constitution in ways that would remove some of the protestant criticisms would improve relations. What Hillery was thinking was that changes in the constitution would strip protestants of their main arguments against a united Ireland and make it easier for Britain to nudge them in that direction.

He said that when both countries were in the Common Market 'the economic fears in the North will vanish'.

Whitelaw said he would welcome any moves Dublin might make. He was having problems himself persuading moderate catholics that he was impartial. He could see that they were afraid of the British army now and hoped to get soldiers out of sensitive areas and have them policed by the RUC. He wanted to persuade people that the army would not behave in a vindictive manner.

Then Hillery came back to trying to coax Whitelaw into making a united Ireland his goal, saying, 'it would greatly help the Taoiseach in giving an appropriate lead if Mr Whitelaw could satisfy him that the initiative will be followed up in a manner which will lead to the desired final solution'.

Whitelaw wouldn't have it. He said he could not prejudge what the constitutional settlement would be. He accepted that there might even be some protestants in the North who wanted a united Ireland but the bottom line appears to have been the avoidance of war. 'There are far too many arms in the hands of Protestants and there is always the risk that they may use them.'

Hillery pressed on. He said that 'in the absence of clarification as to where the initiative is going, the minority must naturally entertain fears that things will again be handed back to Mr Faulkner and that there will be a return to the previous position'.

Whitelaw's refusal was then more emphatic. He said he had no intention of forcing the majority against their will into a united Ireland. He seemed happy that Lynch would make a speech saying that direct rule advanced progress towards a united Ireland, so long as this thinking was not being attributed to himself. Presumably he hoped that such a speech might ease the anger within the nationalist community, the 'minority', without alarming the unionists.

Hillery had tried the same approach in a meeting with Alec Douglas-Home, who had personally advised Heath to set a united Ireland as a policy objective. In Sir Alec's meeting with Hillery he betrayed none of his personal conviction and stuck firmly to the argument that Whitelaw made, that there could be no resolution without unionist consent and that the British would not prejudge the outcome of the process that had begun with direct rule.

*

The death toll was growing and so was the toll of wounded and maimed. While Whitelaw was looking for a way to heal division in Northern Ireland, the McNern sisters were carried along by efforts to heal their broken bodies.

Jennifer and Rosie, after recovering to a degree, were transferred to Musgrave Park Hospital for rehabilitation, to be fitted with prosthetic limbs and trained in how to use them. Strangely, Jennifer looks back on that as a happy time.

'When we went into the ward at first it was very quiet and we were thinking, God, what's going on here? Sister McAdams was an ex-army nurse and she had told everybody not to speak to us and not to annoy us. So we arrived in and people were very quiet. Some had to get their bladders pumped, all this stuff was going on that we weren't used to and quiet. Then we gradually got to know everybody and we used to all just sit in a circle talking. It was lovely. It really was a lovely time. I'm glad we were in a ward like that.'

She was there with people who had been injured in other explosions and shootings. There was John McGuinness who had been shot in a scuffle with republicans in Ballymurphy, and was paralysed from the neck down.

'He was a lovely guy. He said that they wanted to use children in front of the riots so that the army wouldn't shoot and he was against that. He couldn't move anything, only his head. If he had a cigarette you had to put it into his mouth, the same with food and drink. He was able to maintain a sense of humour, absolutely. Out and out. Couldn't move. And he loved gambling, whereas Joe Hall didn't deal with it at all, God help him.

'Joe Hall was from the Crumlin Road. He was paralysed from the neck down. He was shot in the Clifton Street area. He had been at the tech and he was just starting at Queen's when a drive-by just riddled him.

'One Christmas, Rosaleen was still there and I was visiting. A choir came in singing "We Wish You a Merry Christmas", and Joe wasn't out of bed, just lying there, couldn't see his face. It's the only thing I remember him saying, Get those fucking carol singers out of here.

'There was another guy from Lurgan. Another guy from the Donegall Road. The motley crew. We did have fun now. I missed hospital when we left. Aidan Shortt was one of them. Aidan was shot in Carlisle Circus. He's big into music.'

The patients used to get alcohol brought in to them.

'We used to take in drink in lemonade bottles. And it

would be on the corner, V for Vodka and B for Bacardi. We cancelled out breakfast, didn't want breakfast at half six in the morning. We were just in there too long really. We used to sit around and drink. You didn't really think this is because of what happened to me. It was something to do. And then Sister found out that we were slightly tipsy and confiscated it all. But it was replenished.'

They even skived off to the pub together one night. The bar they went to was the Green Briar, on the side of Black Mountain, popular with the Provisional IRA. I went there often myself and one night saw one poor singer booed off the stage because he wouldn't sing rebel songs. Another night I saw the whole crowd cheer at the sound of a distant bomb explosion.

'We were out for the night. There were steps up. We were all lifted up. Some of the staff went as well. And there was music on. All out dancing. And then we came home again, back into the ward.'

One day in Musgrave an ambulance driver who had helped recover her shattered body from the wreckage of the Abercorn joked with her, 'You're looking a lot better than the last time I seen you.'

She says she loves that humour and down the years she has heard other stories from that day. A man told her on the street that he had been born in an army Saracen. His mother was being rushed to hospital but was delayed by the bomb. A woman in a lift told her that her nephew had made Jennifer's leg. 'I found that very difficult then, when you're trying to be discreet. Now I find it funny.'

And she has been accused of being the bomber despite police statements that she was not.

'A friend of mine was on the Dublin train and sparked up a conversation with this girl, not talking about anything in particular. The girl got round to talking about the Abercorn and said, those two deserved everything they got. And this was to a friend of mine and she said, no, you've got it wrong. But she didn't convince her.'

The Building Backlash

May was an horrifically violent month. Undercover soldiers of a secret unit called the Military Reaction Force (MRF) joined the murdering. This unit patrolled republican areas in civilian cars, apparently under orders to spot and kill known activists. They appear to have been the ones who shot and injured an eighteen-year-old man on the Glen Road in Belfast on 6 May, a schoolboy coming out of a disco on 7 May, and who murdered Patsy McVeigh, aged forty-four, in Riverdale, at a barricade just round the corner from my home, on 12 May.

Angelina Fusco was a friend of Patsy McVeigh's daughter. 'I was playing camogie and we were going to Claudy to play a game but our goalkeeper didn't turn up. Her name was Joan McVeigh. I was a full back and I had to play in goal and I was raging, really cross with her because she was a far better goalie than me. Her father had been murdered the night before. He was killed by the MRF.'

The MRF seems to have been inept at selecting targets and willing to shoot people dead with no clear certainty that they posed any threat to anyone. They also recruited agents from within the catholic community, often vulnerable and pliable young men who would be murdered by the IRA when they were found out.

Tommy Gorman took part in one of the biggest gun battles of the whole Troubles period that month after a loyalist bombing of Kelly's Bar on the upper Springfield Road.

I was not sent out as a reporter on such a dangerous assignment, probably because I was so young and inexperienced. I was twenty-one. In fact, many of those who were trying to kill others or save themselves on the streets that day were much younger than I was.

Tommy Andrews, who was fifteen, says his job on the day was to evacuate protestant families from the line of fire.

William Whitelaw told the Commons later that the bomb had been the IRA's. It had gone off prematurely. There was still a reflexive tendency to doubt that loyalists were as dangerous as they were. Or maybe he, or those who briefed him, were trying to cool sectarian passions. Tommy Andrews could have told him who was responsible. He had been warned in advance to expect the blast.

'We were all called, all the junior UDA, to Highfield shops and we were told, you may hear an explosion. Once you hear it, go to the Springmartin Road and clear all the families out from the front of the Springmartin Road.

'When we went to the front of the Springmartin Road, we cleared all the families out. The people left because bullets were whizzing everywhere. Bullets would have been slamming against the front of their houses. We went in through the back of their houses sometimes and got them out and moved them to the back of the Springmartin estate and into Highfield. That gun battle raged for a whole weekend. That was a crazy time. Sometimes, even in daytime, we had to crawl on our bellies to get into the house.'

John Moran, a nineteen-year-old barman in Kelly's, was hit and would die days later. Sixty people were injured and loyalists fired on the ambulance crews arriving to help them. One of those shots killed fifty-year-old Tommy McIlroy from Riverdale.

At first, for Tommy Andrews it was like a game.

'At times we as kids were running from street to street dodging bullets. Like for us at the time it was like playing commandos till the reality kicked in. And I remember one time thinking it was a great thing to hear a crack and a bullet hitting the wall and "look at me, I just got shot at".'

Tommy was there when John Pedlow, a young protestant, was killed. The bullet that hit him had passed through another boy standing beside him. 'It was like a game to us until we saw the reality of it but we still insisted on being around when those gun battles were happening.'

Tommy was given his first chance to fire a gun during that battle. 'I was taken to the bottom of Highfield and given an old Martini Henry rifle. It looked like a cowboy rifle to me. Breech loading. Like a Winchester. You put the bullet in over the top.

'We were shown how to load it. We were brought to the end of the street in a derelict house. Bullets were whizzing all around the place. We were brought up an embankment and just told to point the weapon at a certain place and pull the trigger. The kick of it nearly knocked me on my back and somebody was standing beside me with a handgun giving covering fire so that we could run away.'

Eddie Kinner was there too. 'My brother-in-law was a small fella and two fellas standing beside him were hit with the one bullet.' That was seventeen-year-old John Pedlow and his friend.

Tommy Gorman had gone to join the battle with Tucker Kane.

'It was a fucking joke. We'd get a bucket of bullets. We took the poorest weapons that wouldn't be badly missed. Anywhere there was trouble, I was there. I was shooting at the prods mostly. We got a brit too.'

The 'brit' was twenty-two-year-old Alan Buckley of the King's Own Scottish Borderers. He was married and had one child.

Michael Magee died of a gunshot wound to his chest. *Tírghrá* says he was 'on active service' and was 'accidentally shot'. The tribute to him says that he 'joined the ranks of na Fianna Eireann in an attempt to play his part in the struggle for national liberation' having been 'forced to make decisions that would not normally have been made by teenagers'. The entry in *Tírghrá* says he was 'just 15 years old'. In fact, the date of birth attributed to him in the same entry makes him thirteen.

Political efforts to create political alternatives to this violent shambles included an approach by John Hume to the Irish government to ask for financial help for the Assembly of the Northern Irish People. This was a body to which he had been elected president but it had only met once, the previous October, and had failed to attract interest from other parties.

Hume was in difficulty, however, and he may have felt that keeping the body alive would provide him with authority.

Some of his immediate colleagues were opposed to his close dealings with the Irish government. They were also opposed to the SDLP entering talks with Whitelaw before internment was finally ended. Perhaps he felt that the Assembly of the Northern Ireland People could talk to Whitelaw without being bound by the SDLP boycott. Perhaps he just wanted the leadership of nationalism without usurping his party leader, Gerry Fitt.

To the more left-wing, working-class members of the SDLP, like Fitt and Paddy Devlin, the taoiseach Jack Lynch was a green tory and his party, Fianna Fail, was to be kept at a distance. A by-product of that strategy, however, had been that the advice the Irish government received from Hume was coloured more by events in Derry than those in Belfast.

When Lynch had gone to Chequers to meet Heath and Faulkner the previous September, and said nothing of complaint about the Parachute Regiment's murderous behaviour in Belfast, that might have been put right if Devlin and Fitt had committed themselves to a strong input into talks like that.

Decades later, Lord Saville could conclude that there had been no basis for assuming that the paras would gun down innocent civilians, despite the fact that they had already done this in Belfast.

The Irish government agreed that it had already committed itself to giving money to the now virtually non-existent assembly but doubted the value of doing so since the 'centrifugal forces' within the SDLP made it unlikely that it would meet again.

A discussion paper for the taoiseach asked, 'Does the government wish to gain a political foothold within the North and influence minority politics there, bearing in mind that the Labour and Official Sinn Féin parties are already active in both parts of the country (and that this fact, in some measure, accounts for the internal difficulties within the SDLP)?'[1]

Essentially, Hume wanted to get into talks with Whitelaw and be part of the conference Whitelaw promised so that he could discuss a new constitution for Northern Ireland, but the left wing of Hume's party, competing for credibility with other left-wing parties, was against this.

Whitelaw was building his project, working through the SDLP to coax the IRA into a ceasefire. He had said, 'No one can deny that the IRA has been gaining in support, both active and passive, from the Catholic minority. Yet I am convinced that many of these people… want violence to end and peace to come.'[2]

The loyalists were now building momentum. May would be their most murderous month yet and their strategy was perhaps as much to unnerve Whitelaw as to punish catholics for the actions of the IRA.

Gerry Duddy, twenty, was killed just round the corner from my home on Finaghy Road North. He had walked his girlfriend home and was shot dead by the UDA at about two in the morning. Andrew Brennan, twenty-six, was with his pregnant wife in Sicily Park when UDA men shot and killed him as he got out of his car. These were catholics who were easily spotted because they were living close to protestant areas. If the border provided a retreat for IRA killers, the territorial segregation of Belfast provided shelter for sectarian killers. James Teer, twenty-one, was shot dead from a passing car on

the Springfield Road as he walked near the West Circular Road
that led the trawling UVF killers back home to the Shankill.

This isn't a comprehensive summary of the killing, just a
sampling of it. The violence was now getting worse and building
towards full-scale civil war. Passions were high.

*

Máire Drumm, vice-president of Sinn Féin, was the mother
of a boy I had been to school with and of a girl I had danced
with at ceilis. She went into John Hume's constituency to
excoriate those catholics in Derry who supported his call
for a ceasefire.

In the city of Bloody Sunday, she told them she didn't care
if they were killed by the army: 'If you insist on the truce some
people are calling for, if you refuse to back up the boys who
are fighting the British army, and if the British army comes in
and murders you, I say "good luck to them" for you deserve
to be murdered.'[3]

A protestant backlash was anticipated. Whitelaw himself
had said that Vanguard was armed. The pattern of loyalist
killing so far showed that they were content to take random
catholics off the street, but the catholic nightmare was that
armed men in their hundreds would sweep over them, with
the police and UDR joining in.

This never happened. The protestant backlash was already
under way in the grim despatch of hit squads to find catholics
who had strayed from safe areas and shoot them dead in
back alleys. In the nightmare of a protestant backlash, Short
Strand, a small catholic area near the docks on the east side

of Belfast, was seen as particularly vulnerable. It was talked of as an 'enclave' surrounded by the whole eastern spread of the city which was entirely protestant, as if all those people might one day turn murderous and descend on the little houses and burn them, as others had burnt Bombay Street in the Falls area three years earlier.

A bomb that devastated Anderson Street in Short Strand seemed just what was expected, a massive blast that destroyed two houses and killed eight people. It was another accident. Four IRA men were moving a bomb when it exploded beside a car that had earlier been hijacked in Ardoyne. Two other men and two women died in the blast. The IRA first tried to blame the bomb on loyalists or the SAS and said that IRA men were killed in the explosion because they had moved forward to intercept the bombers. The propaganda depicted them as heroic defenders of the area.

Tírghrá acknowledges that the bomb was an accident and pays tribute to the IRA dead. Edward McDonnell was twenty-nine. Like his father, he was a butcher working in an abattoir. He was a good singer; his rendition of 'Mary from Dungloe' 'brought the house down'. Jackie McIlhone was seventeen. The tribute says that he got his 'first taste of action when he acted as an ammunition runner' during a gun battle in June 1970, when he was fifteen.

Joseph Fitzsimons was seventeen. He had been wounded in an exchange of fire with soldiers who had disrupted a bomb attack he was preparing in Belfast city centre. He also had been an 'ammunition runner' at fifteen. Martin Engelen was eighteen. The story in *Tírghrá* about him is that when he was leaving a hoax car bomb on the Albert Bridge the police stopped to help him, believing that he had run out of petrol.

Mary Clarke who died in the explosion was twenty-seven years old with three children. Geraldine McMahon was seventeen. Jack Nugent was thirty-one. Harry Crawford was thirty-nine and a friend to some of the dead bombers.

The IRA was shown again not to be the slick guerrilla army of the propaganda sheets but so incompetent that it was now killing more of its own members than all other threats against them combined.

Hunger Strikes

Republicans did have a strategy for calling the state to account which was more effective than bombing, and that was hunger striking. In mid-May Provisional IRA prisoners led by Billy McKee started refusing food. They deployed a strategy similar to that of the later 1981 hunger strike in which ten prisoners would starve themselves to death. This strategy was one of a rolling, accumulating protest, prisoners entering the protest at different stages, presumably to prolong the protest beyond the first deaths, if some died.

The direct rule initiative had forced all parties to change strategy. The IRA saw Whitelaw's desire to end internment and bring about political talks as an opportunity to test him with a prison protest. Republicans wanted political status for convicted prisoners and calculated that while negotiating a ceasefire, the British might concede that. They also reinforced barricades in no-go areas like my home estate Riverdale. I came out of the house one evening to see men breaking up the tarmac with a pneumatic drill to prepare for more durable foundations.

Loyalists countered by barricading their own areas, thereby insisting that no deal would be made with the IRA that did not take them into account.

And the security prediction from the previous November that the Officials would call a ceasefire of their own was fulfilled, which was perhaps the only valid insight in that smug document.

The proximate cause of the sticky ceasefire was public protest after the murder of a young soldier, nineteen-year-old Ranger William Best, who was home on leave in Derry. I think their timing may have been influenced by the protests, but I wonder why they didn't see their best advantage in waiting for the outcome of the efforts to get the Provisionals to call a ceasefire. Indeed, I wonder if the provos could have called a ceasefire if the Officials had not and if, secretly, the Officials went first to make it easier for the provos to follow. Or might they have calculated that if their ceasefire coincided with one called by the Provisionals they would be perceived as simply following their lead and losing their distinctiveness?

In the meantime the stickies would put their efforts into political action around the prison hunger strike. It was a huge protest involving dozens of prisoners, both interned and convicted. Bridie McMahon, who had joined the IRA after the killings by soldiers of her friends Dorothy Maguire and Maura Meehan, was now ready to be a martyr for a cause she'd had no part in just months earlier.

We get an insight into Official IRA thinking from a letter sent from Long Kesh by Sean Flynn to 'C Company' in the Markets and lower Ormeau area. Flynn wrote congratulating his comrades on acquiring a new clubroom but expressing his reservations about it having a bar.

Tony Rosato says, 'He understood that his comrades had chosen to sell drink in order to raise money from the local people who at that time did not choose to leave their own district through fear of the ongoing sectarian killing campaign and expressed a fear that this could tempt them away from the road of revolution. Sean suggested that we should give a political lecture to those attending the club in order to maintain a developing level of political consciousness.'

Flynn supported the ceasefire. Tony explains, 'He said that in trying to keep up with the Provisionals we had left the path of revolution. His main point was that the Officials were socialist and not sectarian and he believed we were getting some recognition of that from the UDA. Because nobody wins in a sectarian working-class war.'

The letter said that there was no point in taking up arms again until they had the majority of the people with them.

Flynn promised to continue making handcrafted models of harps and Thompson submachine guns and decorated handkerchiefs for the club that could be then be sold for additional fundraising.

Flynn's optimism may have been based on an understanding that political moves were afoot to bring the British government into negotiations with the IRA. A fellow internee at that time was one of the Provisionals with whom relations were good, Gerry Adams.

*

At the beginning of June, William Whitelaw chaired a meeting at Chequers to discuss the reform of government in Northern Ireland. He thanked the civil service for putting an administration in place and heard suggestions on what form of government Northern Ireland should have. The choice was between some form of devolution and full integration of Northern Ireland into the UK. A mix of the two was also considered, with security powers being retained in Westminster and finance and other powers being devolved.

The problem with integration was that it would be seen as making the 'Protestant position impregnable and making the reunification of Ireland impossible'.[1]

The meeting accepted that 'In the long term the entry of the United Kingdom and the Republic into the European Economic Community would reduce the significance of the Border and, hopefully, lead to a solution of the problems of Ireland.'

There would have to be a conference of all the parties, excluding the two wings of the IRA.

On a security assessment, a diplomat called Philip Woodfield, of whom we will hear more later, proposed that the closure of Holywood Detention Centre should go ahead, if it didn't demoralise the RUC, and that interrogation methods should be more sophisticated.

'Mr Woodfield explained that, since internment, interrogation techniques have aimed more at obtaining intelligence than getting successful prosecutions; there is now a need to change the order of priority. This was generally agreed.' They also agreed that the RUC needed to adopt 'more sophisticated methods'.[2]

The lord chief justice had already ruled that statements made under pressure of interrogation under the Special Powers Act were inadmissible unless the suspect had had time to recover from the effects of interrogation. The controversial Special Powers Act allowed for emergency measures like detention without trial. Its abolition had been a key demand of the civil-rights movement.

The meeting also agreed that there was no need yet for a special court to hear terrorist cases since the acquittal rate for those cases was the same as the general acquittal rate in the rest of the UK, about 40 per cent.

I wonder if Mr Woodfield and Mr Whitelaw had more to discuss outside the main meeting. Woodfield had an assignment. It was to meet with the IRA leadership and arrange for the top men to come to London to meet Whitelaw himself. This meeting would be at the home of another person who was at that Chequers meeting, Paul Channon, a minister of state in the Northern Ireland Office.

Whitelaw had an intermediary who was talking to the Ulster Defence Association on his behalf. Described in the PRONI records as the 'Bishop of Down and Connor' (a Catholic title), this is more likely a reference to the Church of Ireland bishop of Connor, Arthur Hamilton Butler. The bishop had met with 'anonymous high-ranking officials of the UDA' who had been threatening to erect barricades but had persuaded him that they wanted a way out of that commitment.

The secret document entitled 'Conclusions of the Secretary of State's Daily Meeting, June 12 1972' says that the UDA did not want a 'full scale army assault on the Londonderry "No

Go" areas but asked for some definite proposal for firm action sufficient to placate their own extremists'.[3]

This is very odd. The UDA must have felt that it had actual influence over Whitelaw. Or perhaps it was just trying to sound amenable in the hope that a connection would be developed. Even so, the creation of the loyalist 'No Go' areas would continue.

Whitelaw sent a message back through the bishop urging the UDA 'not to play the IRA game; and indicating that their understandable sense of frustration would be given sympathetic notice in his speech later in the day at Westminster'. He also agreed to meet the UDA leaders on the following day. He was hoping to meet the Vanguard leader, William Craig, too.

The next day Whitelaw met officials to discuss how they would approach the meeting with the UDA and 'the best method of participation in the talks by the GOC', Sir Harry Tuzo. He also asked for copies of Hansard in which assurances about the border were made plain. At the same time, Whitelaw was publicly refusing talks with the IRA who had asked him through the SDLP to meet them in 'Free Derry'.

The report of his daily meeting on 14 June says, 'The differences between the two organisations [the UDA and the IRA] and their approach to talks were covered in the discussions which also considered the possibility that the rejection of this IRA approach might tend to lessen in areas like the Bogside and Creggan the signs of a growing disenchantment with the IRA.'[4]

I wonder if they took into consideration that the UDA was actively killing random catholics at this time and had conceded no ceasefire. The day before the message through the bishop they shot dead forty-three-year-old Hugh Madden while he was sweeping up outside his shop on the Oldpark Road. This incident triggered a major gun battle involving the IRA but appears to have had no effect on Whitelaw.

Three days after the talks with Whitelaw the UDA shot and killed Charles Connor, aged thirty-two, and dumped his body at Minnowburn. He had been taken by them while looking for lodgings in a protestant area, the Newtownards Road. Connor had psychiatric problems and one of the gang later said in court that he had prayed repeated 'Hail Mary's' while being taken away to be shot.

It does look as if Whitelaw was much less concerned about sectarian killings between catholics and protestants than about attacks on the army and police, and the outworking of the IRA ceasefire that was shortly to follow would suggest that too.

Whitelaw decided to try to find out through John Hume how the rejection of talks with the IRA was being received in Derry. But given that the IRA had asked for talks without making the ending of internment a precondition, the clever suggestion was made that this now freed up the SDLP to meet with Whitelaw on a similar basis. Until then, the continuation of internment had been the obstacle to the SDLP participating in talks with government. The IRA had, however, made it a precondition of talks that prisoners belonging to its movement be given political status.

Whitelaw also said that there was a growing need to 'consider further firm action in relation to the Londonderry "no go" areas'. He said that it was 'possible that a decision to mount a new containment operation in Londonderry might be taken in the next couple of weeks'. He'd be discussing that with the army later in the day.

I had been to the 'no-go' areas in Derry as a journalist and there was a relaxed and even slightly giddy feeling about moving through streets in which the IRA had control and even issued press passes to journalists.

But I was now living in a 'no-go' area in Belfast myself. I had Tommy Gorman and Tucker Kane and others in their IRA company who had escaped from the *Maidstone* living in safe houses across the street from me. Life in those homes must have been chaotic and dangerous with armed men coming and going and bedding down there while teenage children had their meals or waited to use the bathroom.

Negotiations for a Ceasefire

Gerry Adams was released from internment into the care of the SDLP's Paddy Devlin to prepare for talks with British officials. He was met one morning at the gate of Long Kesh by two sisters who would later be famous for their bombing activities and prison hunger strikes, Dolours and Marian Price. They took him to Devlin's home in north Belfast. Adams now had safe passage through a city that was more militarised than he had seen it since his arrest, with the huge defensive barriers around police stations now raised higher to deter RPG7 missiles. The roads near those stations were made hazardous with ramps that already bore the scars of car exhausts that had not passed smoothly over them.

Adams travelled a few days later to Derry to meet with two diplomats, both experienced in unravelling British colonial entanglements. These were Philip Woodfield and Frank Steele. Woodfield was an old soldier who had helped prepare for Nigerian independence in the fifties. Steele was an MI6 officer who had worked with Jomo Kenyatta in the run-up to Kenyan independence. So, whether Britain was seriously contemplating withdrawal, having already told the Irish that such a policy was inconceivable, it had sent out to deal with the IRA two men who were well experienced in decolonising work.

The IRA was represented by Adams and Dáithí Ó Conaill (or David O'Connell as he is referred to in the British record of the meeting) and was assisted by a solicitor called P. J. McGrory. They all met at the Derry home of Sir Michael McCorkell, a Donegal man who was a colonel in the Territorial Army and an aide de camp to the Queen.

In order to get the IRA to this meeting Whitelaw had already conceded special category status for IRA prisoners and thereby settled the hunger strike.

Philip Woodfield's report of the meeting is fascinating reading. He clearly was impressed by Adams and Ó Conaill and trusted that they both wanted an end to the violence, but the course of the actual negotiations suggests that the IRA was trying hard to outsmart the British and was even ready to jeopardise the secrecy of the talks.

First, the IRA delegates asked to be allowed to speak by phone from McCorkell's house to a senior member of the IRA in the prison to confirm that the hunger strike was over. At another time they asked the British to introduce them to the UDA with an assurance that they would get on a lot better than they might expect. This must have alarmed the British delegates, who were hoping that no information would come out about these talks. Whitelaw would want to deny that they had even happened.

The republicans asked for the right to carry guns during the ceasefire and the British refused a direct answer but said they hoped a situation would be created in which they would not feel the need, but that in any event they would not be stopped during the ceasefire while going about their legitimate business.

Adams and Ó Conaill tried to get a commitment from the army to stay out of no-go areas. They offered to give the British a list of areas they should avoid. Woodfield replied politely that there could be no such undertaking but 'any specific proposal genuinely designed to help would be carefully considered'.[1]

Woodfield was clearly impressed by these men but he worried about another member of the IRA leadership, Seán MacStíofáin, and asked if he could be left off any delegation to meet Whitelaw. Ó Conaill said MacStíofáin probably wouldn't want to come anyway. They'd think about it.

Woodfield also asked that the ceasefire should endure for at least ten days, including two weekends, before the meeting with Whitelaw.

Woodfield wrote in his report to Whitelaw, before the commencement of the ceasefire, 'There is no doubt whatever that these two at least genuinely want a ceasefire and a permanent end to violence. Whatever pressures in Northern Ireland have brought them to this frame of mind there is little doubt that, now that the prospect of peace is there, they have a strong personal incentive to try and get it. They let drop several remarks showing that the life of the Provisional IRA man on the run is not a pleasant one.'

He continued, 'Their appearance and manner were respectable and respectful – they easily referred to Mr Whitelaw as "the Secretary of State" and they addressed me from time to time as "Sir". They made no bombastic defence of their past and made no attacks on the British government, the British Army or any other communities or bodies in Northern Ireland. Their response to every argument put to them was reasonable and moderate. Their behaviour and attitude appeared to bear no relation to the indiscriminate campaigns of bombing and shooting in which they had both been prominent leaders.'

The IRA gave four days' notice of its ceasefire, killing five more soldiers and an RUC man between the meeting with Woodfield and Steele and the start of the cessation. The leadership timed the ceasefire to start on a Monday, perhaps specifically to deny the British their requirement that two weekends should pass in the ten days before the meeting with Whitelaw.

Announcing the ceasefire in the House of Commons, Whitelaw dodged questions from Ian Paisley about a deal with the IRA: 'Will the Secretary of State define a little more clearly, in order that the majority people of Northern Ireland will be under no misapprehension, the question of the reciprocation of the IRA truce?'[2]

Paisley said that Irish radio had reported that concessions had been made. Had conditions changed for prisoners in the Crumlin Road Gaol?

Whitelaw responded that he had already made clear that the army and police would continue to maintain the security of the people of Northern Ireland. 'Regarding the arrangements that I have made for prisoners in the Crumlin Road prison, I should make it clear that these arrangements, which I have made in a difficult situation, are in line with what is already carried out in the special security wings at Leicester and Parkhurst prisons.'

He was plainly hiding the fact that he had sent Woodfield and Steele to negotiate the ceasefire terms with Adams and Ó Conaill and that he had accorded special category status to IRA prisoners as a minimal concession simply to secure that meeting. And he inserted his routine assurance to the protestant community, congratulating them on their forbearance.

That community, he said, 'has been extremely-long suffering. It has seen its country destroyed in front of its eyes and life made extremely difficult over many years. It has borne this with great restraint and patience, and I am sure that the House and everyone else commends it. I believe that the people of Northern Ireland, like everybody else, will pray urgently that this really will mean an end of the violence.'

On the morning of 26 June Whitelaw expressed his anxiety about the fragility of the ceasefire arrangement at his morning meeting which was attended by Frank Steele and the GOC. He said he feared that every incident and every rumour could lead to a disruption of the peace that he hoped would follow the Provisional IRA ceasefire due to begin at midnight.

The report of the meeting says that Lord Windlesham, a minister of state in the Northern Ireland Office, 'stressed that it would be in the interests of all concerned for the IRA to disclose the whereabouts of booby-traps etc so that the Army could render them harmless as otherwise their accidental explosion after the ceasefire could be construed as a breach of faith'.[3]

The report is interesting in the way it has been corrected. The writer struggled in particular with one line, whose first draft was amended three times. In the scored-out part Whitelaw is reported as having originally said it was still his intention, during the ceasefire, 'that persons seen to or suspected of committing offences under the Special Powers Act were to be apprehended'. Even this, before it was scored out, was written over a version that had been redacted with Tippex and is unreadable. The final version is, 'any breach in the criminal law would still [with 'still' then deleted] result in prosecution'.

The IRA has often referred to the ceasefire as a truce but this line has been worked on to make clear that there would be no change in the application of the law while avoiding reference to the Special Powers Act, which Whitelaw perhaps understood as not being strictly part of the 'criminal law'. The easy inference is that he had decided that the Special Powers Act would not be used during the ceasefire.

Then he asked his officials to 'obtain the necessary legal guidance so that the GOC and the Chief Constable could issue appropriate instructions'. It is hard to see why they would need 'appropriate instructions' if the ceasefire was not to change the way in which the security forces would respond to the IRA.

Tommy Gorman told me that he attended a 'battalion briefing' from the IRA chief of staff, Seán MacStíofáin, who told them not to expect the ceasefire to last long or to produce a political result.

The two weeks of the provo ceasefire were, in fact, more violent than those which preceded it, but this violence was mostly sectarian. The IRA did not attack the army or bomb commercial property and the British conceded that this satisfied their conditions for a meeting with the secretary of state in London.

The army changed its entire profile on the streets. Instead of soldiers carrying their rifles in readiness to return fire, they wore them slung over their shoulders and vehicle patrols used open-top canvas-covered jeeps rather than the armoured ones that had become more common.

In effect, they were expressing their faith in the IRA's promise not to fire on them.

The loyalists were not party to the agreement, were unsettled by it and increased their killing rate against catholic civilians. Both wings of the IRA retaliated in kind, killing random protestants.

After loyalists killed two catholics and dumped their bodies in Westway Drive, republicans shot two protestants and dumped their bodies on waste ground off the Cliftonville Road. In the two weeks of the ceasefire, loyalists and republicans (including Officials) killed sixteen people between them, but Whitelaw accepted that the IRA was still on ceasefire despite this and his meeting with the leaders went ahead.

He was now fearful that the loyalists were 'on the point of exploding'. That is the phrase used by the Irish ambassador Donal O'Sullivan in a letter to the Department of Foreign Affairs after a brief meeting with Whitelaw on 30 June.[4]

One of Whitelaw's measures for appeasing the protestants was a promise of a plebiscite on Northern Ireland's membership of the UK. He was also pleading now with people in Derry to use their influence to have the no-go areas opened up.

On the same day, the UDA issued a bizarre statement inviting catholics who were intimidated by the IRA to come and join them and receive 'the hospitality of protestant homes'.

There were tense moments in which the stability of the fairly limited ceasefire was endangered, as Tommy Gorman, who was stopped by the army in Bingnian Drive, recalls: 'I was getting back into the car and they came up and stopped me and stood round the car. They started being – not cheeky – but nasty. And I says, you're breaking the agreement.

'They said, what agreement's that?

'I said, away and fuck.

'I had a weapon in the car. There was a fella not too far away and I gave him the nod and he came in and got the weapon and he got behind one of them and he said, right, there's a ceasefire or there's not a ceasefire, What's it going to be?'

Gorman thinks they didn't see the weapon but that they understood that they could on no account take the matter further and arrest him. But he did not believe the ceasefire was going to last. 'I didn't believe it was for real. The volunteers were all running about and laughing. I says to them, it's not over.'

I got a message from Tony Rosato's brother Martin on the first Saturday of the provo ceasefire that if I went to the Markets area that evening I would see something I could make a story out of for the paper. He suggested I bring a photographer. The staff photographers I worked with then were wary of going into dangerous republican areas. Most of them were protestant and more used to covering stories for our sister paper, the *News Letter*, which was ardently unionist. Some of them were even a bit sniffy about working with this catholic from Andersonstown. One of them had said to me one day, 'We only want hundred percenters here, Malachi.'

And I was sympathetic to their wariness of me because I was living in an IRA-controlled no-go area and they were entitled to fear that I was close enough to the IRA, at least physically, to endanger them, if only through careless talk.

At that time an American journalist called Marc Crawford was in Belfast and we were working closely together, so I invited Marc to come to the Markets with me and see what this story was. I knew some of the Official IRA men there. One was an affable and slightly tubby man called Tommy Conlon who had helped me with stories. I would meet him in the drinking club they ran there.

Marc and I went to the designated location at about seven on that Saturday evening. While we were waiting, a grey Land Rover approached. Four armed men in balaclavas sat in the back with a variety of weapons. Tommy Conlon was one of them. He said they were going to patrol the area to protect the people from loyalist attacks. It seemed to me from some of the mutterings among them about men watching us from a distance that they were more concerned about the provos.

Marc and I got into the jeep and were taken on a tour of the area. Each man in turn showed me his gun and described it. They had a Luger, a hunting rifle and an M1 carbine. Children ran playfully alongside us cheering.

But wasn't this a breach of their own ceasefire? They said that the army was not coming into the area any more so it fell to them to provide protection, 'against any aggression, be it the UDA, the Provisionals or the British'.

It was a stunt, a reckless one which relied on an assumption that the British army would not open fire on them.

I was delighted with the story, though I didn't have a picture. When I got back to the office, Ric, one of the senior reporters who monitored the police radio, told me that we had been spotted and there had been some discussion on how to deal with the gunmen in the jeep.

On the same night the UDA in different parts of the city killed two men, one of them a nineteen-year-old English visitor, Paul Jobling, the other Daniel Hayes, thirty-four. Jobling had been volunteering for work with deprived children. Poor Hayes had been kidnapped by the UDA and beaten, tied up and gagged, then shot in the head.

There were six sectarian murders in the first two days of July, four of them by loyalists and two by republicans. Hugh Clawson and David Fisher, both in their thirties, had been out drinking and wandered into a catholic part of Ardoyne and were probably killed in direct vengeance for the killings of Jobling and Hayes, though there is no suggestion that the killers knew any of them personally.

And now the UDA was erecting barricades in earnest around the city.

In those bloody days it was rarely clear who was killing and why. Two brothers, Malcolm and Peter Orr, aged twenty and nineteen, were shot dead and dumped on the road out towards the airport. They might have been killed by republicans for being protestant or by loyalists for going out with catholic girls.

As was often the case, the most likely people to be killed in a sectarian attack were people with the least sectarian inclination themselves.

This was not a ceasefire at all in any meaningful sense.

The bottom line for Adams and Ó Conaill had been that the IRA could conduct itself as the lawful authority in republican areas. The government and the army did not then contest them on this.

The Provisionals set up roadblocks. They shot dead two people who tried to drive through them, just as the British had done. Bernard Norney, thirty-eight, was killed in Ballymurphy and Samuel Robinson, nineteen, in Cavendish Street. This was on the very day that the IRA leaders flew to London to meet Whitelaw, and he had not regarded this as a breach of the ceasefire, despite having told parliament that the army would continue to be deployed for the protection of the people.

Seán MacStíofáin, Dáithí Ó Conaill, Seamus Twomey, Ivor Bell, Martin McGuinness and Gerry Adams gathered in Derry to be flown by helicopter to an RAF flight out of Aldergrove. The IRA had disregarded Woodfield's request that MacStíofáin not be included. They also brought Myles Shevlin, a solicitor, as a note taker.

The meeting was held at 96 Cheyne Walk, Chelsea, the home of Paul Channon. The house was on a T-junction, facing Chelsea Embankment, which meant it was easy to secure. Whitelaw and Channon were accompanied by Woodfield and Steele.

MacStíofáin read the republican position paper, requiring the British to make a public declaration of the right of the

Irish people, acting as a unit, to decide the future of Ireland and to withdraw all forces from Irish soil by 1 January 1975. They demanded an amnesty for all political prisoners in both countries, for internees and detainees and all who were on the run. They also wanted an end to oaths of allegiance to the crown and proportional representation for all elections in the North.

The IRA delegates were lowering their demand, opting for a political compromise short of immediate Irish unity. The leaders absurdly understood themselves to be the legitimate government of the whole of Ireland, drawing their authority from the 1918 general election which Sinn Féin, at the time, had interpreted as giving them the right to establish a breakaway parliament. But neither the British nor Irish government nor any of the Northern Irish political parties would acknowledge that they had that status and would defer to them in it. They had nothing to barter with other than their power to end the IRA campaign and thereby enable others to negotiate a political settlement that would inevitably fall short of their aims. Unelected republicans would have had no seats by right at those negotiations.

But both sides had had a good look at each other and connections had been established between them and would endure. The British knew now that the IRA had total control over its organisation and some talented members in the leadership. The IRA knew that the British would negotiate again some day and that they would compromise on principle to do it. It had seen that it could murder during a ceasefire and still be regarded as not having broken it. That was enough for now.

Two days later the IRA would collapse the ceasefire with a major gun battle and four sectarian murders. The year of chaos was suffering its most chaotic month.

Breakdown

Lenadoon Avenue is a winding downhill street through a housing estate on the lower western slope of Black Mountain. Before Lenadoon was built the area was open fields that we as children scrambled through at the start of many Sunday afternoon climbs of the grassy mountain, up towards the quarry and the television mast.

This was a bright Sunday afternoon, two days after the IRA meeting with Whitelaw, and the ceasefire had served its purpose. Whether consciously contrived as such, it was the device that would enable the SDLP to ward off criticism when it entered talks with Whitelaw on proposals for giving nationalists a right to sit in the government of Northern Ireland.

This was the formula that John Hume and his colleagues would bring to a constitutional conference in Darlington, County Durham, in September. It was what would be agreed on the following year with the British, the Irish and Faulkner's unionists at the table. It was the essence of the Good Friday Agreement that it would take another twenty-six years to win adequate support for.

But there was a long way to go and a lot more people would die, many of them on that Sunday. None of them died in Lenadoon, however, though battle lines were drawn there and there would be much shooting. The interesting thing about the IRA's plan to end its ceasefire in Lenadoon was that it was not predicated on political ideology. Two days earlier, the leadership had met with Whitelaw in Paul Channon's house in Chelsea and, presuming to speak for the Irish people, had demanded self-determination and progress towards a British withdrawal.

Whitelaw had already told the Irish government that it was inconceivable that Irish unity should be British policy, so he was in no position to concede more to an unelected terrorist organisation than to a government that was soon to be its partner in the EEC. But the IRA did not come home to announce that it was returning to war because peace talks had failed. Why not? Probably because most people, even in their own communities, would not have agreed with that as an excuse for more bombs and killings. What they might agree with was a demonstration of the need for an IRA that could confront loyalist aggression and British partiality.

Lenadoon Avenue was filled with people waiting. They were watching a furniture lorry approach Horn Drive at the bottom. The IRA had said that it would support catholic families who wanted to move into vacant houses that had been previously occupied by protestants. The UDA had said it would resist this. The army said it would keep the peace by blocking access to the houses. So a confrontation was inevitable.

A row of houses at the top of Lenadoon Avenue had IRA gunmen waiting at the windows. Tommy Gorman was at the bottom of the hill, by the army barrier. His job would be to signal to the gunmen that the way had been barred to the lorry and they would then open fire. Had I known that at the time, I would have positioned myself more carefully, as would probably hundreds of other people around me.

Seamus Twomey, a member of the IRA army council and one of those who had met Whitelaw days earlier, was talking to the soldiers. I was far enough back not to see clearly what was happening. I was closer to the IRA guns than to the army.

When the shooting started I felt a jolt of terror and ran as the cascade of gunfire erupted behind me. I ran into someone's garden, between houses out the back and through hedges into another street, still just yards from the ongoing prattle of weaponry.

Those weapons included a Lewis gun fired by Jimmy Bryson. Tommy Gorman later told me that Bryson, when taking up his position in a bedroom window, had smashed the glass. 'There was no need for that,' he said, meaning that if someone is going to let you use their bedroom for a firing position then you owe them the courtesy of not vandalising their home.

A friend of mine told me later that he was on a rooftop firing a Thompson submachine gun into the air and praying that he wasn't hurting anyone when the bullets came back down again. That would have added considerably to the noise.

I got out onto the Shaw's Road and walked the mile home with the gunfire continuing and echoing across the mountain. Much of that shooting was for show. At least that seems the most likely explanation why no one was killed there. I went home and sank down speechless into an armchair, utterly deflated, and my father handed me a large whiskey.

Republican gunmen had already killed three men in another part of town before the attack that formally ended the ceasefire by shooting at soldiers. Joseph Fleming, thirty, Brian McMillan, twenty-one, and Alan Meehan, eighteen, had gone to a party the night before and were warned by friends as they left to be wary of sensitive areas. Two of them were protestants. Fleming, a catholic, was a staff sergeant in the Territorial Army so killing him was an actual breach of a ceasefire hours before the gunplay at Lenadoon. A milkman found their bodies in the car on the Sunday morning. McMillan was dead and had been squeezed into the boot. Fleming and Meehan were still alive at that point, though with head wounds. Someone had driven the car to the Grosvenor Road and tried to burn it with the men inside. Fleming would die later that day, Meehan three days later.

Loyalists killed David Andrews, aged thirty-one. He was found shot dead at the Waterworks by the Cavehill Road. He had been kicked and beaten before being finished off with a bullet.

And the day wasn't over. British soldiers would kill five more during a gun battle at Springhill, near Ballymurphy. Overlooking Springhill there was a big timber yard owned by a company called J. P. Corry. When I went later as a reporter to try to get some sense of what happened, a local man pointed out little rectangles cut into the facade of the timber yard and claimed these were firing positions used by loyalists. Others argue that the shootings were carried out by the army. It was all horror.

Five dead. One of them a sixteen-year-old member of the Fianna, the junior IRA. The Parachute Regiment claimed to have hit fourteen gunmen, resorting to the familiar theory that the IRA was disguising its losses. As in Ballymurphy during internment week, one of the dead was a priest, Noel Fitzpatrick. Three of them were children, Margaret Gargan, thirteen, John Dougal, sixteen, and David McCafferty, fourteen.

That was nine dead in the one day. By my count ninety-two people were killed that month. Loyalists killed twenty-three people; republicans killed fifty; the army killed nineteen. Other counts differ slightly but that gives a close approximation of the carnage.

Whitelaw's pitch for peace had failed. It is hardly fair to blame him for the escalation that followed. He had alarmed the loyalists but they had been gearing up for sectarian attacks since the previous September when the UDA was formed and Tommy Andrews had joined. Once they got involved, both wings of the IRA, the Officials and the Provisionals, indulged in sectarian killing of protestants. Both had announced ceasefires but had carried on this killing. The ceasefires had simply redirected their energies against other targets, uninvolved civilians, killing innocent for innocent.

Even in such a grotesque month there were bloody highlights. Some of the deaths came singly, some in clusters. Seven dead on 13 July, mostly in separate incidents, apart from two killed by the army in a gun battle. Six dead on the following day, four killed by the IRA and two by the army. Yet the incidents most remembered from that month are Bloody Friday, 21 July, in which ten died, and the Claudy bomb of 31 July in which nine died. You have a better chance of being remembered if you die in a full-blown atrocity than if you die alone.

Riverdale was expected to be where the IRA would make

its last stand in defence of the no-go areas. That's what former soldier Harry Beaves says in his book *Down Among the Weeds.*

The IRA was now looking for other houses to operate from and my father stupidly agreed to allow them to use ours. I let them in and just as stupidly said, 'No guns.' That night I lay in bed and listened to them coming and going and bringing back the smell of cordite and clearing their rifles. I came down in the morning to see them sleeping on the sofa and floor. I moved out until they stopped using the house. I don't know what brought them to the decision to leave. My mother told me that when cleaning up after them she found a pistol under a cushion and took it to the safe house across the street and gave it to Tucker Kane. If our house had been raided then, as it was later, and that gun had been found, at least one of us would have gone to jail for a long time.

Before the army got round to dealing with Riverdale it had to pacify Lenadoon. I watched one evening as a convoy of military vehicles, Pigs and Saracens, went up Finaghy Road North to occupy the estate. Soldiers moved into residential flats and established billets and were fired on by the IRA.

On a Saturday evening I stood with a group of reporters on the Shaw's Road anticipating action. One of them was an affable guy called Christopher Hitchens. Later I walked around the area. On the Glen Road I dived for cover as a pillion rider on a passing motorbike opened fire. At least, I think that's what happened. You don't get a clear picture when you have your face in grass.

The provos organised a mass evacuation of Lenadoon and families paraded down the road with basic domestic belongings, swearing they would not go back until the army had left. They first held a mass rally in Casement Park. Then some went back home, while others bedded down that night in a local school. I went there to see if I could do some interviews and met Gerry O'Hare and Máire Drumm's husband Jimmy, himself a senior member of the IRA. They were driving round the area in a large black Ford Zephyr, the kind of car a priest would drive, and they took me with them on a tour of the estate. There did not seem to be much purpose to the tour other than perhaps to create an opportunity for us to talk, away from others. When we got back to the school there was an armed guard on the gate. Gerry thought this was inappropriate. He said: 'What's that fucking eejit doing there with a weapon? Who gave that order?'

Later they took me to the house of Tom Conaty. He had been a member of a citizens' defence committee and had been co-author with Fr Padraig Murphy of the letter to Jack Lynch arguing that the catholics could be weaned from supporting the IRA if internment was ended. I think at this stage he was probably mediating to Whitelaw about the feelings of the catholic community. O'Hare and Drumm didn't introduce me to him or tell him that I was a reporter so I assume he took me for an IRA man. If Conaty was relaying messages from the IRA to Whitelaw, I doubt they were now being received with much interest. The invasion of Lenadoon was the beginning of a progressive assault against the no-go areas.

The army was escalating its war on the IRA and the IRA was escalating too.

Bloody Friday

21 July was a beautiful day. I went out for a walk up Royal Avenue with Eddie, one of the other reporters. The outsider might not understand that even among such routine murder normal life continued. We were not all worn down by it so much that we couldn't enjoy the summer heat, browsing the shop windows after lunch, spending a little money.

Nor had the city yet adapted, as it did later, to the influx of bombs. Soon there would be barriers closing the whole city centre to traffic, and checkpoints on footpaths for pedestrians. Bombs were part of our lives, and yet more so as hoaxes, so there were times in the office when the alarm went off and everyone would groan with exasperation at having to leave the building again. One might just sit on and finish typing a story, too well used to there not really being a bomb in the building anyway. And what chance was there, if a bomb had been planted, that anyone would find it in a brief half-hour search, given the clutter we worked in?

I saw a suede jacket in a shop window, priced at £9. I thought it looked very smart, with its two-tone colouring and the little breast pockets that opened like slices. Not quite a cowboy jacket; I wouldn't have wanted that. I went in, tried it on, wrote the cheque and, when the bombs started going off, I even harboured the evil thought that my cheque might end up under rubble and no money would leave my account to pay for this lovely addition to my wardrobe.

We heard the first as we walked back along Royal Avenue towards the office.

You might think that if you heard a bomb blast in a city street you would rush for cover, that people around you would be screaming. It wasn't like that yet. One bomb. Unfortunate for someone, perhaps calamitous, but you had heard it and you were spared. When we got back to the office we would find out what had happened.

Then there was another explosion. And another.

Beano Niblock says he was in the Ormeau Park at the time, on the other side of the River Lagan: 'I heard this bomb. I think it may have been from Botanic direction. I'm not sure. I saw the puff of smoke. And then over the next hours you had this perfect view of it. And you're thinking, there's something serious here.'

He too remembers the beautiful summer weather: 'It was a lovely day and you had the Lagan in front of you and right across from where I was standing there was a boat club and there must have been a band practising for the weekend gig, and you could hear the music very clearly across the water. And then these bombs started to go off and the music stopped. It was like a moment.'

Tommy Gorman says, 'We were tasked to do stuff out at Shaw's Bridge, the old bridge. We didn't do any damage. It was a fucking joke. I said, this is fucking bad. We were all up at the Green Briar, and the bombs were going off and I says, fuck me pink. Afterwards I was fucking crying for fuck's sake. That can never be justified.

'To the people around me in the Green Briar every boom was a good un.'

In the newspaper office we felt we were in danger. The realisation was settling that the scale of the bombing was new to us and we had no idea what to expect or how to react. A journalist from the Press Association who was there looked at me and said, 'Are you OK?'

'Yeah, sure, fine.' But he had seen the fear in my face and I really didn't have to pretend. We were evacuated down into the print room. A woman who had previously been injured by a bomb at another job, a woman I smiled and joked with when I passed her on the stairs, was screaming. She was flailing her arms in panic. Her friends were carrying her.

When we were below just waiting, my colleague Stephen nudged me and looked up. This grim dusty workspace was lit from high above by a series of skylights, glass. In the stupid way in which you prefer not to alarm people or draw attention to yourself, even to save your life, we said nothing.

Harry Beaves says in his book that he dealt with a bomb under the M1 bridge on Finaghy Road North, about half a mile from my home. Then he and his men were fired on from waste ground nearby.

Beano Niblock says, 'I thought shit, there's something happening here. And basically went home. As a tartan gang we always stood at a corner of two streets with an Ulster flag on it and that was our corner. If you were first out of the house you just stood there and people came, and as it happened I got a sandwich in the house and went round and there was a couple already there. And sooner or later everybody came. We go into somebody's house. We have a meeting here. A guy who lived a couple of doors away. He had a parlour house. We went into his parlour. By that stage you knew what had happened. The consensus was, right, we'll do something. We'll retaliate. And a couple of ones who were in senior positions said, listen, no. That's not going to happen.'

They wanted to consult with the other loyalist paramilitaries first.

Eamon Hanna was in North Street. His wife Carmel was nursing in the Mater Hospital and dealing with the injured and dead coming in.

'It was rather a nice day. Making my way home and the horror of it. I was very close to a guy called Tom Donnelly. His sister was killed at the Cavehill shops, Margaret Mary O'Hare. He rang me later that night to say that they had discovered that Margaret Mary was dead. He had been down at the morgue. He had passed by the bodies and said, no, it's not her because she was wearing a white dress. And then he realised that it was the blood. She was blown to bits.'

Jennifer and Rosie McNern were still in Musgrave learning to work with their new artificial limbs.

'We used to get home for the weekend and one Friday we were going home and it was Bloody Friday. My God, it was a nightmare. I was saying, I want to go back to the hospital, just take me back. It was just chaos really.'

She felt that the mood of the city was not as she had known it in the relatively more peaceful days of three months earlier: 'Our house was just the same. But the whole atmosphere seemed to have changed.'

Eddie Kinner recalls, 'A couple of us headed into town when we heard the bombs going off. Four or five of us from Highfield heading down into the town to see where all this was happening. In Union Street a crowd had been rioting there. At the corner of Union Street there was a couple of nineteen year olds standing and as we were getting drawn further into Union Street, these two guys had run up and grabbed one of ours and held him and yelled for guys from Unity Flats to come and take him. While they were holding him, our crowd had pulled back, so I ran in then and hit the main one a punch on the side of the head and they let go of our guy and he bolted. And then they turned on me, grabbed me by the shirt and I stood back and said, come on ahead, and he turned and went.'

Anthony McIntyre was rioting too: 'My mother was down the town and all you heard all day was these bangs of explosions and I was worried. And then that night there was a lot of tension in the town and we went down to garages on Shaftesbury Avenue and took all the lorries out. And we barricaded the place.'

The worst bomb was at Oxford Street bus station. Six died there. Young firemen on parade because they had just completed their training were directed to the scene. You can see them in the old footage, in dress uniform, shovelling torn flesh. Another fire engine passing on the way to a different bomb swerved to avoid a woman's head lying in the road.

There were nineteen bomb explosions in the city between 2.10 p.m. and 3.15 p.m. That first one that Eddie and I heard while still on the street had been at Smithfield bus station. The targets were other bus and railway stations at Oxford Street and York Road, Great Victoria Street and the terminus for the Liverpool ferry. Taxi companies, garages and hotels were hit, as were busy junctions and bridges.

There were twenty-seven explosions across Northern Ireland that day. In addition to the nine dead, 130 people were injured. Whitelaw in parliament would list them as 'at least 40 were Roman Catholics, 53 were men and boys, 77 women and children'.[1]

When the bombs stopped we went back to the office to resume work, trying to find out the scale of what had happened. Jim, the news editor, phoned to say that if his wife called we were to say he was all right, though he had been blown off his feet by the bomb that killed Margaret Mary O'Hare. He was grim when he got back but settled behind his typewriter and started writing.

I took a phone call. It was Gerry O'Hare, the press officer for the Provisional IRA's brigade staff. 'What the fuck was the point of all that?' I said.

Jim took the phone from me and dealt with him more professionally.

*

That night gunmen called at the home of Tony Rosato's father on the Deerpark Road. They asked to speak to one of his other sons. Joseph Rosato closed the door and pressed his foot hard against it to hold them back. One of the men fired a shot which tore an artery in his leg. He bled to death.

At first this seemed to be a loyalist attack on a republican household. Tony believes that other members of the Official IRA killed his father in a dispute with his brother. Liam McMillen, the Belfast commander, then stood down all the Rosato men who were in his Official IRA, ostensibly on compassionate grounds. Stickies actually attended the funeral but Tony believes that internal divisions were behind it and it was not meant to culminate in a killing, least of all the killing of his father.

Two days later, the UDA killed three catholics. Rose McCartney was a twenty-seven-year-old singer who performed in the Old House, a bar favoured by the Officials. They kidnapped her and her boyfriend, who was a year younger, and shot them dead, side by side in a car. When they were found, she was dead, with a cloth covering her face. Her boyfriend Patrick O'Neill was still barely alive and groaning as the life slipped out of him. Rose's head was resting on his shoulder. One of the two had seen a lover shot in the face before taking a bullet too.

Francis Arthurs had been travelling home to Ardoyne in a taxi with other people. UDA men stopped the car, checked everyone's identity and took Francis away and shot him. The police, asked at the inquest about allegations that they hadn't done enough to find him, said that there had been five murders in that division that night, so they were overstretched.

Tommy Andrews, who was in the UDA, then says he later committed himself to working for peace because of some of the things he saw during this awful time: 'Once I was in a club where a catholic was being tortured and I heard the screams and even smelt flesh burning. Horrific.'

But despite the other killings it was Bloody Friday that preoccupied the Sunday papers that week. An editorial in Dublin's *Sunday Independent* said the whole country had a share of the blame: 'There is a black sin on the face of Irish Republicanism today that will never be erased. Murder now lies at the feet of the Irish nation and there is no gain-saying that fact.'

Whitelaw thought the carnage was a massive mistake by the IRA that would finish off popular support for them: 'Even those sections of Roman Catholic opinion throughout the world which have traditionally identified themselves with, and, perhaps, sometimes given the benefit of the doubt to any group of men who claimed to speak for the Irish Republican movement, can surely no longer continue to uphold the men who were responsible for Friday's horrible catalogue of slaughter.'[2]

The ceasefire and negotiations had failed so he concluded that the IRA had no interest in advancing its cause through politics: 'They have degraded the human race, and it must now be clear to all that their sole object is to promote their aims by violence and by violence alone.'

And he signalled that he now intended to crush the IRA: 'No one can deny that Her Majesty's Government have now an absolutely unchallengeable right to ask this House, this country and, indeed, the whole world for their support in an absolute determination to destroy the capacity of the Provisional IRA for further acts of inhumanity.'

Motorman

Our family home in Riverdale was close to the M1 running west towards Dungannon. On the other side of it at that time the population was predominantly protestant and there had been exchanges of fire across the motorway and adjacent waste ground. The IRA posted a warning notice in a local shop saying that it had mined the waste ground, still called McAlpine's Yard after a company that had used it. I wrote up a story about this for the *Sunday News* and the national news picked up on it and reported it that night.

In his book *Down Among the Weeds*, Harry Beaves says that he and his men in the Royal Artillery were then ordered through the supposedly mined area. He worried about that and one of his mates didn't help put his mind at ease: 'I reckon you're in big trouble, mate.' He didn't want to question orders or 'to seem chicken' but he went back to his senior officer, David Storrey, in the Ops Room.[1]

Storrey said, 'I've thought about it and we've seen kids playing on that grass regularly.' He thought the message about the mines was a bluff, 'so I'd like you to carry on as planned'.

At 11 p.m., Beaves and his men moved out from Musgrave Park Hospital where they were based and headed towards the motorway and a culvert that ran under it. There, he says, he was faced with the question of whether to send another man in front of him to face any possible booby traps. In these cases, the commander would send someone more expendable ahead.

Storrey was treating Beaves as expendable but Beaves was more considerate of his men than his commander had been of him. So he led from the front into the culvert, trusting also in his greater expertise. Beaves wrote, 'The tunnel would have been a great place for a bomb.'

Once through to the other side the men fanned out on their stomachs on the bank of the river. They edged up to get a view of the houses in Riverdale. There was nothing of interest to see.

'Riverdale went to sleep and we watched the whole drama unfold!'

And at 3 a.m. they edged back down the stream and into the culvert and laughed with relief.

'Nothing to make you think there were mines or anything there?' asked their colonel. 'That's fine, well worth knowing.' Beaves didn't complain about having been sent out as a potential sacrifice to test the ground. He trusted the officer's judgement and 'got on with the job'.

Harry Beaves also took part in operations to dismantle barricades, first in relatively safe estates. On the night of 26 July his company provided protection for the Royal Engineers at eight locations around Andersonstown where they expected little or no resistance. This was part of a strategy to pare away at the defences established by the IRA before a major assault on the barricades in the toughest areas. Then the army was able to get foot patrols into those streets.

On that same day, the Prime Minister's Office received draft changes in guidance from the Ministry of Defence on 'rules of engagement', the circumstances in which a soldier might open fire. The particular amendment to the rules concerned the use of heavy weapons, such as the Carl Gustav – an anti-tank weapon. The IRA didn't have tanks. The guidance began: 'For this operation only...'

The army was planning Operation Motorman, its invasion of the no-go areas, expecting it to be its biggest operation in Northern Ireland and of a scale not to be repeated. GOC Sir Harry Tuzo had anticipated a major battle in which the Carl Gustav would be used in housing estates in Belfast and Derry. On July 26 the Ministry of Defence confirmed temporary amendments to the Draft Rules of Engagement.

> For this operation only, a company commander may order the firing of heavy weapons (such as Carl Gustav) against positions from which there is sustained hostile firing, if he believes that this is necessary for the preservation of the lives of soldiers or of other persons who it is his duty to protect. In deciding whether or not to use heavy weapons full account must be taken of the risk that the opening of fire may endanger the lives of innocent persons.[2]

Tuzo had written to Whitelaw to say that he believed the IRA had gained in strength during the ceasefire and that the two wings between them might have 2,000 men that they could mobilise. So the army should prepare for a major 'fire fight'. It should move to neutralise the IRA now because British public opinion, he believed, would not tolerate a long campaign. It was therefore necessary to finish the job: 'It is unrealistic to think in terms of total elimination; complete demoralisation and surrender is the best we can hope for.'[3]

Alongside the mass invasion of the no-go areas and the anticipated last stand at Riverdale, which is on my own family home's doorstep, Tuzo said there would have to be an information campaign to assure us that this was all in our best interests: 'Indeed our Information Policy would aim to attract support from Catholics in the North as well as in the Republic for ridding society of a force which would otherwise bring about a civil war, with dire consequences for Catholics in Ulster, and every likelihood of spreading south of the border. The fact that low key military operations and sincere political proposals have been tried and failed must be emphasised.'

Did he really think that people like me and my neighbours would be willing to see the army killing innocent civilians on our streets as a price to be paid for getting rid of the provos? He was mad if he thought that. Army excesses against civilians had drawn recruits to the IRA, not deterred them. Had he learnt nothing?

Harry Beaves's men were told on 30 July that a big operation was ahead and that they would be leaving their base in the bus depot opposite Milltown Cemetery. He wasn't told what the operation would be, but expected that it would be an assault on Riverdale where the army believed that gunmen were waiting for them in readiness for a battle.

That night I was drinking in the Official IRA club in Lagan Street when Tommy Conlon told me and my friends that we should go home. Whitelaw had just broadcast an announcement that the army would move to dismantle the barricades and Conlon feared that if we didn't leave straight away we might get trapped in that area.

Beaves got his orders at 1 a.m. One body of soldiers was going to seize the GAA sports ground and pavilion at Casement Park. Others would move to protect sappers deployed to dismantle the barricades at Riverdale Park South and Riverdale Park Avenue. These both faced onto Finaghy Road North. It's creepy reading this account of a plan to invade my own street while I was in bed. '6 Troop would enter Riverdale between 61 and 63 Riverdale North and establish a cordon around numbers 40 to 62 Riverdale Drive which would be searched by the Battery's search teams.'[4]

This cordon would end right next door to me. Beaves says he expected 'stiff resistance'. His book describes events which I did not see, 'a constant stream of abuse and sporadic stone throwing' as search teams 'charged into the houses'.

At 10 a.m. the soldiers moved into Casement Park to establish their billets.

I woke up the next morning to my mother making breakfast. She told me there was a soldier standing on our porch at the front door. There was no rioting, no shootings.

Tuzo's vision of an IRA last stand was grounded on a misunderstanding. The IRA did not need to stand and fight when the soldiers crashed through the barricades, nor did they. All they had to do was stash their weaponry and those who were known to the police could clear off south of the border. In Derry they hadn't far to go to be in Donegal where they could watch the whole operation on television in the pub. And those who were not known as activists could stay at home or take the kids to the park.

Tuzo had envisaged that Whitelaw would make an appeal to the people of Northern Ireland to assure them that this mass invasion and the anticipated battles were in their own interests. Whitelaw was smoother than that. He gave the IRA time to move out of the no-go areas and evade a colossal battle with huge losses through the simple expedient of declining to turn up.

Two boys were killed in Derry by the army but they were not part of a resistance. Onc, Seamus Bradley, was a nineteen-year-old member of the IRA who shot himself in the leg and bled to death. Another, Danny Hegarty, aged sixteen, had apparently gone out with his cousin to watch the action in the early hours when an alarm was sounded that the army was coming in. The soldier who shot him later said he appeared to be armed. As in so many other cases of its kind his companions said he was not armed and no weapon was found. His cousin was wounded in the same incident.

The clever thing to do when an army overwhelms your territory and drives your forces away is to strike behind enemy lines. The IRA bombed the village of Claudy, south of Derry.

This was not a military target. It was a sleepy village in the Sperrin Mountains. There was no sense in attacking Claudy other than simply to demonstrate that you could do it, even as your home base was surrounded by the British army. The plan did not work. It had been to destroy commercial property, a small hotel, some shops, but to give due warning so that people could get to safety before the bombs went off. The South Derry IRA had mobilised three car bombs with scouting teams to get them into the main street. They had alibis set up to cover themselves against prosecution. However, there was one little detail in the slick operation that no one had properly taken care of: how were they going to deliver the message to the people living there that they were now about to be blown up if they didn't get off the streets?

The IRA team left the cars in the town with the primed bombs and went to look for a phone so that they could call in a warning. But the same IRA had previously bombed the telephone exchange and none of the phones in the area were working. They called at the house of a local supporter: 'Sorry, lads.'

They belted out the road and stopped at a shop. By then the first bomb had gone off.

Nine people died in Claudy. The youngest was nine-year-old Kathryn Eakin. The oldest was sixty-five-year-old James McClelland. Joseph Connolly was fifteen, William Temple, seventeen. Joseph McCloskey was thirty-eight, Arthur Hone, forty. Rosemary McLaughlin was fifty-one, Elizabeth McElhinney was fifty-nine, David Miller was sixty. A July morning, far from the tumbling barricades and the Donegal pubs and safe houses that the IRA men had retreated to. You might turn off the Derry road to pass through Claudy if you take the mountain route through to Strabane and suddenly you are out of the heavy traffic and into a little valley surrounded by the Derry hills. You may have to stop at the crossroads to let a tractor pass. Then on your right is the Beaufort Hotel, which was one of the targets.

It wasn't a sectarian attack, at least in its outcomes. Five of the dead were protestants, four were catholics. It had been an ordinary lovely summer morning.

It would have made sense for the Troubles to end there. The British had recovered control of the no-go areas and succeeded in doing it without major atrocities. The SDLP was ready for talks and Whitelaw was planning a conference that would direct efforts towards the Hume plan for power sharing. The loyalists had been assured that the Union was safe until a majority wanted out of it. The IRA had been pushed out of its main operational bases, and if defeat wasn't enough to make the point that it was time to give up, the organisation had disgraced itself with the Claudy bomb.

We were still twenty-six years away from the Good Friday Agreement and a settlement between nationalism and unionism. There would never be a year as bad as that between internment and Motorman, though thousands more would die.

Conclusion:
Not Like Other Wars

The year of chaos was like a cross-section of the whole Troubles period. It had all the elements: sectarian murder, the murder of neighbours, barricades, army excesses, government fumbling, even hunger strikes and ceasefires and a peace process. But leaders were still clinging to ideas that would only get in the way of peace, such as London first backing Faulkner and a security crackdown and bristling against the Irish Republic. They were defending soldiers who murdered. In Belfast, Faulkner imagined that bringing unionist-minded catholics into government would appease nationalist aspirations, and Dublin thought that every catholic in the North wanted a united Ireland.

The Troubles did not end after Operation Motorman. The killing would continue at a reduced rate over two and a half decades of further paramilitary campaigns, and there would be more occasions when the stresses would seem barely manageable and the prospect of stability remote. But the army's invasion of the no-go areas was a far more successful operation than the internment raids of the previous August which cost lives and exacerbated the whole problem. Not that the army hadn't been prepared to kill an awful lot of people if the IRA had organised armed resistance. The IRA had seen no point in offering its volunteers up as targets for an overwhelming force. It didn't really do battlefield warfare.

We congratulate ourselves now on a peace process that managed division, but long before that, the violence through the late seventies and eighties and into the nineties had mostly settled into a routine that, though onerous and bloody, lacked the incendiary potential of the year of chaos, largely because the violent groups could not rally sufficient popular support to grow into armies that could assert their demands.

Though it seemed likely in 1972, Northern Ireland did not fall apart like Bosnia would. And while political violence created a climate in which political compromises and necessary agreements could not be made and secured, it never had the potential to achieve its declared aim of enforcing a united Ireland on the republican side, or quelling republican ardour on the loyalist side, or even just of wrapping up the whole bloody thing on the government side. We had arrived at a point of balance.

So why did Northern Ireland not tip over into full civil war? What held it together?

One explanation favoured by some is that the country held together because it was Christian. Although religious divisions were implicated in the trouble, both communities were deeply religious. Church attendance at that time was high. But other countries with strong Christian cultures fought bloody and ruthless wars before then and since.

The authority of the Churches was compromised by their failure to wholly uncouple their traditions and theologies from the arguments of the militants. The Catholic Church had endorsed the IRA in the war of independence. Throughout the Troubles it refused to concede to arguments from unionists that dead IRA members should be excommunicated and denied church funerals.

Within the Protestant Churches there were some pastors who fomented sectarian dissension, presented the whole conflict as being about the need to curtail the expansion of the Catholic Church.

Appeals to moral conscience by religious leaders and politicians after major atrocities may have seemed to speak for the majority of people at the time of their utterance, in the shocked aftermath of a mass killing, but the horror and revulsion didn't last. Many times down the years we heard moral excoriation of the killers such as Whitelaw gave vent to after Bloody Friday. That most people did not want the killing to continue seemed obvious. Still there was no way in which their disapproval could translate into an actual restraint on the killers.

The broader society did not rise up in anger at the killing, but its low level of support for the paramilitaries must have produced an environment in which it was difficult for the paramilitaries to operate. Anthony McIntyre and Beano Niblock and others have spoken of the high level of community support they experienced during riots, doors left open for them to escape through, for instance. But that kind of support was localised.

And people may have felt unable to criticise the paramilitaries who presumed to represent them for fear of seeming to excuse the state or the political or paramilitary forces of another community. The newspaper office I worked in was bombed and the young woman on the reception desk suffered a leg injury. When she returned to work I approached her to offer my sympathy, but it was embarrassing because she was a protestant and I was a catholic, and the unsayable for her was the reasonable suspicion that I, living in Riverdale, might have known those who had left that bomb.

When we commiserate we resort to reassuring simplifications and there were none. The unsayable for me was that when I was back in the pub I'd be among friends who would delight in the bombing of a newspaper office.

Sympathy and perhaps the ability to receive it were compromised by community background, for on each side suspicion extended beyond the actual bombers and killers to the ordinary uninvolved who might be sympathetic.

One might suppose that the paramilitaries in Northern Ireland were ultimately suppressed by the forces of the state, and the success of Operation Motorman might support that theory. The year of chaos had begun, however, with the army exacerbating tensions and violence through the brutal conduct of the internment raids. Then again, the army made things worse on Bloody Sunday when an ill-disciplined and trigger-happy regiment was deployed against civilians. But Operation Motorman appears to have been the fruit of lessons learnt.

But that didn't end the Troubles and for more than twenty years after the operation the state would try different security and judicial remedies, from special courts to infiltration of the armed groups and even, apparently, selective assassination, the facilitating or ignoring of killers whose targeting served the state's interests. (See, for example, the De Silva Report into the loyalist murder of lawyer Pat Finucane, published in 2012.)

Foreign allies like American sympathisers and the Libyan government poured in weaponry such as would equip an army, but the Irish version of a Tet offensive never came, perhaps because even the IRA leaders saw that there was no point. They were getting nowhere. Crucially, the state held itself intact despite the killings and destruction, and it was always going to. War becomes mayhem when people flee their homes, when disorder is so great that the state cannot function. In Syria the hospitals got bombed and refugees took to the roads. In Northern Ireland the NHS was always there. It wasn't just the police and the army who stalled the revolutionary effort of the IRA; it was the postman and the dole clerk, the shopkeeper and the district nurse, the journalist and the social worker, the bus driver, the fruit importer and the brewer.

*

When I returned to Belfast after taking a week's refuge in Donegal after the internment raids in August 1971, I was perplexed and a little annoyed by the response of the dole clerk when I went in a week late to sign on.

'Where were you last week?' he said.

I had to provide a written excuse for not having made my way into town, past rioting and burning buildings, when the buses were off, to declare my availability for work and pick up my money.

I wrote, 'Bombs and bullets,' and handed his slip back to him.

He had the manner of a teacher sniffing at a faked note from a parent. But he stamped the dole form, slid it across for me to sign and I collected my cash.

That incident stayed in my mind and I retold it many times over the years to illustrate what I took for obduracy, and probably sectarian obduracy, evidence that some people were oblivious to the horror around them and probably blamed every working-class catholic for the trouble. But the guy took my excuse and stamped my form and enabled me to get my money, so why had he been momentarily difficult about it? What was he saying? What reason did he have to present himself righteously to me?

I could have told him the fuller truth, that I had fled in fear from my home. Actually, I had stayed through most of internment day, listening to distant cracks of gunfire, hearing the rumours from neighbours that the cathedral was burning, that 'they' – whoever they were – were coming up the Falls. And in the evening my mother and father, who had been on holiday in Donegal, had managed to drive over the mountain from the north, down into the city and tell their story of how most of the country was OK but how they had seen burning and barricades in Derry.

I went back to the safety of Donegal with them and it was

remarkable crossing the whole of Northern Ireland to see how little of it was touched by the chaos.

Maybe that had been a day off for the dole clerk. Maybe he lived in Ballymena or somewhere untouched and had only seen the trouble on the television news. Or maybe he had meant something else by his momentary challenge to me. Maybe he just wanted to say, I turned up for work, and if I hadn't, you wouldn't be getting your dole money.

It was a strange kind of war, if it was a war at all. What normally happens when communities turn against each other, when the army moves against the people, when houses burn and people flee, when civilians arm themselves into militias and attack the state, is something different from what happened in Belfast.

We know it now from having watched the collapse of Yugoslavia on television, from having seen the wars of the Middle East. The social order breaks down. The hospitals clog up. The army and police are no longer there to help or protect you. The centre does not hold.

But Northern Ireland was only a region of the UK. Belfast is about the size of Hull. The centre was London and the IRA was no challenge to its administration of the country. The state, being so much bigger than the war zone, remained stable, was able to absorb the violence and continue to function. So, the IRA wasn't really an army fighting a war but a protest movement expressing itself through murder and vandalism. It could disrupt the local functioning of the state but could not stop it.

Real war escalates by the logic of fear.

The men who turn up to chase you from your home and then move in with their families are not driven always by hatred of you; they just need somewhere to shelter and bed down their children and cook a meal, and since you and your neighbours are of the other community, you can go somewhere else. Ethnic cleansing, as we came to call it, may be driven by practical considerations.

There was something of that in the early eruption of violence in Belfast, catholics and protestants being scattered to go and take the houses of other protestants and catholics who had been evicted by hostile neighbours elsewhere.

And a strange thing happened then. The state approved the house grabs with new tenancy arrangements and issued rent books. Anne Tannahill had refused to be part of that and had demanded that the newly formed Housing Executive give her a home rather than leave it to the loyalist paramilitaries to get one for her.

And no one took over the house that the Fuscos had fled from because it was a private house that the family owned and no one but the Fuscos could have transferred the ownership or accorded a tenancy to it. The squatter wouldn't have got a rent book. But that is not how it works in a real war. Nor do refugees come back home after a week and sign on the dole.

Indeed, many of the IRA men and loyalists were on the dole too, supported by the state in their wars against the state. And businesspeople like Diljit Rana whose restaurants were bombed received compensation for their losses from the state.

That week in August 1971 was the beginning of the year of chaos. It was a period of massive escalation of the violence, a period in which we would anticipate civil war as something far worse than what we were actually living through.

Different people had different perceptions of how it would happen but the talk was of whether we were on the brink, whether there would be a protestant backlash, whether in the heat of naked warfare we would all have to fight or flee.

It didn't happen as badly as we feared and I wonder why. Much has been written about the forces that almost tore Northern Ireland apart but we should acknowledge the forces that held it together.

And perhaps that smug civil servant turning up for work was one of them.

The early days of the Troubles, before the escalation in August 1971 into a year of chaos, suggest that the disruption of life and the spread of political violence might have evolved differently. The main violent forces of that time were small and unpopular.

The revolutionary tendencies were diverse. The Provisional IRA was sneered at by many of the other groups and did not seem likely to emerge as the predominant revolutionary force, let alone the predominant political expression of nationalism in later years.

The radicals of the time were young, enthusiastic and inexperienced. Many were much more interested in the camaraderie of protest than the more solitary and dangerous pursuits of sniping at an army foot patrol from a window or transporting a bomb. The energy, as I recall it, was more enthusiastic than angry at that stage.

The paramilitary organisations that were formed in protestant and catholic working-class areas quickly made themselves part of the social fabric. They set up drinking clubs where the booze was cheaper. These clubs were popular because people were more wary of travelling into the city centre and taking the risk of encountering a riot or getting caught up in a bomb scare or actual explosion. A visiting journalist seeing a large hut packed with people drinking while a singer sang IRA rebel songs might easily have gathered the impression that all these people were supporters of the IRA – or the UDA on the other side. The paramilitaries themselves might have gathered the same impression.

When the collection box went round for the Green Cross, a fund to support IRA prisoners' families, it was more politic to drop a penny in it than announce by a refusal that you were happy to take their cheap drink but didn't agree with the cause. Curiously, the Green Cross shared a name with a road safety campaign for children at the time called the Green Cross Code. After internment there would be hundreds of prisoner families to support and the IRA would extend its reach further as a sort of social service, gathering money to help transport families on prison visits, to give them food parcels for Christmas. And how were you to know where your penny went, for a turkey or for guns from America?

With this degree of immersion in communities the paramilitary groups were already establishing patterns that would preserve them into the future. They had an organic connection to communities that might look and feel like endorsement. Institutions quickly became more concerned with preserving themselves intact than with pursuing their declared goals.

But there was a logic in the situation that ultimately asserted itself. That logic was that nationalism and unionism in Northern Ireland had to make space for each other.

The IRA had failed to recognise the balance of attitudes within Northern Ireland and imagined that it could force Britain out of Ireland on behalf of the Northern Irish catholics. This was militarily impossible and incapable of attracting sufficient popular support.

Vanguard and the loyalist paramilitaries indulged an equally ludicrous fantasy that killing catholics would alienate that community from the IRA or that a military crackdown on the IRA would destroy it without at the same time jeopardising the Union.

Ted Heath in the autumn of '71, along with the army, believed that a military crackdown could end the IRA campaign and that then the catholics, as good citizens, would settle down and accept a unionist-led, democratically elected Stormont government.

Sir Alec Douglas-Home was right in his observation that the Northern Irish were not like the Welsh or the Scots of that time, and would never settle down as fully British. Consequently, they would never thank a British government for deploying the army to kill other catholics on their behalf. That reality came into sharp focus after Bloody Sunday.

The catholics, or the minority or the nationalists, had not been named for what they were. They were not British. They were not unionists, but many were not really nationalists either in the sense of being people who wanted a united Irish nation and wanted it now. The SDLP were the ones who had taken the pulse of that community and understood that it did not support the IRA or its aspirations but identified as Irish and not British. They have still not been properly named, though they can no longer be called the 'minority'.

One reason they did not want to push for Irish unity of course was the avoidance of civil war. But that doesn't mean simply that they were being cowed by a loyalist threat. They had little sense of belonging to Dublin. They were economically better off than the citizens of the Republic, and that might be part of why they didn't want a united Ireland, but perhaps they also had a sense that they were at home in the North and just didn't want the disruption.

The catholics would encourage their children to seek jobs in the civil service or to go to England and live there and raise families there. What Hume and the SDLP grasped was that they would settle for justice and a share of power in the North. Faulkner could give cabinet seats to nationalists and be safe because they weren't really nationalists as he understood the term. They didn't want to rock the boat but to stabilise it.

And the evidence of that was that through fifty years of the Northern Ireland state, despite discrimination, there had been no significant uprising or protest movement to displace it. What produced violence was state violence and that arose from a paranoia about a growing section of the population not being British in the way that the unionists were. They were not Orange. They were not monarchists. But then, an awful lot of British people living in England aren't those things either.

In the late sixties and early seventies and especially in the year of chaos, division was exacerbated by conflicting forces.

And in time, when things settled down, the logic of the

situation would prevail, that the Irish in Northern Ireland would prefer stability and good governance and would contribute to both, so long as they were not treated as an alien threat, which they weren't.

The numerous pleas by catholic leaders to give justice to catholics and thereby alienate the IRA sounded to some back then like a protection racket, or a naive and absurdly ambitious boast, but it was simply a way of stating the key reality that the IRA would never be able to claim to speak for even a majority of catholics if there was justice and fairness in governance. Hume got that.

Yet in the heat of that crazy time that simple logic could not assert itself. Maybe part of the problem was the want of a name for the Irish in Northern Ireland. Today they are routinely called nationalists for they are secularising and the word 'catholic' applies less. They don't like to be called the Irish because that implies that the unionists are not Irish and they want them to be comfortable in feeling and saying that they are. If we had a precise word it would only sharpen the division, so perhaps we are better off without one. The more sectarian loyalists have words for us like fenian and taig and deploy these words because they want the division to remain.

In time, community division may dissolve altogether, though a paranoid unionist will worry about a majority 'catholic' population that doesn't share the unionist sense of being British. That's a worry, as Brexit is a worry. But the question I asked was not what tore Northern Ireland apart but what held it together? And the answer is that it never really wanted to be torn apart in the first place.

Leabharlanna Poiblí Chathair Baile Átha Cliath
Dublin City Pub

Notes

In the references that follow, 'proni' stands for Public Record Office of Northern Ireland and 'nai' stands for National Archive of Ireland.

Gearing Up
1 *Tírghrá* (Dublin: Republican Publications, 2002).

Internment
1 proni_HA-32-2-54_1971-nd_b.pdf.
2 Potter, John, *A Testimony to Courage: The History of the Ulster Defence Regiment, 1969–1992* (London: Leo Cooper, 2001).
3 proni_HA-32-2-54_1971-08-18.pdf.
4 *United Irishman*, September 1971, as quoted in McKittrick, David, Kelters, Seamus, Feeney, Brian, Thornton, Chris and McVea, David, *Lost Lives: The Stories of the Men, Women and Children Who Died as a Result of the Northern Ireland Troubles* (Edinburgh: Mainstream Publishing, 1999), entry 102 for William McKavanagh.
5 nai_TSCH-2002-8-483_1971-10-16.pdf.
6 nai_TSCH-2002-8-483_1971-10-07.pdf.
7 nai_TSCH-2002-8-494_1971-11-16.pdf.
8 nai_TSCH-2002-8-483_1971-10-07.pdf.
9 nai_TSCH-2002-8-494_1971-11-01.pdf.

One of Those Things That Happen in War
1 Hansard HC Deb 16 February 1922 vol 150 c1270.

Summitry
1 nai_DFA-2003-13-6_1971-09-09.pdf.
2 nai_TSCH-2002-8-483_1971-09-29.pdf.
3 Hansard HC Deb 22 September 1971 vol 83 cc14–15.
4 nai_DFA-2002-19-457_1971-09-28.pdf.

Shooting Women
1 Part of Corporal Raymond Beadon's statement reproduced by Relatives for Justice in its submission to the Council of Europe's Commissioner for Human Rights.
2 Walsh, Roseleen, *Bridget's Daughters* (Relatives for Justice, 2001).
3 McKittrick et al., p. 108.

The Army Gets It Wrong
1 proni_HA-32-2-51_1971-nd.pdf.
2 Corbett, Steve, *A Tough Nut to Crack: Andersonstown – Voices from 9 Battery Royal Artillery in Northern Ireland, November 1971–March 1972* (Solihull: Helion & Co., 2015).
3 Radden Keefe, Patrick, *Say Nothing: A True Story of Murder and Memory in Northern Ireland* (London: William Collins, 2019), p. 44.

Deepening Deadlock
1 nai_TSCH-2002-8-483_1971-10-27.pdf.
2 nai_TSCH-2002-8-508_1971-11-26_b.pdf.
3 nai_TSCH-2002-8-483_1971-10-08_b.pdf.
4 nai_TSCH-2002-8-417_1971-11-05.pdf.
5 nai_TSCH-2002-8-417_1971-10-29.pdf.
6 nai_TSCH-2002-8-484_1971-11-15.pdf.
7 nai_TSCH-2002-8-416_1971-10-07.pdf.

Living in the Middle of It
1 Corbett, p. 241.

Routines of Murder
1 nai_TSCH-2002-8-252_1971-12-15.pdf.

A New Year
1 proni_HA-32-3-7_1972-01-27.pdf.

Bloody Sunday
1 Kelly, Henry, *How Stormont Fell* (Dublin: Gill and Macmillan; London: Macmillan, 1972), p. 119.
2 Hansard HC Deb 01 February 1972 vol 830 c296.
3 Hansard HC Deb 01 February 1972 vol 830 c298.
4 Hansard HC Deb 31 January 1972 vol 830 c32–33.
5 nai_TSCH-2003-16-462_1972-02-01.pdf.
6 Hansard HC Deb 01 February 1972 vol 830 c298.
7 Hansard HC Deb 01 February 1972 vol 830 c310.
8 proni_CAB-9-R-238-7_1972-02-04.pdf.

Britain Is Now the Problem
1 proni_PM-5-169-13_1972-02-01.pdf.
2 proni_HA-32-3-7_1972-02-03.pdf.
3 Hansard HC Deb 01 February 1972 vol 830 c299.
4 Hansard HC Deb 01 February 1972 vol 830 c298.
5 Hansard HC Deb 01 February 1972 vol 830 c310–311.
6 Kelly, p. 124.
7 Ibid.
8 Ibid., p. 125.
9 Ibid., p. 126.

The Abercorn
1 proni_PM-5-169-13_1972-03-07.pdf.
2 Adams, Gerry, *Before the Dawn: An Autobiography* (New York: William Morrow & Co., 1996), p. 188.
3 O'Doherty, Malachi, *The Telling Year* (Dublin: Gill & Macmillan, 2007), p. 114.
4 Ibid.

London Takes Control
1 National Archives, Kew, Thursday 3 February 1972, Document reference: CAB 128/48, Cabinet Minutes Confidential Annex.
2 Kelly, Gerry, *Playing My Part* (G & M Publications, 2019), p. 42.

Dublin's Pitch for Unity
1 nai_DFA-2003-13-16_1972-04-21_b.pdf.
2 nai_DFA-2003-13-16_1972-04-27_a.pdf.

The Building Backlash

1 nai_TSCH-2003-16-502_1972-05-09.pdf.
2 Hansard HC Deb 28 March 1972 vol 834 c239.
3 O'Doherty, p. 132.

Hunger Strikes

1 proni_FIN-30-R-1-8_1972-06-03.pdf.
2 proni_FIN-30-R-1-8_1972-nd.pdf.
3 proni_CAB-9-G-27-6-2_1972-06-12.pdf.
4 proni_CAB-9-G-27-6-2_1972-06-14.pdf.

Negotiations for a Ceasefire

1 National Archives, Kew, Wednesday 21 June 1972, Document reference: PREM 15/1009, Note of a Meeting with Representatives of the Provisional IRA.
2 Hansard HC Deb 22 June 1972 vol 839 c725.
3 proni_CAB-9-G-27-6-2_1972-06-26.pdf.
4 nai_TSCH-2003-16-561_1972-06-30_a.pdf.

Bloody Friday

1 Hansard HC Deb 24 July vol 841 c1326.
2 Hansard HC Deb 24 July vol 841 c1327.

Motorman

1 Beaves, Harry, *Down Among the Weeds* (Kibworth Beauchamp: Matador, 2018), pp. 69–71.
2 National Archives, Kew, Wednesday 26 July 1972, Document reference: PREM 15/1011 Annex A to CGS/828, Northern Ireland: Draft Rules of Engagement.
3 https://thebrokenelbow.com/2015/06/17/the-tuzo-plan-1972-extirpate-the-ira-and-turn-a-blind-eye-to-uda-guns/ Sir Harry Tuzo's report is in the National Archives at Kew.
4 Beaves, p. 75.

Acknowledgements

I would like to thank the many people who helped me with this book. Some of them were former paramilitaries who spoke frankly about their past and about the evolution of their thinking since the days they terrorised the people of Northern Ireland. They are named throughout the book so no list is needed here.

I would like to acknowledge the invaluable resource of the CAIN (Conflict Archive on the Internet) website at the University of Ulster and the records of the National Archives of Ireland and the Public Record Office of Northern Ireland.

I received permission from Jean Bleakney to quote from her poem 'The Sunday After Bloody Sunday' from her collection *No Remedy* and from the family of Seamus Heaney and Faber and Faber to quote from Heaney's Bloody Sunday song.

The book was started at a time when I was receiving funding from the Arts Council of Northern Ireland through a Major Artist Award.

Most of it was written during the Covid-19 pandemic lockdown which brought its advantages and hindrances, providing peace and quiet for a writer but complicating access to interviewees.

Thanks for support go also to my agent, Lisa Moylett, and, more than anyone, to my wife Maureen Boyle.

Since the completion of the book an inquest into ten killings by soldiers in the Ballymurphy estate, in one of the bloodiest periods in Northern Ireland, just after the introduction of internment, determined that all ten victims were innocent.

A trial of two soldiers for the alleged murder of Joe McCann was dismissed by the judge.

Picture credits

British Army troops in Belfast (*Rolls Press/Popperfoto*); Children playing in the streets, Belfast (*Alain Le Garsmeur 'The Troubles' Archive/Alamy Stock Photo*); Members of the UDA in Belfast (*David Lomax/Hulton Archive/Getty Images*); IRA gunmen in Derry (*Leif Skoogfors/Corbis Historical/Getty Images*); Brian Faulkner and Edward Heath (© *Keystone Pictures USA/ZUMAPRESS.com/ Mary Evans*); Jack Lynch (*Rolls Press/Popperfoto/Getty Images*); Reginald Maudling (*Rolls Press/Popperfoto/Getty Images*); Peter Sellers and Swami Vishnu meet Irene Gallagher (*Mirrorpix/Getty Images*); Lieutenant General Sir Harry Tuzo (*PA/Alamy Stock Photo*); Wounded man carried away by friends on Bloody Sunday (*William L. Rukeyser/Hulton Archive/Getty Images*); Protesters are rounded up by British troops on Bloody Sunday (*William L. Rukeyser/Hulton Archive/Getty Images*); IRA men who escaped from the prison ship HMS *Maidstone* give a press conference (*PA/Alamy Stock Photo*); Gerry Adams (*PA/Alamy Stock Photo*); Ruairi O Bradaigh (*John Walters/ANL/Shutterstock*); Bernadette Devlin (*Michel Laurent/AP/Shutterstock*); Gerry Fitt (*Rolls Press/Popperfoto/Getty Images*); Ian Paisley (*Heinz Ducklau/AP/ Shutterstock*); John Hume (*Mirrorpix/Getty Images*); Bloody Friday, 21 July 1972 (*Mirrorpix/Getty Images*); Julie Cockburn (*Roger O'Doherty*). All other photographs are taken by the author.

Index

A Note About the Author

Malachi O'Doherty is a writer and broadcaster based in Belfast. He is a regular contributor to the *Belfast Telegraph* and to several BBC radio programmes. He covered the Troubles and the peace process as a journalist and has written for several Irish and British newspapers and magazines, including the *Irish Times*, the *New Statesman*, the *Scotsman* and the *Guardian*.